A Short History of Western Ideology

A Short History of Western Ideology

A critical account

ROLF PETRI

Bloomsbury Academic
An imprint of Bloomsbury Publishing Plc

BLOOMSBURY
LONDON · OXFORD · NEW YORK · NEW DELHI · SYDNEY

Bloomsbury Academic
An imprint of Bloomsbury Publishing Plc

50 Bedford Square	1385 Broadway
London	New York
WC1B 3DP	NY 10018
UK	USA

www.bloomsbury.com

BLOOMSBURY and the Diana logo are trademarks of Bloomsbury Publishing Plc

First published 2018

© Rolf Petri, 2018

Rolf Petri has asserted his right under the Copyright, Designs and Patents Act, 1988, to be identified as Author of this work.

All rights reserved. No part of this publication may be reproduced or transmitted in any form or by any means, electronic or mechanical, including photocopying, recording, or any information storage or retrieval system, without prior permission in writing from the publishers.

No responsibility for loss caused to any individual or organization acting on or refraining from action as a result of the material in this publication can be accepted by Bloomsbury or the author.

British Library Cataloguing-in-Publication Data
A catalogue record for this book is available from the British Library.

ISBN: HB: 978-1-3500-2609-4
PB: 978-1-3500-2610-0
ePDF: 978-1-3500-2607-0
eBook: 978-1-3500-2608-7

Library of Congress Cataloging-in-Publication Data
A catalog record for this book is available from the Library of Congress.

Cover image © Bibliothèque nationale de France

Typeset by Deanta Global Publishing Services, Chennai, India

To find out more about our authors and books visit www.bloomsbury.com. Here you will find extracts, author interviews, details of forthcoming events and the option to sign up for our newsletters.

Contents

Acknowledgments vii

Introduction 1

1 Europe and history 17
    1.1 *Christianitas* 20
    1.2 Civilize or make disappear 25
    1.3 Philosophies of history 30
    1.4 A somewhat gloomy utopia 41

2 Freedom and sovereignty 47
    2.1 Liberty and liberalism 49
    2.2 A chosen people in a promised land 60
    2.3 The religion of the people 71
    2.4 Democracy and the rule of law 90

3 Hierarchy among equals 101
    3.1 European spaces 102
    3.2 Human races 111
    3.3 World cultures 121
    3.4 Global rights 128

4 A craving for goodness 149
    4.1 A fair amount of killing 153
    4.2 An over-accumulation of benevolence 158
    4.3 A rescue from the limbo of history 163
    4.4 Imperialism: A popular sentiment 167

5 Ecology and apocalypse 171
    5.1 Nature 174
    5.2 Identity 180
    5.3 Alienation 187
    5.4 Apocalypse 192

Afterword 201
References 203
Index 227

Acknowledgments

It is impossible to acknowledge adequately the intellectual stimulation I have received over many years from so many colleagues and friends. It was sometimes agreement and other times disagreement with their ideas that greatly helped me in elaborating the present book. I wish to thank in particular Franz J. Bauer, Antonio Benci, Giulia Bonazza, Jordi Catalan, Monica Centanni, Matthew D'Auria, Claudia De Martino, Marco Doria, Anna Maria Falchero, Nobert Götz, Heinz-Gerhard Haupt, Peter Hertner, Janne Holmén, Mario Isnenghi, Paolo Jedlowski, Jussi Kurunmäki, Antonis Liakos, Giacomo Marramao, Matthias Middell, Michele Mioni, Michael G. Müller, Deborah Paci, Vasilis Petrogiannis, Hartmut R. Peter, Stefano Petrungaro, Armando Pitassio, Camilla Poesio, Thomas Rahlf, Maurizio Reberschak, Massimiliane Rieder, Omar Salani-Favaro, Antonella Salomoni, Marianna Scarfone, Dirk Schaal, Hannes Siegrist, Anastasia Stouraiti, Bo Stråth, Jan Vermeiren, Massimo Tomasutti, Larry Wolff, Stuart Woolf, Rolf Wörsdörfer, Giovanni Vian, and Konstantina Zanou. I am very grateful also to the colleagues of the history journal *Memoria e Ricerca*, and to the participants of the congresses and workshops I attended or co-organized; in particular, those of our "Spaces of Expectation" research group and the workshop on "Nostalgia" of 2008. They gave me the opportunity to take part in exciting debates and learn so many things from outstanding scholars. I would have loved to list all of them here, but will recall just two by name—Svetlana Boym and Franco Rizzi—who passed away prematurely.

For advice regarding the present book, I owe many thanks to the anonymous reviewers, as well as to Antonis Liakos, Axel Körner, Domenico Losurdo, Matthias Middell, and Larry Wolff. I thank Giusy Chidichimo and Maximilian Stoib for help. I happened also to have brief conversations regarding aspects of this project with Joanna de Groot, Masayuki Sato, Meghan Sutherland, and Jacopo Zanella, which were more important to my work than they may imagine. I thank Emily Drewe, Beatriz Lopez, and the other staff of Bloomsbury Academics for their excellent cooperation.

I express my gratitude to Megan Elisabeth Rae of Ca' Foscari University for the flawless translation of the original text.

I had already published some parts of the first chapter in 2004, in the article "Europa? Ein Zitatensystem," *Comparativ* 14 (3): 14–49. Parts of the fourth chapter appeared in 2012 in the chapter "Geopolitica dei sentimenti, ieri e oggi," of the book M. Isnenghi (ed), *Pensare la nazione. Silvio Lanaro e l'Italia contemporanea*, 29–47 (Rome: Donzelli Editore). I am very grateful to the publishers for granting permission to reuse these passages.

As a sign of gratitude to my family, I dedicate this book to Emiliano Friederici, great-grandson to history professor Hans Jürgen Friederici and grandson to the author of this book. I hope he will have a good life without someone charging him with history as a burden.

Introduction

i

"It is my hypothesis that the fundamental source of conflict in this new world will not be primarily ideological or primarily economic. The great divisions among humankind and the dominating source of conflict will be cultural," wrote Samuel P. Huntington (1993: 22–23) in his famous article on the "clash of civilizations." He went on to state that "with the end of the Cold War, international politics moves out of its Western phase, and its centerpiece becomes the interaction between the West and non-Western civilizations and among non-Western civilizations."

The present book aims to clarify the core elements of western ideology. Although it will hint at the self-ascertaining function of "the West," which construes a Self through the imaginary gaze of an Other, it will not dwell much on the fact that "the West was originally a European concept" but then "migrated to America" (Gamble 2006: 1–2), or on "the problematic relationship between the *two halves of the Occident*: the Anglo-American *oceanic model* and the European *Continental model*" (Marramao 2012: 10). As contemporary geographers explain, it was teleology that shaped the classical geographical description of the Earth's surface and not the other way round (Schultz 2007: 20). Therefore, this study scrutinizes geographically varying Wests only insofar as it is necessary to understand how they affect teleology. The "West" of this book fundamentally is a spatial metaphor, the core meaning of which does not vary with the places to which it applies. Nor is the book particularly committed to investigating the political variety of "contemporary western ideologies" (Gamble 2009: 3). This is not to deny that there are important political differences, nor that they deserve investigation. Here, however, they will be considered only to the extent to which it is necessary for the understanding of the general argument. And the general argument of this book is not variety, it is singularity. Throughout the book, "western ideology" will be used mostly in the singular form.

My central thesis is similar to John Gray's statement, according to which if anything defines the west, "it is the pursuit of salvation in history. It is historical teleology—the belief that history has a built-in purpose or goal—rather than traditions of democracy or tolerance, that sets western civilization apart from all others" (Gray 2008: 103). Consequently, I will not distinguish between contingent variants of western ideology and "genuinely universal" aspects, which, according to Andrew Gamble, "need to be accepted as the common basis for all societies that make the transition to modernity" (Gamble 2009: 19).

I will argue instead that within the conceptual framework of civilization and modernization theories, or any other form of universalistic and eschatological thinking, the critical comprehension of western ideology is destined to remain limited and in a certain sense fallacious. As the focus of this book is on the singularity of the eschatological vision of past and future, it will not even go deeply into the truly important discussion regarding the various substitutions of specific revelations and utopias with others, for example the substitution of the secular Enlightenment utopia with apocalyptic religion which, according to Gray, is presently under way. Antonis Liakos (2011: 15) rightly points out how "the utopias that have gone astray, utopias that transformed into dystopias, and realities that proved to be post-utopian" marked profound changes in western society's views of the past and its expectations for the future. We should admit indeed that there exists a "plurality of modern historicities and their underlying structures" (Trüper, Chakrabarty, and Subrahmanyam 2015: xi), and that it is important to understand each of them in its own right. This said, what I claimed regarding western ideology, I repeat here for its conceptual skeleton. The purpose of this book is not to investigate the multiplicity of, and changes in, the meanings attributed to history, or the plural forms of teleology and eschatology. It is, instead, to highlight the very singular idea that history must have a purpose and its translation into a secularized ideological corpus. We should keep in mind that, as a consequence of millennia-old education and indoctrination, a large share of humans simply seems to take for granted the idea that history must have a purpose, and lacks awareness of the fact that another conspicuous portion would probably feel it is abstruse. This particular aspect should emerge with sufficient clarity.

I hope to offer the reader not only a synthetic but also a comprehensive investigation of western concepts. The book will not limit itself to highlighting how the eighteenth-century neologism "civilization" is a product of western eschatology. It also will mention that the same holds, although perhaps less obviously, for the semantic transpositions of other terms in frequent use, such as "humanity," "reason," "nature," and "identity," among others. Take, for example, the term "culture" (Petri 2012a: 26–32) to which Huntington refers. Most authors seem to overlook that, in its contrast with "nature," "culture" itself is also relatively new. During the seventeenth and eighteenth centuries, its uses became intimately interwoven with the beginnings of a secularized western ideology. Over this period, a fundamental alteration in the semantics of the term took place whereby, from its distant original Latin roots, which contained a normative provision for the education of individuals, it transformed into an analytical term for collective practices, ideas, and behaviors. It was in particular Voltaire who contrasted "'nature,' upon which the unity of mankind depends, with 'culture' (made up of 'customs' and 'usages'), which, on the other hand, has scattered variety all over the world" (Remotti 1992: 642). It was around the same time that Adam Ferguson and others merged the concepts underlying the adjective "civil," the noun "civility," and the verb "to civilize," the use of which had already spread into the neologism "civilization," with the intention of designating another central aspect of the historical process. Therefore, the neologisms "civilization" and "culture" in their revised understandings are two outstanding examples of concepts that characterize the core of western ideology.

ii

"Ideology," the word that presents the main subject of this book, has an Enlightenment background as well. More precisely, it was coined on the threshold of the post-Enlightenment period. Around 1800 the French liberal Destutt de Tracy used it to denote an objectifying "science of ideas" (Kennedy 1979: 353), but Napoleon had already assigned two predominantly negative meanings to ideology: as theory devoid of practical relevance and as a set of untrustworthy dogmas. For Karl Marx, however, ideology was not simply a false consciousness of reality; as he pointed out, it "can mislead even when nothing in its claims is strictly speaking false; it might, for instance, misdirect critical attention by concentrating on a part rather than the whole of a truth" (Leopold 2013: 24).

Almost from the outset, ideology was associated with social hierarchy and power structures, and often it is seen as a major stabilizing factor for existing power settings, thanks to its consent-producing psychological pervasiveness. According to Clifford Geertz (1973: 218), it is also an agent of change. Ideology, in his view, is a symptom of modernization as it frees the political realm from received religious tradition, making "an autonomous politics possible by providing the authoritative concepts that render it meaningful." Those who consider modernization to be positive should therefore acknowledge ideology's positive function. Many critics, especially of the post–Second World War period, did not share the same view. On the contrary, for Karl Popper and others, ideology remained dishonest partisan speech apt to undermine what Habermas (1984: 18) would call the "communicative rationality" of modern societies. The optimists among the modernization theorists maintained that ideology is residual, however. Edward Shils predicted the "end of ideology" in the west, because western society is too complex and empirical to accept ideological infatuations any longer (Shils 1968: 14). After 1989, claims regarding the post-ideological era that had dawned intensified, notwithstanding that the evidence to the contrary was crushing—at least for all those who were not blinded by ideology.

What then do I mean, after all, by "ideology"? According to Bo Stråth, the term escapes definition because as a concept it "has a history." The author prefers a conceptual history approach, which "is about discursive struggles aimed at appropriating positions of interpretative power." The historian should therefore ask who uses key concepts like ideology, what meanings they confer on them, and how "struggles about the occupation of semantic fields change the meaning of key concepts over time" (Stråth 2013: 19). It seems that ideology as a definable phenomenon relates to the reality of language, whereas its connections with the world narrated by the means of language remain unavoidably vague and contradictory. The linguists Gunther Kress and Bob Hodge went even further when they wrote: "Ideology involves a systematically organized presentation of reality. How then can ideology be defined without a prior description of the truth? All such descriptions involve language, and presenting anything in or through language involves selection." These three laconic-sounding sentences are dense enough to refute any acceptance, at least as ultimate "definitions," of either the independent life of ideas that Destutt de Tracy meant to study, or his detractors' interpretation of ideology as illusion or false consciousness. They also imply that language itself can be interpreted "as ideology" (Kress and Hodge 1979: 15). The understanding of ideology to which this book adheres starts from similar insights. It is particularly close to what Bob Hodge stated elsewhere, that ideology "identifies a unitary object that incorporates complex sets of meanings with the social agents and processes that produced them." He goes on to explain why ideology's time is not up yet:

> No other term captures this object as well as "ideology." Foucault's "episteme" is too narrow and abstract, not social enough. His "discourse," popular because it covers some of "ideology's" terrain with less baggage, is too confined to verbal systems. "Worldview" is too metaphysical, "propaganda" too loaded. Despite or because of its contradictions, "ideology" still plays a key role in semiotics oriented to social, political life. (Hodge n.d.)

Given the role of social agency in the performance of speech and the attribution of meaning, Andrew Vincent maintains that the symbols constituting ideology "*are* the social and political reality. All social action is therefore symbolically mediated and ideology performs that mediating role. It is the language of *actual political life*. Ideology therefore authorizes, legitimates, and enables everyday human understanding" (Vincent 2012: 172). It is precisely according to their everyday understanding that many westerners will doubt that any such thing as a western ideology can exist. In their view, only marginal extremisms in the west or anachronistic worldviews expressed by backward societies outside the west can be labeled as ideological, whereas at the core of modern western societies "communicative rationality" prevails. Yet terms such as "culture" or "civilization," when used to describe the wider world and its history, are far from being aseptic analytical terms. As I previously stated, they carry meanings derived from other meanings, which refer to one and the same ideology. The single elements of this ideology are part of a complex elaboration of "metaphors that embody social meanings" (Vincent 2012: 171), which create political reality rather than just represent it (Žižek 2008: 15).

The acknowledgment that writing down a concept or uttering an idea possesses a performative and reality-changing property is one of the achievements of the Cambridge School of intellectual history. The scholars who in the 1960s and 1970s formed that group set ideas free, so to speak, of the isolated life where earlier *Ideengeschichte* had confined them by inserting language into the general frame of human action. Quentin Skinner (2002: 4) made Ludwig Wittgenstein's statement, according to which "words are also deeds," a programmatic starting point for explorations in the history of political thought. Texts of the past have to be examined in light of the linguistic conventions of the period during which they were written, that is, under the constraints that shaped the beliefs of authors and influenced their intention when writing. However, Foucault's "discursive regime," which underlines such constraints, is not an absolute one, according to Skinner, because language is also a resource as the acts of writing and speaking have a performative character. Any "successful alteration in the use of a concept," therefore, "will at the same time constitute a change in our social world." Similar shifting conceptualizations "constitute the very stuff of ideological debate" (Skinner 2002: 118, 176–77). John Pocock (2009: 74) called the relatively more stable formations of political discourse "languages of politics." These "must be thought of as plural, flexible and non-final; each must permit of both responses and other speech acts which will modify it from within, and of various forms of interaction with other language-structures which will modify it from without." While the present study can be situated within this general frame of propositions, I argue that western ideology possesses a more enduring character than "languages of politics" normally do.

The Cambridge School has been criticized for adhering too closely to verbal linguistic forms instead of appreciating the influence that the social context also exerts in other ways. Patrick Boucheron, for example, highlights how artistic visual codes can superimpose over linguistic codes and contribute to create an ideology in their own right (Boucheron 2005, quoted in Brice 2012: 59–60). German *Begriffsgeschichte* started its major editorial project in 1972 (Brunner, Conze, and Koselleck 1984). It investigated concepts central to "political and social language" from the point of view of semantic changes which occurred under the influence not only of intellectual debate but also of other social processes. As French historian Pierre Rosanvallon explained, conceptual history "borrows from the history of mentalities the desire for incorporating all the elements that make up the complex object that is a political culture: its ways of reading the major theoretical works, its literature, press and opinion movements, its pamphlets, ritual speeches, emblems and signs." At the same time, conceptual history should study the history of words and the evolution of language. "More broadly, the history of events and institutions must be taken into account permanently. There are not so much specific materials to collect for conceptual history, but rather all the materials which in a different manner the historians of ideas, mentalities, institutions and events also rely on." (Rosanvallon 1986: 100–1). To this list, already long, one could easily add the study of communication, print, and diffusion techniques, as well as aspects of sociability and the de-codification of nonverbal languages such as music, visual art, or architecture. The list is endless and it is difficult not to agree with any of its entries.

Generic principles like those outlined above certainly inspire this book as well, although it lacks most of the requirements of conceptual history as listed by Rosanvallon, especially the requirement to study all the various aspects simultaneously. Skinner expressed appreciation for conceptual history because a "whole society may eventually come to alter its attitude towards some fundamental value or practice and alter its normative vocabulary accordingly," but he also underlined the arduous challenge of the "kind of social history that would be required" to meet the necessities of a similar research program (Skinner 2002: 181). There is in effect a methodological ambition behind certain formulations of the conceptual history approach that is almost impossible to meet in practice. Regarding ideology, Michael Freeden indicated research objectives that appear much more realistic. They are not just motivated by pragmatic considerations, but also take into account the epistemological limits that the subject matter presents to the researcher. According to Freeden, the purpose of a history of ideology

> is to explain, to interpret, to decode, and to categorize. In so doing, it does not claim to offer a correct description of the world of ideologies, nor a complete account of the patterns of political thinking that world incorporates, nor the promise of an archimedal vista of social relations beyond the tarnished sphere of ideologies. It must rest content with holding out the possibility of a plausible, generally applicable, and

reasonably comprehensive framework of analysis that is both intellectually and culturally satisfying, but that acknowledges the multiplicity of available perspectives on ideological thought as well as the inevitable gaps in recreating so intricate a phenomenon. (Freeden 1996: 6)

The present text should be located in a similar scenario of methodological considerations. I shall not, however, try to shield the flaws in my own work behind such appropriate procedural and epistemological cautions. Rather, I will attempt to defend my own choices and also admit the text's undeniable lacunae.

iii

In his monumental studies on the Enlightenment and the French Revolution, Jonathan Israel proposes a "new intellectual history" of thought to succeed in "fusing the advantages and shedding the disadvantages" of the Cambridge School, *histoire des mentalités*, and *Begriffsgeschichte*. As a possible method, he indicates his own "controversialist" approach as it offers the possibility "to see in a reasonably objective light how structures of belief and sensibility in society interact dialectically with the evolution of philosophical ideas" (Israel 2006: 23, 26). In this way, he argues, documentable intellectual controversies of the past place themselves in the time–space frame of social changes, instead of being located there by researchers who adopt a too strictly language-related analysis or, on the contrary, proceed by abstract deductions regarding the influence of social structures. For example, in his history of the French Revolution Israel indicates the "royal financial crisis" as the only "major tangible, material factor" of the Revolution which, however, cannot really explain it, while he ascribes even less explanatory value to the "too long-standing, slow-moving, marginal, and insufficiently specific" economic, social, and cultural changes. Rather, a "revolution of ideas" was necessary before a political revolution could start, during which radical enlightened *philosophes* took the lead of the process (Israel 2014: 8–10, 15). Israel's volumes raise relevant questions of method relating to the epistemological status of language and the role of ideas in the process of social change. His reflections also refer to explanatory factors and the problem of causality. He finally concludes that philosophers have a great impact on society and its political dynamics.

This book is also particularly based on the works of the "great thinkers." They are not seen here as demiurges of collective ideologies. If anything, their gift is their capacity to gather and translate what circulates within the social ether of their time. Contrary to Israel's studies, this book contains no systematic investigation of the flow of ideas in the political and social realms, apart from some short references in the fourth chapter and the hope that readers can directly appreciate the ideological impact on politics by comparing the concepts discussed with the political language of everyday life. According to Rosanvallon (1986: 100), proceeding in that way means following in the tracks of outdated *Ideengeschichte*. He argues that, contrary to an old-style history of ideas, "the conceptual history of the political cannot be limited to the analysis of great works and their commentary, although in some cases they may be correctly seen as crystallization poles for the questions that an epoch raises and the answers it attempts to give."

As a response, we must not necessarily argue that the study of the "sophisticated and elitist world in which the actions of authors produce texts and modify the contexts and structures they do reach" is the only thing achievable, since deeper grammatical structures of language as well as deeper geophysical conditions of social life have a *longue durée* rather than a history, and therefore do not pertain "to the history of consciousness" (Pocock 2009: 107–08). I think that describing the flow of ideas as a flow in the continuum of physical and social conditions also adheres typically to the realm of consciousness when it goes beyond self-reflection. At the same time, I believe that the impossibility of grasping the complex entirety of all interrelated conditions and elements of the process should not create exaggerated methodological concerns, especially if they are based on unreliable metaphysics of thought, or concepts of causal concatenation that fall short.

Is it not telling that scholars who intend to borrow their methods from *histoire des mentalités* have been called "diffusionists"? The word suggests that individual human thinkers, however "great" or "minor," would retain the exclusive copyright on ideas. In accordance with William James's statement that the "thought is itself the thinker" (James 1890: 401), I would suggest that the generation and transformation of ideas irreverently crosses all the borders we establish out of analytical necessity when we accurately distinguish, for example, authors, audiences, critics, media, individual intentions, social interests, political movements, techniques of transmission, and so forth. Without restoring autonomous life to the "spirit" in the tradition of idealism, James's statement frees ideas from the cage of individual subjectivity. This makes it not unimportant, but still less important, from which window we survey the process. The "great-thinker" window is not the only one. It has a specific angle that differs from others. Each window offers specific insights into the same process. If I prefer to open the "great-thinker" window it is because compared with the others it appears to be the picture window. The idea–material processed, however, is the same from whatever angle we look at it: not in the sense that it would display no variants or modifications, but in the sense that it is an illusion to believe that somewhere—for example, in the forgotten diary of a "great thinker"—we can find this same idea in an uncontaminated "true" form.

To be sure, this does not solve the problem, again highlighted by Rosanvallon (1986: 101), that one does not hear in the same way "in 1789 or in 1793 when someone talks about democracy, for example." Even more, we do not read the same either when reading about democracy in texts from the nineteenth century and from the twenty-first. But we do not hear the same in utterances on democracy made by different speakers in one and the same conversation that is just minutes long. Therefore, the above statement only dissolves the illusion that there might be any "perennial" meanings, as Skinner called them. This, for me, is an even greater incentive to observe the semantic transformations from the picture window, and simultaneously to agree that a history "in which the major theorists of the past still figure prominently" should lay its emphasis "less on thinkers and theories than on 'thinking' and debates" (Israel 2006: 23).

If the present text does not go much into the details of debates and controversies it is because it prefers to dwell on concepts, most of which have hardly altered their position in the internal semantic economy of western ideology over the last four centuries. That is not to say that other meanings did not become ambiguous or varied. For example, the imaginary complexions of a "barbarous" person may greatly differ in the present from those of the days of Robinson Crusoe. Still, it is a difference that hardly affects the position of the word "barbarian" in the hierarchy of teleological significances, and this is what matters here. Conceptual settings that display a certain stability over a longer period are not "perennial," as we have said. Some four hundred years of western ideology is still not a historically long period. Therefore, the intention behind this book is not to show that important philosophical works of the past are parts of a perennial philosophical debate (Lamb 2009: 51–73). On the contrary, one should be aware that concepts taken from the contemporary conceptual toolbox cannot "fully grasp the specificity of historical doctrines" (Gut 2014: 54). One should also recognize that language "is a dynamic whole" in which meanings do not just change but also "are first stretched, made . . . ambiguous by extended usage itself, and are invested with nuances, overtones, and connotations that they did not have before" (Parekh and Berki 1973: 167). By recalling the changes in the concept of "culture," I have already given one such example. However, there are many concepts that have hardly changed over the whole period of observation, while others changed at early stages of that period, and still others did so only recently.

Why do concepts change at all? Regarding causality, I suggest updating Heraclitus's motto Τα παντα ρει by imagining the historical process in terms of a thermodynamic metaphor. In effect, not unlike thermodynamics, in history unpredictable and irreversible changes occur in a complex and multilayered unstable environment. Chaos theory is not about the beat of an African butterfly's wing that causes rain in China, it is about the fallacy of univocal causal explanations, both at the factual and probabilistic levels regarding the "effective" or "most probable" cause of a single event such as a rain shower or, say, a political revolution, or any other singular phenomenon that we circumscribe in time and space. Whatever explanatory value we attribute to long-standing or short-lived, slow-moving or hurried, marginal or central, phenomena that precede the event—the occurrence that is of interest to us to explain—any logically univocal explanation will produce a misrepresentation of the very mode of change in complex environments. This is why I have suggested elsewhere that the concepts of time and transition elaborated by twentieth-century science could offer us a useful analogue for a non-teleological dialectical understanding of change in history, which might be able to tackle causality and change in a more appropriate way (Petri 1999: 37–68). For that matter, "non-causal explanations of action" (Skinner 2002: 4) are distinctly possible. Yet since our scholarly narrative is conventionally grounded on noncontradictory statements, establishing explanatory relations between cause and effect will not be completely avoided. What matters is that we make transparent both the limited reach of our explanations and the arbitrary character of the logical presuppositions which are necessary to make them work.

The unavoidably arbitrary character of the assumptions on which we ground our explanations is justification enough for a plurality of coexisting approaches and procedures. It legitimates, for example, Skinner's claim for the methodological correctness of an approach that does not pretend to embrace "the entire process of conceptual change" (Skinner 2002: 187). It also sustains Pocock's point that our awareness regarding histories alternative to our own which "can be traced as having actually have happened" should not prevent us from recounting "another history" (Pocock 2003: 562). For the same reason Israel's effort to demonstrate that only one macro-controversy characterizes the political legacy of the Enlightenment in the west deserves full methodological recognition, although critics are probably also right in pointing out that his approach selectively oversimplifies a number of other philosophical controversies and conceptual differences in order to safeguard his own thesis (La Vopa 2009: 717–38).

Similar objections can be raised against this present work, with even more grounds. I am fully aware that the effort to communicate what I see to the reader, that is, the possibility of carving out the enduring core elements of a western ideology in the singular form, and the arduous pretension of synthesizing these elements into a "short history," requires a degree of oversimplification of intellectual controversies that would be indefensible when it comes to the analysis of particular philosophical disputes or political struggles located on a narrower scale of space and time. But since the choice of scale, scope, and sources should be defined by the research problem and not the other way round, I consider my opting to recount "another history" perfectly legitimate.

Admittedly, a sense of incompleteness remains. One may wonder, for example, whether it is admissible not to dwell more on the pre-Christian roots of the republican ideal of civic virtue, instead of underlining the apocalyptic political rhetoric; or not to go into more detail on the controversy among "moderate," "radical," and "counter" Enlightenment thinkers, but rather mix them together although they were engaged in a deadly clash during the French Revolution. Is it acceptable not to spend many words in this book on opposing confessional factions, the fights between democratic movements and reactionary forces, class struggles and the fierce clashes between national movements, and all the other conflicts, which for at least four centuries upset the west-dominated world with bloodshed on a sometimes catastrophic scale? Does it make sense to ignore the variants, differences, and conflicts that have brought about the deaths of countless people? Is it not a lack of respect to their memory to make their ideas, expectations, emotions, and myths converge toward a unique, simplified scheme of ideological commonality among them? I do not deny the importance of variety and differentiation. However, I underline once again that the specific purpose of *this* book is, for once, to prevent the multifaceted landscape of controversies from obstructing the reader's view of western ideology's core constituents. If a loss of differentiation were indeed unsatisfying, I would argue that in a short history of western ideology getting lost in differentiation would be less acceptable still.

Pocock explains why at a certain point in his reflection he abandoned the Kuhnian concept of "paradigm" in favor of "languages." If one single paradigm defines a community, a place "where several paradigms were being rhetorically urged at the same time, and were in debate and interaction with one another," could hardly be conceived as a community. Society happens to evolve "within a multiplicity of problem-situations so great that no one 'paradigm' can long succeed in excluding or occluding its alternatives" (Pocock 2009: xii, 73). In the event that we accept this distinction, I think we should admit that western ideology displays many characteristics of a paradigm. The belief that history has a purpose or meaning did in fact long succeed in excluding or occluding its alternatives. For centuries, an overwhelming number of philosophical, religious, and political controversies revolved around the question of *what* was the end or meaning of human history, and *how* its purpose can be deciphered most appropriately. Not many debates, however, come to mind regarding the possibility that there might be no meaning at all. Not even those who mourn, or protest against, the loss of meaning, have been capable of conceiving of meaninglessness as an acceptable condition.

iv

The lacunae that derive from a similar choice nevertheless remain, and it seems appropriate to mention them in advance. If I suppress the intellectual regret of incompleteness when faced with the task of bundling together such boundless subject matter, it is not only because "recounting another history" is legitimized by epistemological and methodological considerations. I also do so from the necessity of reacting to the crude ideological reality that surrounds us, and which we observe on a daily basis. When you tune into the television news and you hear a political leader talk about "advanced" countries, and a geopolitical pundit suggests armed "humanitarian" intervention, and the sober presenter qualifies a murder as "barbaric," you know that coarse undertones of western ideology truly exist. It is not immediately dismissed as propaganda by the public because the underlying ideology has swamped minds over the centuries thanks to a hypnotic repetition of concepts not necessarily invented, but surely consecrated, by the founding works of western culture.

This state of things, I feel, requires, rather than allows, at least every now and then, an explanation equally coarse and schematic. This is why the following pages positively refer to what has been called Karl Löwith's "rather woodcut history of eschatology and its secularization" (Trüper 2014: 54), and to other texts that carve out the conceptual nucleus of western ideology with clarity. The urge that the conceptual nucleus should not be "differentiated away" comes not only from the desire to make a contribution to the understanding of the present, but also from the perception of political dangers that emanate from eschatological thinking. To be honest, it can hardly be felt without a certain presumption of knowing better, and of opposing the social success of an ideology that "implies that the individuals 'do not know what they are doing.'" (Žižek 2008: 16). The views of Kress and Hodge I referred to affirmatively above in fact also imply, at least indirectly, that a nonideological critique of ideology is difficult to attain. Therefore, I owe the reader some final elucidations regarding the inadequacy of western ideology according to *my own view* of the present world. In order to do so, I propose to return to Huntington.

In the citation at the beginning of this chapter, Huntington highlighted an important aspect of the situation that emerged following the Cold War: that the main lines of conflict up until that moment could be attributed to disputes that were in some way internal to the framework of western "civilization." Gray (2008: 41) even observes that in intellectual terms "the Cold War was a competition between two ideologies, Marxism and Liberalism, which had a great deal in common." This does not mean that the Soviet Union's social and political models, as well as its geopolitical interests, were not in radical opposition to those of the NATO member states. In the field of military and foreign policy, something similar can be said also for Russia's present Eurasian aspirations (Bassin 2008), which stand in the way of the Atlanticist's efforts to gain influence in Central Asia. When the iron curtain was lifted and the land east of it liberalized, an "unspecifiable barrier" (Wolff 2016b: 44) between East and West remained in place. Among other consequences, this imaginary barrier made Bolshevism appear in retrospect like an earlier manifestation of "eastness," which was easy to replace with other targets of criticism and Russophobia.

The stigma of eastern backwardness, however, is a rhetoric device of frequent use *within* the western community of discourse, and the Russian intellectual elites' indignant reaction confirmed their belonging to that community. Over the last centuries, the struggle around the primacy in the representation of some of the western ideological cornerstones, such as "civilization," "modernity," and "progress," spared hardly any place of what commonly is considered "the West." For a long period, for example, the Irish were harassed with de-westernizing adjectives such as "wild" by their eastern neighbors, that is, by the same Englishmen who together with the Russians were excluded from the honors of European belonging by *their* eastern neighbor (Hugo 1845: 229–36). From the general scenario of rhetoric in/exclusions, Russia may stand out for its macroscopic dimension, which undermines the Atlantic-centered idea of "the West" and boosts the visibility of its actual and alleged peculiarities, but it hardly stands out for a lack of eschatological mindset. Whatever "clash" may have taken place between the Atlantic alliance and Russia, according to Huntington's intuition, it could not be defined as one of "civilizations."

His theory may be doubted for other reasons than the inclusion of Russia. The most important is that the very word "civilization" is inadequate to analyze any complex reality or the multiple experiences and conflicts that lie within it. A similar observation can be applied to other very basic terms of world description, such as "culture," which I have already mentioned, or "religion." The latter, for example, despite being a term "thought and conceived of a priori as universal" (Dubuisson 2003: 10), has become one of the major definitions of Us and of the Other. It has eventually come to serve "others" as a representation of their own experience. Following five hundred years of colonial, imperial, economic, and communicative hegemony, the elements of western ideology have become a part of non-western vocabularies and non-western cognitive, descriptive, and analytical tools. It has therefore become increasingly difficult to break free of them, even for those intent on developing an alternative vision, because "every ontology is made unattainable in a colonized and civilized society," as Franz Fanon ([1952] 1986: 109) wrote. As Daniel Dubuisson (2003: 10) argues, a similar risk of deception and self-deception can be attributed to categories through which "we conceive of others, and . . . these others, who are most often subject to our influence, conceive of themselves." It is because of its long-lasting hegemony that the west's hypertrophic consideration of itself has been inflated even further, given that westerners tend to believe their philosophical, religious, and ethical thought to be particularly profound and of unlimited value, whereas the ideas and notions of others are downgraded to "beliefs" or "ideologies." It is commonplace in history for an excess of power to cause blindness. No excess of power, however, can hinder the eventual development of contradictions, tensions, antagonisms, and breaches.

The theory of a "clash of civilizations" is also dubious because, leaving Islam aside, there is to my knowledge no other corpus of ideas with which to clash productively on the same level of universalistic self-confidence. In fact, there is no other that promotes an equally fanatical idea of a universal mission for the Good of humankind. As, for example, Masayuki Sato observes, East Asians "did not posit an omnipotent deity, as seen in revelatory religions." Consequently, they refuted teleological representations of history because "the dramatization or fictionalization of the past would have amounted to a repudiation of their fundamental philosophy" (Sato 2007: 228–9). In a world seen "as an ever changing phenomenon," the absolute and the supreme, according to this philosophy, was not in the revelation of an eschatological purpose for the future. It was instead located only in the past, insofar as "human beings could not alter that which had already happened" (Sato 2015: 48). To an unprejudiced observer these may seem pragmatic and plausible, even easily understandable, conclusions. Not so for many western intellectuals, for whom the absence of transcendent purpose, or the "lacking" aim as Nietzsche put it, is a matter of profound concern. Whether a "nihilistic interpretation" of the Buddhist concept of *śūnyatā* is viable (Jackson 1993: 57–60), and whether the "nihilistic despair over the human condition" (Heisig 2001: 191) that unavoidably derives from it can be healed by a syncretic blend of Buddhist principles and Heidegger's philosophy, are among the fields of ongoing passionate reflection and enquiry.

Meanwhile, western elites driven by Mackinderian nightmares are working hard, and more profanely, on the geopolitical frontline to reinforce their position and obtain China's strategic containment and encirclement. Functional to this effort would be a stronger negative characterization of that country, but things appear not to work out so easily. If western media and political elites once again downgrade Russia to its centuries-old role of the despotic aggressor (Mettan 2015; Hofbauer 2016), in the case of China they seem to suffer from the difficulty to make out a "system of antithetical categories or principles" (Dubuisson 2003: 105) that would fit with their interpretative schemes, for which reason they sense a rising "ambiguity over Beijing's long-term plans" (Johnson 2014: 66). The growth of a power into a size of worldwide relevance that "lacks" an analogous missionary agenda is nothing that they could easily cope with. Unfortunately, for the west, in that increasingly important Asian part of the world, which resisted the influence of monotheistic religion and enlightened philosophy more successfully than other areas, there is no universalistic eschatology to compete with. This creates interpretative embarrassment. It may one day even represent a major ideological threat to the western worldview.

Perhaps it is not accidental that the west, in order to find an enemy worthy of the term in the collective imagination, chose "extremist Islamism"—as familiar and as close to its own ideological horizon as communism was, although in a different direction. As Subrahmanyam observes, it is historically difficult to make out clearly distinguishable eschatological patterns outside the range of influence of the three Abrahamic religions and the Zoroastrian one, with the exception perhaps of certain strands in Hindu belief regarding the "controversial figure of Kalki." Little doubt seems to exist, however, regarding the similarities between the two principal monotheistic religions' areas of influence. They even appear to display a certain simultaneity if we consider, for example, that "political eschatology took a powerful and significant form in the Islamic world in the sixteenth century" (Subrahmanyam 2015: 31, 34). Faisal Devji (2015: 302) highlights also the universalistic "claim to mankind itself as an ideal" put forward by political Islam since the nineteenth century. To the scores of examples quoted by Devji we might add Sayyid Qutb ([1964] 2005: 2), who underlined that the universal message of Islam should be "a guide for all the inhabitants of this planet in all their affairs until the end of time." Besides the differences and similarities in the theological and philosophical foundations, which deserve profound consideration in their own right, it is difficult not to notice that the very presence of an eschatological and universalistic worldview nurtures expectations of historical fulfillment. As Gray (2008: 99) argues, "Christianity and Islam are integral parts of western monotheism, and as such they share a view of history that marks them off from the rest of the world." Under similar premises, the battle between Good and Evil seems to be destined to drag on for quite a while, perhaps allowing western ideology to be strengthened again by that conflict, and permitting it to legitimize preparations on land, sea, sky, and even in space, for Armageddon.

The conflict between members of the Abrahamic family may eventually stabilize it once again in the political arena, just as the Cold War confrontation with the Soviet Union, another insubordinate family member, functioned as an ideological cement of Western Europe and America, and reinforced the traditionally Atlantic-centered imaginative geography of "the West." For western ideology as such, the true hidden danger is most probably another. It may one day come from a world in which political, economic, and military power is distributed equally enough to impose an authentically plural scenario made up of multiple visions of humans, and their rights and responsibilities; multiple meanings attributed to Good and Evil; a variety of models of polity and statehood; effectively impartial international institutions, rather than executors only of dominant ideas; and hopefully impartial, consensual, and nonviolent mediations and methods of conflict regulation. In summary, it is a scenario that comprises the reciprocal recognition of the other's truth as a legitimate statement, and a conception "of what constitutes us" that relies not on a "unity of differences" but on differences that are allowed to be different (Marramao 2012: 197). Would it represent a catastrophe for our species to live in a world in which the pretension that the "universal values" of the west must be imposed on the universe as the lowest common denominator has to be abandoned? I am not ready to believe it, but readers should make their own judgment.

1

Europe and history

there will be a new generation and consequently the possibility of attaining the aim in the next generation. If the next one does not attain it, then the next after that may, and so on, till the aim is attained, the prophecies fulfilled, and mankind attains unity.

LEV TOLSTOY,
THE KREUTZER SONATA (1889)

For a good part of the past as investigated by archeologists and historians, the name of Europe held no meaning for the people who happened to live in and travel the lands and waters stretching from the strait of Gibraltar to the forests of Karelia, from the shores of the Aegean to the geysers of Iceland. It is also true that the ancient Greek *poleis* already had an idea of Europe, the spatial vagueness, mythical origin, and political uses of which made it similar to ours. We should emphasize, however, that ancient "Europe" was geographically different from the Europe of today. We should also highlight that there was no continuity in its political uses. In the transition to the Middle Ages, "Europe" was pillaged of its symbolic value and reduced to a vague geographical expression, the northern and northeastern extensions of which remained nebulous. Following the Carolingian era the word disappeared almost completely from documents. Its political recuperation came about around halfway through the fifteenth century, whereas a loose agreement between geographers on where to draw the eastern boundaries of the pseudo continent was only made possible during the eighteenth century, even if some of its aspects continued to be a matter of debate up until recent years.

The revitalization of the concept of Europe did not come about during the golden years of the Renaissance humanism by chance. Through its reinterpretation, the term "Europe" was recovered on behalf of a revisited conception of culture and politics, similarly to what happened to other elements of the philosophical, scientific, and cultural heritage of ancient Greece. It should therefore not be too surprising if, for example, certain metaphorical virtues of the European Us already present among the ancient Greeks were to be reactivated, such as the conflict between Asia and Europe being metaphorically intended as a dispute between despotism and freedom. However, a deceiving sense of millennial continuity was then grafted onto the revitalization, and onto the adjustment to the new needs of what was in fact a reinvented tradition.

What was the restoration of Europe all about? Similar to modern Europe, ancient Europe was a container of multiple meanings and attributes that were partially contradictory, yet variable and reciprocally intertwined. Ancient Europe was in many ways evasive in terms of geographical boundaries and spiritual contents but like our current Europe the ancient version also seemed to draw from its evasiveness a remarkable strength of attraction within the realm of the political. Not so different from the impotence of today's criticism of the European myths—whereby, like the critique developed in these pages—in Antiquity little to nothing was able to oppose the communicative strength of symbols. Not even the historical–critical objections of Herodotus had much success:

> As for Europe, no one can say whether it is surrounded by the sea or not, neither is it known whence the name of Europe was derived, nor who gave it name, unless we say that Europe was so called after the Tyrian Europe, and before her time was nameless, like the other divisions. But it is certain that Europe was an Asiatic, and never even set foot on the land which the Greeks now call Europe, only sailing from Phoenicia to Crete, and from Crete to Lycia. (Herodotus [~ 450 BC] 1942: 496)

It seems that, under the geographic definition, continental Greece was initially identified with Europe, and it was only over time that the concept and its opposites widened geographically, entering into the emerging conflict between Greece and Persia. Ultimately, it seems the name Europe included the world of Greek language and culture on the northern shores of the Mediterranean, except for Asia Minor. The bordering barbaric lands were also in some way included, in fact sometimes so as to distinguish the "true" Greece from Europe. "My intent is to throw a bridge over the Hellespont and march an army through Europe against Greece," Herodotus ([~ 450 BC] 1942: 308) made Xerxes say. It may also be a recurring topic—perhaps because it is unavoidable in every collective identification process—in the identification of modern Europe: the Us, which at times is at the same time the Them.

It is more than likely that representations of tragedies, epics, and historical narrations of war with the Persians contributed to the handing down of the vision of Europe as opposed to Asia. The Greek conceptions of Asia, of the East, and of the Persian Empire alternated between admiration and rivalry, and between a sense of affiliation and of unfamiliarity. At times they were seen on an equal level, at times the other was inferior, and at others, superior. During the Persian wars, and with the aid of their poetic representations, this overall tipsy and contradictory attribute would be reorganized in the way of a clear and irreducible conflict. Europe versus Asia now meant almost exclusively civility and freedom against rudeness and despotic rule (Barcellona 2001: 146).

Poetic representations placed Europe where the sun sets, that is, in the west or in the Occident. This interpretation receives some support from etymological speculations that trace the contrast between Europe and Asia not to Greek mythology but to the semantics of Akkadian. Hence, Europe may derive from *erebu* for the dimming of the sun in the west, Asia from *asu* for the rising of the sun in the east. A critique similar to Herodotus' would here apply, as it is only from the east that *others* can see the sun set where *we* live and say to us, "you are the Westerners." Therefore, whether the primary source of the spatial metaphor is mythology, poetry, or etymology, "Europe" apparently cannot escape the dynamics which generally distinguish the phenomena that are today expressed by the term "identity," and which necessitate incorporating the other's gaze in order to define the self (Remotti 1996: 63; Graumann 1999: 63–67). In all cases, however, the other, compared with Europe, was identified with a threatening and despotic East, which at the same time was also the place of ancient origins, the destinies of which remained indissolubly entwined with those of Europe. Today, as back then, the East—or Asia, or the Levant, or the Orient, or however we want to call it—is indispensable for European or western self-identification. As Said (1978: 1–2) pointed out, "the Orient has helped to define Europe (or the West) as its contrasting image, idea, personality, experience." The apparent endurance of the East–West opposition seems to be owing to the fact that neither of the two juxtaposed concepts has ever signified a well-defined geographical historical object independent from fantasy, and thus neither could ever be scrutinized with objective certainty. Hence the Europe of today, despite being spatially dislocated elsewhere, can view itself to be in some ways close to the "classical" version. It is not for this reason, however, that it is impossible to sketch a tradition that hails from ancient times to today without succumbing to mystification. It is impossible because modern Europe, beyond the similarities outlined here, was not at all reborn equal to the ancient version. If ancient Europe was particularistic, succumbing to the universalism of empires and monotheistic religion, modern Europe has instead become a symbol of missionary universalism.

1.1 *Christianitas*

The breach occurred indeed in the most radical of ways: an oriental import in the way of a monotheist religion which took hold in the Roman Empire, infiltrating it so thoroughly as to eventually become its state religion. The arena in which European rhetoric was to become politically worthless, however, had in fact been prepared for some time through the "universal" ambitions of Alexander the Great and the pagan Roman Empire itself, in as much as the concept of Europe gave meager ideological support for expansion and the integration of new peoples coming under its control. It is likely that it was because of this increasing symbolic political futility that Europe found itself downgraded to a vague geographic indication (Cortelazzo 1988: 50). The pairing of Europe and the Middle Ages, which is today in vogue in exhibitions and tourist itineraries, therefore appears to be a mystifying representation which lacks documentary support. If Arab and Lusitanian sources spoke of "European armies" during the times of Charles Martel, they were more than likely referencing the geographical specification in order to mark the presence of groups other than Christians among the enemy ranks (Mikkeli 1998: 17–20). Only Charlemagne in fact vindicated a more political conception of Europe. Significantly, however, he needed to refer to geography in order to prefigure his power to be less spiritual and rather territorial. Europe, therefore, was not a land superposed to Christianity for him either, and neither was it linked with the Christian mission to spread the word of God. In Michael Wintle's (2009: 155) words, the Carolingian effort signed "the end of an era in the ideology of Europe, rather than the launch of a new one." Later, "Europe" seems to have almost disappeared from the documents, with a few exceptions. Since the twelfth century, rare sources refer Europe to "religion and saintliness" and describe it as Christianity's "last refuge" (Oschema 2017: 12). On the whole, however, medieval historians appear to agree on the rarity of coming across this term in sources of the period, if not occasionally, whereas to point out the frequent use of *Christianitas* and other similar concepts is not difficult at all.

> It was precisely in this environment in which the Europe of the High Middle Ages might have been able to perceive of itself and in which it was already acting more or less as a single unity, that it had no role at all, if not perhaps an all but marginal one. This applies to all of the Crusades, the Europeanization of western science and the universal expectations of the Church and the Empire. The fact that Arab sources did not refer to "Europeans," but instead spoke of "Franks" is further evidence. (Schneidmüller 1997: 11)

The centrality of *Christianitas* also borrowed from the Augustinian vision, which was prevalent for a long time, according to which Christianity could only establish itself within a universal perspective that was entirely separate from any territorial constraints. Indeed, the idea of *fines Christianitatis* found agonizing theological acceptance no earlier than the eleventh century (Mikkeli 1998: 22–23). It would have of course been idealistic to think that for a mere theological prescription the image of *Christianitas* would have been all but cut off entirely from any spatial representation. In some way, demarcations between Christianity and anything that was non-Christian inevitably already existed, even geographically. Most, however, did not initially have anything to do with a "Eurocentric" concept. If the Islamic West, or the Maghreb—much more western than most of Europe—is to be indexed under "Orient," then this type of metaphorical coding of geographical spaces was the result of a slow and more recent process. Moreover, even after the Arab conquests, multitudes of Christians from various liturgies and denominations lived in areas from northern to eastern Africa, Asia Minor, the Levant, Mesopotamia, and the Caucasus, often among populations that had converted to Islam. Vice versa, the geographic location of the Other or the unbeliever could also be the north, pagan and nonetheless "European" (Borgolte 2001: 13–27).

In Christian and Muslim nautical maps the south, or "midday," the solar zenith, was generally represented at the top, and the night of the north at the bottom. The stylized and symbolic cartography of the Middle Ages, however, retained the late ancient three-way partitioning of the *orbis terrarum*. Indeed, the circle of the O was divided by a T, interpretable as the symbol for the cross of Christ. The largest chunk, Asia, was at the top while the other two smaller areas, Europe and Africa, were underneath to the left and the right, respectively. These three continents were thought to be divided by the Mediterranean Sea and the waters of the Nile and the Don. Rome was inscribed in some of these representations, in others it was not. Jerusalem, which was clearly placed on the Asian coast at the top of the Mediterranean, and slightly higher than the geometric center, was, however, assigned great prominence (Nagel 1994: 9–20, 73–96; Sammet 1990: 74–139). Even in the world maps of the twelfth and thirteenth centuries, halfway between religious symbolic stylization and topographical representation, the center was not fixed at Rome, or in the lower left quadrant in Europe, but in Asia, centered on Jerusalem, which was envisaged as being the sacred heart of the world. *Christianitas* therefore was positioned around the Middle Sea, centered on the Holy Land, pushing out toward Asia (Milanesi 1988: 13–46).

The tensions between the Roman papacy and Constantinople, and then the religious schisms, would also weaken a unitary and geographically solid vision of *Christianitas*. The Roman Empire, as perceived by the followers of the bishops of Rome, ended in 476. In fact, it finally succumbed only a thousand years later at the hand of the Turks. Militarily speaking, the Ottoman conquest of Constantinople was more than anything a matter of the formalization of a long secular agony. Nonetheless, no earlier than half a century before its end, the ancient capital of Constantine's patriarch—by now almost stripped bare of dominium, but still entrapped in the illusion of representing the center of Christianity—proudly declined to pass the universal representation of Christian and Roman values on to Moscow, an Orthodox power which had emerged following victory over the Tartars. Due to its symbolic value and the apparent end to Christian polycentrism—if viewed from Rome—the fall of Constantinople in 1453 was one of the main catalysts for the birth of modern Europe, as was colonialism on the other side, including the later discovery of the American continent.

On first approximation, the rebirth of Europe was therefore also a political and psychological consequence of the Islamic and Turkish threat, at least as much it was perceived as such, given that "at other times, almost all the Christian princes, under the pretense of a holy war, entered into a league to invade this metropolis and bulwark of Christendom; and now when it was attacked by the Turks, not one of them appeared to defend it," as Voltaire (1759b: 238) criticized. The fall of the "bastion of Christianity" in Latin western eyes in some ways Europeanized a posteriori the "Byzantine" Empire, at least partially overcoming the previous pejorative vision of the *Rhomaioi*, which over time had even become difficult to include in the western idea of *Christianitas*, increasingly centered around the papal throne of Rome. However, the "Levantine" image of the late Roman Empire was probably only established later, particularly in the eighteenth century, likely due also to the profound impact of Gibbon's *The History of the Decline and Fall of the Roman Empire* (Runciman 1976: 103–07; Jordan 1969: 71–96). It was because of such purported diversity that the Latin–Catholic West believed it was the only legitimate heir to the classical tradition achieved by ancient Greece. It was the heritage of *that* Greece, and not the Christian Empire, to which Voltaire (1759b: 247) referred (even moderating his prejudice against Byzantines and Ottomans) when he wrote that under the Turks "the country of the Miltiades's, the Leonidas's, the Alexanders's, the Sophocles's, and the Plato's, soon relapsed into barbarism."

Christianity and Europe were therefore not congruent at all in the medieval imagination. The term "Europe" was almost completely out of use, and had lost the mythical and ideological connotations that had distinguished it in the Greece of the *poleis*. During the early Italian Renaissance, which was a period of return to the ancient sources, "the myth of Europe and the Bull became more popular than it had been for nearly a millennium" in figurative representations (Wintle 2009: 109). However, Europe was fully restored as a political program only in the fifteenth century (Vogler 1997: 293), not by marginal thinkers but by powerful men from the Catholic Church, such as Nicholas of Cusa and Enea Silvio de' Piccolomini, the latter enthroned as Pope Pius II in 1458, five years after the fall of Constantinople. It almost seems as if the dispute over the Ottoman advance in the Mediterranean and the Balkans required a new and different projection over the Orient to be translated into a defense of Christianity. But why was it necessary to mobilize and gather the great Christian kingdoms of the west under the banner of Europe? Why, after so many centuries of coexistence and conflict with followers of Islam, could that unity no longer be completely encapsulated in the symbol of the cross?

There were numerous reasons. The unity of the Catholic world was now being evoked within a very different context from the Hun invasions in the fifth century, or the period of Arab expansion in the Mediterranean and what we now call the Middle East. Something had also significantly changed with respect to the more recent era of the Crusades. New secular and territorial powers had emerged and, in addition to being more attracted by the Atlantic, they were also becoming increasingly autonomous of the Church because of their increasing resources. Equally, new centers of knowledge were emerging beyond the walls of the monasteries, and gradually surpassed the realm of Christian dogma. Humanism and the new sciences were emerging, and the colonial discoveries became a source of wonder and encounter with an unexpected exotic reality. Religious apprehensions hoping for *renovatio* were permeating Catholic Christianity. All of this was apparently in need of a broader and more ecumenical definition while at the same time being more "worldly," less religiously fervent, and more explicitly aligned with interests of power, before being functional to an anti-Ottoman alliance that would be able to resist the assault. This alliance, although inherently unstable, would be upheld by thinkers such as Nicolò Machiavelli and Torquato Tasso in the following century, and would symbolically culminate in the naval battle of Lepanto in 1571. Religious causes were of course also needed to meet the challenge, although politically they had become increasingly prickly with the post-Reformation wars. An expression such as "Europe" could mean that, despite everything, and beyond interconfessional hatred, a unity should be sought to face external threats. Such unity, however, was never reached, not even in approaches toward the "infidels."

It is important to underline that the restoration of a classical and pre-Christian concept—such as was that of Europe—was in line with the humanist taste of the period. Despite that restoration, in the Quattrocento an attempt at drafting up a type of "secularized" Europe had not yet been prefigured. The leaders who relaunched "Europe" were conspicuous exponents of the Catholic Church. Their reprisal of a "forgotten" concept can be interpreted as an attempt to provide an updated Latin and Catholic geography. As Franco Cardini (1997: 11) stated, it was in this precise set of circumstances that a Christian Europe emerged. The narrative in terms of a Christian Medieval Europe would only be coined later, "beginning from the fall of the western empire, the independent power of the Roman Church, and the settlement of the barbarian kingdoms, and continuing through a history 'as well ecclesiastical as civil' to the end of the Latin Middle Ages" (Pocock 2007: 44).

As I have already pointed out, it was not at all insignificant that, other than already being slightly Nordic and Atlantic, and not only Greek–Latin and Mediterranean, modern Europe was to be reborn Christian: during its second life, in fact, Europe did not reemerge so as to simply re-invoke the ancient metaphor between West and East. In being reborn Christian, it received an unprecedented missionary, historical, and eschatological investiture from the hands of its masterminds, which had been unknown to ancient Europe. Where did this mission stem from? We read in Saint Paul's first Epistle to the Romans (Rom. 1:13–16):

> I want you to know, brothers and sisters, that I have often intended to come to you (but thus far have been prevented), in order that I may reap some harvest among you as I have among the rest of the Gentiles. I am a debtor both to Greeks and to barbarians, both to the wise and to the foolish—hence my eagerness to proclaim the gospel to you also who are in Rome. For I am not ashamed of the gospel; it is the power of God for salvation to everyone who has faith, to the Jew first and also to the Greek.

The great news was that the divine power of salvation was extended to literally everyone. "Never before had a man thought of expounding a wisdom, a conception of the world, beyond his country and his people, and also of converting all humanity to a new mode of life and thought by going forth to meet them" (Dubuisson 2003: 104). Saint Paul's decision to evangelize the heathen and go to the center of the pagan empire had far-reaching consequences: "Without doubt this decision, which inaugurated what in its further propagation would be transformed into a veritable world conquest, must be seen as one of the founding acts of the West, one of those of which we can say with certainty that it influenced the fate of humanity" (Dubuisson 2003: 103).

In being reborn Christian, the Europe of a millennium and a half later indissolubly linked its name to this arduous missionary consignment. The European universalism that ensued, in addition to being spiritually grounded, would produce many further implications. "The step from a universalist goal to the spirit of conquest is probably no longer than that which leads from doctrinal rigor to intolerance. Thus we see in the West these dogmatic, conquest-oriented tendencies taking form both on the intellectual level and on the institutional level, in a Church whose power and hegemony they reinforced" (Dubuisson 2003: 104). The colonial conquest was understood and experienced, at least initially, by the powerful western—in particular the Iberian—maritime kingdoms of the fifteenth and sixteenth centuries as a Christian mission. No distinction was made between business and spreading the word of God, as perhaps would be required by retrospective moralist criticism, given that on both fronts the church was particularly active—as shown, for example, by its fervent economic and religious activities that brought about the destruction of Goa's Hindu and Buddhist shrines in its fight against "idolatry" (Magalhaes Godinho 2001: 55–56). Nevertheless, as religious conversion extorted with the persuasive power of the sword does have its limits, the control over non-Christian populations required additional legitimization that transcended the raw violence of armed enforcement. To western eyes the new banner of Europe—Christian, universal, and bringing messages of love—seemed to be the most suitable solution for luring that barbaric and multicolored humanity into waking up from their lethargy.

1.2 Civilize or make disappear

During the sixteenth and seventeenth centuries, extra-religious elements of distinction started to permeate and eventually dominate colonial discourses and practices. These mostly concerned techniques, the sciences, commerce, finance, political systems, and good governance, all fields in which the Europeans were claiming to provide a model. Although the *forma mentis* was preformed by religion on the whole, it was only through these extra-religious practices that during the eighteenth century the Christian universalism linked to the name of Europe definitely merged with other claims and arguments for European superiority. It was a superiority that was experienced and interpreted not so much as a privilege but as a burden. The Europeans felt themselves to be charged with the dissemination of the "universal" values they had acquired through their worldly experience over the ages of history. In the eighteenth century, this missionary vision would go on to meet with the neologism of "civilization," and later also with other expressions.

One of the most tangible signs of this evolution was the rotation of the medieval world maps by the seventeenth century. They now placed Asia on the right, Europe at the top, and Africa in an inferior position. As mentioned above, in previous symbolic maps north was usually located on the left, whereas Jerusalem dominated the center of the world. The sacred city had now slipped into an almost peripheral position, while it was Europe that dominated the center. But which Europe? Scientific surveying of the geographical outline of Europe can be considered to have concluded around 1600 when Willem

Barents returned from his exploration along the coasts of the northern seas. This did not, however, mean that the mental representation of Europe coincided with the current mapping. Some of the charts created continued to exclude not only the Tartar lands, but also the Scandinavian Peninsula. In the meantime, the science of cartography had made great progress, urged on in the interests of power. When Moscow demanded to be recognized as the Third Rome following the fall of Constantinople, maps that showed the enormous extension of the grand duchy were submitted to the pope. Especially during the long and harrowing Thirty Years War, which ended in 1648 with the Peace of Westphalia, geographical maps were transformed into a sort of identification card for the main powers not only as a representational and contractual object, but also as a practical tool for bordering and for exercising sovereign power over the territory. For fear of being marginalized by the policies of the European powers, the Polish and the Swedish rulers produced detailed geographical maps which documented their membership of Europe, enabling them to lay claim to sovereignty over their land at the same time.

In its projection abroad toward the world outside during the seventeenth and eighteenth centuries, however, European rhetoric remained dominated by the Christian Europe. Jan Amos Komenský wrote in 1645 that the supreme purpose of Europe was to announce Christ to all populations and thus "the light must be taken to other peoples in the name of our fatherland of Europe" (quoted from Perkins 2004: 79). At the height of the century of Enlightenment, for Giambattista Vico ([1744] 1816: 141) also, Europe was to posit itself to the world united behind the flag of Christian religion "since also for human purposes the Christian one is the best of all religions in the world, because it unites commanded wisdom with reasoned knowledge." We do not need to recall here that for Kant and other philosophers reason also finds its place and its transcendent meaning in the soul inspired by God. The transition to a fully secularized, perhaps even atheist, concept of "Europe" remained hesitant, even more so than the philosophical innovations for which the Enlightenment era was renowned would have us suppose. According to what Lucien Febvre ([1945] 1999: 206) would tell his students during lessons on *L'Europe, genèse d'une civilisation* at the Collège de France in 1944–45, the middle of the eighteenth century was "the moment in which the French commonly started to utter humanity, where an old word that was no longer spoken said Christianity." The same author needed nonetheless to admit the importance of the religious cause in the genesis of the concept of "European civilization." In the words of Voltaire ([1751] 1779: 7):

> Christian Europe, all except Russia, might for a long time have been considered as a sort of great Republic, divided into several States, some monarchical, others mixt. Of the latter, some were aristocratical, and

others popular; but all connected with one another; all professing the same system of religion, though divided into several sects; all acknowledging the same principles of public justice and policies, unknown to the other nations of the world.

Febvre ([1945] 1999: 203) commented: "It is a curious passage, in which Voltaire does not omit religion, 'the same system of religion' (which is not, however, referred to by its name). But he passes quickly over it." In fact, the passage can appear to be less of a single instance if we consider that other coeval thinkers believed that Europe—differently from Asia or Africa—was not an abstract geographical grouping of populations, but a society which was truly united by religion and "reason," as well as by common customs, habits, and laws: "Except for the Turks, an associative relationship exists between all European populations, which is imperfect, but tighter than the loose generic bonds of humanity" (Rousseau 1761: 55–56).

For Rousseau, Europe was held together in some way by its underlying ideas, despite manifesting a plurality of Christian denominations and other agonizing situations and circumstances. For the same reason he considered it a society which could still be perfected, but which was already differentiated—"complex" would be used today—while the rest of humanity lay idle in magmatic vagueness. This same point of view was shared by two representatives of the Scottish Enlightenment, David Hume in *On the Original Contract* of 1748, and Adam Ferguson in *Essay on the History of Civil Society* of 1767. Human advancement for them, and in some ways also for Montesquieu, meant not so much an informed pact as, above all, the acquisition of customs, virtues, and behaviors diffused among individuals of a society, which could then, on the basis of this *esprit général*, edify a "rational" form of government.

As long ago as the fifteenth century the word *civilité* was being used to define honesty, courtesy, and polite manners, or urban behaviors rather than boorish ones, as well as respect for the rules and laws of the *civilitas*. Contrasting expressions such as "uncivilized" later emerged, and the opposites "civility" and "barbarity" can be traced back to the sixteenth century. In the early seventeenth century, a western traveler to the former Greek lands of the Ottoman Levant could observe the "deplored spectacles of extreme miserie [sic]; the wild beasts of mankind having broken in upon them [the Greeks], and rooted out all civilitie" (Sandys 1621: Preface). In *Robinson Crusoe* by Defoe ([1719] 2010: 167, 181), some of the laconic subtitles embrace the essential points of the program: "Discover five Canoes of Savages on Shore . . . Observe two taken to be eaten . . . I save the life of one . . . Christen him Friday, and make him my Servant . . . I civilise Friday . . . Begins to talk English . . . I instruct him in Religion." According to Pietro Rossi (1991: 794), however, "weighing on *civilité* was an affinity with *politesse*, the primary reference to exterior behavior and the manners of a refined society. In order to express the new idea a new word was needed, even if it was an old concept; what was needed was a neologism. And this was found in *civilisation*." Although the verb "to civilize" had been used for some time, the noun "civilization" seems to date back not earlier than the central decades of the eighteenth century, for instance, in the abovementioned work of Ferguson ([1767] 1773: 2), who stated, "Not only the individual advances from infancy to manhood, but the species itself from rudeness to civilization."

The term "Europe" also stands for "reasonable" forms of government, justice, culture, and science instead of injustice, instinct, and ignorance. William Eton, a British expert on Ottoman affairs, with regard to conquering, stated that "happily for modern ages it has generally, in Europe, given place to political equality; but Turkey is the refuge of fanatical ignorance, the chosen feat where she has unfurled her bloody banner, and where, though torpid with age, she still grasps her iron scepter" (Eton 1799: 12). Between the seventeenth and eighteenth centuries in Western Europe and the Mediterranean, "the Ottoman empire inspired a balance of fear, interest, curiosity, titillation, entertainment, and even sympathy" (Wolff 2016a: 2). "The Turks" represented a particularly gratifying projection surface; notwithstanding them, there were also the Tartars, the Arabs, the Greeks, the Morlachs, the Irish, and other "barbarians" and "savages" for pointing out—with an ambiguous mixture of disgust and attraction—the differences between civilized Europe and the immediate despotic, cruel, inhumane, impulsive, lascivious, poor, indolent, or savage, surroundings.

The geographers of the Enlightenment nonetheless tried to separate cartography from the grave preconceptions of its imagination, in seeking "natural" and objective, safer, criteria for defining the outer borders of Europe. These were to be found along the Urals, in the mountain chain and the homonymous river, which from north to south almost entirely "closed" (at least with some imagination) the plains to the east. Other geographers observed at the time that if "continent" was to have a logically consistent meaning, there could be no geographical reason that would divide the Eurasian landmass in two. Instead, the mental map of the Europeans prevailed over the homogeneity of the Eurasian landmass, since—thanks to "civilization"— the Europeans considered themselves antithetical to what the word Asia represented to them.

As far as the transoceanic projection of Europe was concerned, the criticisms of the colonial regime, such as that raised by Condorcet, were aimed at reforming rather than overcoming it. Withdrawal from the colonies would in fact have appeared to be irresponsible since it would have thrown the indigenous people back into a perpetual state of backwardness, hibernation, obscurantism, and barbarianism. It was therefore necessary to remain, for humanitarian reasons prescribed by the European mission, in order to export human progress.

> Can it be supposed that either the wisdom or the senseless feuds of European nations, co-operating with the slow but certain effects of the progress of their colonies, will not shortly produce the independence of the entire new world; and that then, European population, lending its aid, will fail to civilize or cause to disappear, even without conquest, those savage nations still occupying there immense tracts of country? (Condorcet 1796: 253–54)

"Civilize" or "make disappear" that which you cannot change: this is Europe's mission in the colonies of the New World, in the mind of the most prominent philosopher of human progress. According to Condorcet (1796: 255), following the revolution in Europe, reasonable governments would also deprive other colonies of the avid merchants and governors installed by the *ancien régime*, as well as of the influence of monks who inculcated the most shameful superstitions in the natives; "and those settlements of robbers will then become colonies of citizens, by whom will be planted in Africa and Asia the principles and example of the freedom, reason, and illumination of Europe." According to Voltaire (1761: 149), that aspect of western character which most resembled the oriental was

> propensity to war, slaughter, and destruction, which has always depopulated the face of the earth. It must be owned, however, that this rage has taken much less possession of the minds of the people of India and China, than of ours. In particular, we have no instance of the Indians or Chinese having made war upon the inhabitants of the North. In this respect, they are much better members of society than ourselves; but then, on the other hand, this very virtue, or rather meekness, of theirs, has been their ruin; for they have all been enslaved.

While not necessarily being virtuous, according to Gibbon ([1776–89] 1907: 292), Europe had much to take care of in the way of menaces to its primacy and superiority: "The savage nations of the globe are the common enemies of civilised society; and we may inquire with anxious curiosity, whether Europe is still threatened with a repetition of those calamities which formerly oppressed the arms and institutions of Rome." This question reveals one of the reasons that Gibbon's work met with such great success: his work retrospectively "Europeanized" the Roman Empire in order to explain the gap between progress and backwardness in his present as a long-term effect of the fatal Roman decline. From this narrative construct, he arrived at a kind of justification of the anxieties in his present and a warning for the future. Indeed, for Gibbon the happiness of European progress was threatened. "If a savage conqueror should issue from the deserts of Tartary, he must repeatedly vanquish the robust peasants of Russia, the numerous armies of Germany, the gallant nobles of France, and the intrepid freemen of Britain; who, perhaps, might confederate for their common defence." But Europe—which ultimately was a mission, an idea, and as such geographically mobile—had already found refuge: "Should the victorious Barbarians carry slavery and desolation as far as the Atlantic Ocean, ten thousand vessels would transport beyond their pursuit the remains of civilised society; and Europe would revive and flourish in the American world, which is already filled with her colonies and institutions" (Gibbon [1776–89] 1907: 294–95).

Looking back from the twenty-first century, we may say that in the eighteenth century the production of endlessly varying spatial metaphors alongside the progress–backwardness divide was only just beginning. We can nevertheless provide evidence to show how the spatial and semantic contours of a modern western ideology were already well defined in that century. Most, if not all, of the metaphors invented during the following two centuries would follow the same basic rule that Edward Said has pointed out for the "Orient": it was not "an unlimited extension beyond the familiar European world, but rather a closed field, a theatrical stage affixed to Europe" (Said 1978: 63). The imagined geography of a "continent" that was not even a continent offered a platform for the affirmation of European superiority and the civilizing mission of Europe. It exalted the uncertain European boundary toward the Orient in the Russian regions, and the contrast with the Ottoman Empire, which was characterized as obscurantist and tyrannical. It classified native populations in the colonies as savage. Finally, yet importantly, it invested utopian hope in the American "New World" where European settlers were already freeing themselves from the despotic dominium of dynastic rule and could legitimately aspire to become the avant-garde of a historical universal mission.

1.3 Philosophies of history

It was in this same European intellectual environment that from the second half of the eighteenth century "the concept of 'history pure and simple' laid the foundation for a historical philosophy, within which the transcendental meaning of history as space of consciousness became contaminated with history as space of action" (Koselleck 2004: 93). Historical consciousness no longer meant awareness of the will of God, but of human capacity and duty to intervene in history in order to determine its progress. According to

Reinhard Koselleck, this invalidated and eventually annulled the transcendental meaning of the concept of history. During this same transitional period, which the German historian calls *Sattelzeit*, a process of a new type started: modernization. According to Giacomo Marramao, this new process moves within "the continuum of Western rationalism, to the progressive rationalization of means." It was the completion of a process that had begun with the discovery of America, the passage west, as Alexander von Humboldt had written, and which under the conditions of globalization is destined to become a "*passage to the Occident* of all cultures. That is, a passage to modernity destined to produce profound transformations in the economy, society, lifestyles and codes of behavior not only of 'other' civilizations but of Western civilization itself" (Marramao 2012: 15, 123). According to Michael Lang (2011: 754), however, this process does not de-westernize western universalism. Since "every concept of 'progress' implies a universal history," he maintains that modernization theory is also a variant, or at least a legitimate heir, of earlier western philosophies of history.

It is clearly impossible to account adequately for the various philosophies of history within these pages, neither is it possible to cover the remarkable differences that distinguished one from the other. In providing a summary of western ideology, it is just as impossible to neglect their fundamental contribution without resorting to necessary generalizations—such as that advanced by Koselleck when he observes the transition to a concept of history no longer based on divine providence. With this in mind, we can ask whether replacing God with Man was truly enough to substitute transcendence with immanence.

Eighteenth-century philosophies sought to develop an overall view of history, articulating the course of humankind in a variable number of past and future phases. All started with an idea of prehistory, or a "state of nature," in order to give indications as to the character acquired by humankind in the separation from its animal origin, revealing a purpose of humans' actions in history. They referred to philosophical considerations, which had emerged in the two or three previous centuries regarding "God," "Nature," and "Man." Simplified greatly, in discussing the concept of "nature," for example, Francis Bacon, Galileo Galilei, René Descartes, Gottfried Wilhelm von Leibniz, and Isaac Newton depicted a world created by God, which was governed by mechanical and mathematical laws with so much perfection as to be able to function alone. In this kingdom of nature only humans were an exception in as much as, thanks to reason and the faculty of doubt bestowed on them, their understanding of such laws was not precluded. Advocated in the seventeenth century by Huig de Groot (Grotius) and others, within the perspective of innate individual rights, the theory of rights compliant with nature that belonged to humankind was fundamental. Grotius is also credited as the first to formulate a theory of the "social contract," which led him into the mutual relations of society based on the nature of humans. Finally, we cannot forget the debate around a perfect society, conceived of for the supreme happiness of humankind and called "Utopia" by Thomas More (and reflected on by Tommaso Campanella and others). Leibniz maintains that although a perfect society cannot be attained, this was the liminal objective of history toward which humankind should strive.

From Benedict de Spinoza's partly exceptional position in the panorama of seventeenth-century proto-Enlightenment philosophy, Jonathan Israel (2001: vi) derived "the intellectual backbone of the European Radical Enlightenment." In the eighteenth century, Spinozism became a "widespread growing and socially (and politically) menacing force"; this "radical strain" was then opposed by "moderate" Enlighteners. "Spinoza stood for many things Voltaire disdained," in particular, his materialism and alleged atheism. According to Israel, Spinoza "spurns all teleology, Stoic, Aristotelian, or any other, in depicting nature" and rejects teleology in general (Israel 2006: 47, 466, 767). In fact, Spinoza ([1677] 2003: 247) stated that the "eternal and infinite being called God, *or* Nature . . . exists for the sake of no end" and that "he also acts for the sake of no end"; he added that what is called "a final cause is nothing but a human appetite" and that perfection and imperfection "are only modes of thinking." At first sight, similar utterances may appear perfectly inherent to what Koselleck would call an "immanent" view. We certainly can read them as a premature step toward secularization. Not for that, however, does Spinoza's philosophy lack purpose and transcendence. Generally, in Christian, Humanist and Enlightened philosophy it is not God or Nature that has to follow a "higher" purpose, as they already represent that purpose in themselves. Who has to follow a purpose that transcends his original condition of beast is man. Regarding this decisive point, Spinoza makes no exception. His "naturalism cannot be associated with the idea of the reduction of man to a material being" (Gut 2014: 54). Following his *Ethics*, good is what approaches man "nearer to the model of human nature," whereas evil is what "prevents us from becoming like that model." His scheme of psychological development, according to which "men are born in complete ignorance" and must then be educated to "act in accordance with the rules and laws of reason," delivers a blueprint for the Enlightenment teleology of civilization (Spinoza ([1670] 2003: 244–48). On many other occasions, the same teleological narrative would turn to relate psychological development to history and vice versa.

We can thus see how the philosophies of history of the late eighteenth century drew on many previously elaborated elements, which made it possible to build an overall vision of history. In the seminal work of Edward Gibbon ([1776–89] 1907: 163–64), for example, we find sentences such as "Reason might subdue, or passion might suspend, their influence; but they acted most forcibly on the infirm minds of children and females"; or "the credulous maid was betrayed by vanity to violate the laws of nature." Something similar to the attribution of an eschatological meaning to human history can also be depicted:

> The Romans themselves, the most powerful and enlightened nation of the globe, had renounced their ancient superstition; . . . Christianity, which opened the gates of Heaven to the Barbarians, introduced an important change in their moral and political condition . . . while they studied the divine truth, their minds were insensibly enlarged by the distant view of history, of nature, of the arts, and of society. (Gibbon [1776–89] 1907: 184)

Gibbon's account of *The Decline and Fall of the Roman Empire* was neither a sketch of universal history nor was it yet a philosophy of history in the proper sense of the term. It can be interpreted, however, as an attempt at revaluating the civic virtues of Rome, which had been celebrated by Machiavelli ([1531] 1971: 105, 222). So it can be seen as a part of what Tricoire (2015: 27) characterizes as a "movement for *self-colonization*" by the means of which influential intellectual elites strove to recover the "culture of the former Roman colonizer" to overcome the ignorance and servile mentality of their fellow Europeans, a claim that prefigured the Enlightenment "program of civilization."

Giambattista Vico meant to contribute to a "new science" of man-made things: historiography. Under the particular influence of Grotius, he was one of the first to develop a coherent theory of phases, which all the people of all lands would have to go through eventually from their savage infancy or prehistory, due to historical law, in analogy with the development of the individual from infancy to adulthood. This passage occurred because "as proud beasts they did not know how to stay in society with its infamous communalization of goods, and therefore remained isolated until they weakened, and finally became miserable and unhappy, because needy of all those goods which eased a more certain conservation of life." If this happened next to neighboring populations that were already in a tribal and sedentary state, the savages "with their escape from evil experimented in brawls typical of their ferocious community, sought after salvation in the lands cultivated by the pious, chaste, strong and also powerful, that is those who were already united in family societies" (Vico [1744] 1816: 83).

Once peoples had become sedentary and had entered into the first phase of their "gentling," they would believe that they could be directly governed by the will of divinities; the heroic age of aristocratic government followed, which would eventually reach the age of human history in which all are recognized as being equal in nature. In this assembly, the *res publica* conforms to the human right as dictated by reason. Vico referred to the ideal republic of Plato as the "Eternal Natural Republic, optimal in all its best aspects, ordered by Divine Providence." The reason which prevails in the age of Man, however, is not capable of blending with divine providence unless through faith. A natural republic could conceive of itself as eternal only if "the new World of the peoples returns to simplicity, and among them is compassion, faith, truth which are the natural foundations of justice, and are graces and beauties of the Eternal order of God." The opposite choice—that of pursuing only the splendors and sheer utilities of earthly life—was also left to human discretion. In this case "religion gets lost among the peoples, nothing remains for them in living in society, neither a shield for defending themselves, nor a way for consolation, not even a plant to lean on, nor any other way for them to be in the World" (Vico [1744] 1816: 143, 153–54).

If Vico paved the way for an Enlightenment philosophy of history, it was Voltaire's historical writing that, according to Sreedharan, marked the first practical attempt toward a comprehensive history of civilization. The author quotes Voltaire, stating that the principal purpose of his writing was not political or military history but the history of the arts and commerce, seen as expressions of the human mind (Sreedharan 2004: 115–18). Voltaire's *The Age of Louis XIV* of 1751, however, still follows a simplified scheme of human development, according to which prior-to-modern times appear as the mere "opposite of modern when a total lack of Enlightenment ('défaut de lumières') permeates all aspects of life" (O'Brien 1997: 35). It is with his *Essay on the Customs and the Spirit of the Nations* of 1756 that the universalistic teleological criteria, which help one to discriminate among the countless facts of the past, become more sophisticated. "In this immense prospect you seek only what is worth your notice, namely, the spirit, the manners, and customs of the most considerable nations," Voltaire writes. He ponders his "consideration" against the more-or-less outstanding capacity of these nations to interpret the purpose of universal history. That same purpose helps him to corroborate the foundational space metaphor of western historical thinking: "When you consider this globe as a philosopher, you first direct your attention to the east, the nursery of all arts, and from whence they have been communicated to the west" (Voltaire 1759a: 1–3).

For Hobbes the state of nature is one of perpetual war, for Grotius and Vico it makes humans miserable and unhappy. For Rousseau, on the contrary, it is the age of highest happiness, based on the essentiality of needs and intelligence. "Nature," which had already been conceived of by the philosophers of law and political philosophy as an irrevocable manifestation of a superior intention, was definitively depicted by Rousseau to be a sacred essence and therefore intrinsically legitimate, as well as pure and unobjectionable. According to the

Genevan philosopher, the term brings about a reminiscence in humans, one of a lost happiness that has become a memento of human perfectibility. The natural man only knows his own instincts of love and his feelings of compassion toward those who suffer. He does not have, however, moral categories that can position him between good and evil, as he does not have any drive toward sociality. Consequently, neither can "utopia" as a state be described in social terms, as the human of history is unhappy and perfectible, whereas in the non-place beyond history a godlike perfection reigns:

> We are told that a people of true Christians would form the most perfect society imaginable. I see in this supposition only one great difficulty: that a society of true Christians would not be a society of men. I say further that such a society, with all its perfection, would be neither the strongest nor the most lasting: the very fact that it was perfect would rob it of its bond of union; the flaw that would destroy it would lie in its very perfection. (Rousseau [1762] 1913: 118)

Before attaining utopia, the historical human who has left the state of nature can reasonably lean toward a more equal social contract that allows for the sovereignty of the people, and which hinders the consequences of a disproportionate distribution of property (while nonetheless protecting property, which Rousseau considers a positive right and not a natural one). The free will of humans, in contrast, is innate and unalienable; it is that faculty of choice and intervention in one's own destiny that distinguishes a human being from other animals, transforming him into a moral being. The person who renounces liberty renounces being a human, and refutes the rights and duties of humanity; "to remove all liberty from his will is to remove all morality from his acts" (Rousseau [1762] 1913: 10). Through free will, nature confers upon humans not only the right but also the duty of defending the prerogatives of humanity. Morally, one is not free to renounce one's freedom.

Similarly to Rousseau, for Kant the moral laws that distinguish the human rational being consist of "impediments of feelings, inclinations, and passions to which men are more or less subjected." A will "is purely *animal* (*arbitrium brutum*) when it is determined by sensuous impulses or instincts only, that is, when it is determined in a *pathological* manner. A will, which can be determined independently of sensuous impulses, consequently by motives presented by reason alone, is called a *free will* (*arbitrium liberum*)" (Kant [1781] 1855: 49, 486). Reason, free will, and moral law is what differentiates the former beast from the rest of creation, crowning it with a divine assignment: "It is only as a moral being that the human being can be a final end of creation" (Kant [1790] 2002: 309). This means that only reflectivity of being, reason, free will, and moral law can confer a meaning to existence. "All the many creatures, no matter how great the artistry of their arrangement and how manifold the purposive interconnections by which they are related to each other may be, indeed the whole of so many systems of them, which we incorrectly call worlds, would exist for nothing if there were not among them human beings (rational beings in general)" (Kant [1790] 2002: 308). The worst that might happen to a creature, it seems, is to exist for nothing, which indeed would contradict the transcendent purpose of the creator (as well as the predetermining axiom of the philosopher).

> Now we have in the world only a single sort of beings whose causality is teleological, i.e., aimed at ends and yet at the same time so constituted that the law in accordance with which they have to determine ends is represented by themselves as unconditioned and independent of natural conditions but yet as necessary in itself. The being of this sort is the human being, though considered as noumenon: the only natural being in which we can nevertheless cognize, on the basis of its own constitution, a supersensible faculty (freedom) and even the law of the causality together with the object that it can set for itself as the highest end (the highest good in the world). (Kant [1790] 2002: 302)

Since reason, free will, and moral laws are divine gifts bestowed upon the human species, this species, when it enters into history with the assignment of overcoming its own bestiality, does so in order to help "nature" to fulfill its inherent purpose. It also means that by emancipating itself from the mere fulfillment of providence, and setting itself as the highest end of history, "humanity" ultimately obeys the divine design.

Johann Gottfried Herder offered one of the most comprehensive examples of philosophy of history. It is also one of the most comprehensible, and consequently one of the most popularized. In his main work Herder delineated the course of humankind across phases and stages, and the extension of "humanity and reason" from Europe to the entire globe, ultimately arriving at the full objectification of universal humanity, and therefore of the divine principle which humankind carries out on earth. "We have seen that the purpose of our current existence is the formation of Humanity, which all low earthly needs must serve and strive for." However, before attaining complete unity with the divine, man must get rid of his bestial traits, because what from our species can pass over to that world "is nothing other than our Humanity, almost resembling God, the closed bud of the true form of mankind" (Herder [1784–91] 1914: 52–53).

For Herder, history is like a river that cannot go back to its source. His "humanity" represents an Otherworld, which is redemptive and should be desired, but the contours of which we must struggle hard merely to glimpse. In contrast, "Man must not have visions of his future state, but should rather believe in himself. In as much the infinite is certainly inherent in all his strength, it is only that here it cannot be explicated as it is inhibited by other forces, from the senses and impulses of the beast, and from bonds with earthly life." According to Herder, it is not mere daydreaming

> to hope that, wherever men should live, happy and honest men with reason shall one day live; happy not only thanks to their reason, but thanks to the collective reason of all brotherhood of mankind. I bow in front of this grand design that the general wisdom of nature has reserved for my kind, more willingly as this is the design of all nature. (Herder [1784–91] 1914: 54–5, 215)

According to Kant ([1784] 1914: 333), "the history of mankind can overall be seen as the execution of nature's hidden plan." Kant, however, would prefer to translate Herder's thinking in more explicit terms regarding this crucial point. In his review of Herder's philosophy of history of 1785, Kant writes that "the destiny of mankind is, on the whole, to make incessant progress, whereas the completion of such is nothing but a mere yet useful idea of the goal, to which we much dedicate our efforts because of the will of Providence" (Kant [1785] 1914: 319). He then specifies that the unattainable dream of happiness and the progressive and incessant improvement of human society that comes from it is the work of humankind. The divine providence is limited to determining this capability and behavior of humans, but it does not interfere with its outcome.

In Condorcet's atheist philosophy, history is not a divine design, not even as a mere but useful idea; nor is divine providence the ultimate foundation of human freedom of will and historical action, as conceived by Kant and Herder. Human freedom and its intrinsic drift to progress is in the exclusive design of nature. Condorcet's "picture of history" was intended to outline "the order in which the changes have taken place, explain the influence of every period upon that which follows, and thus show, by the modifications which the human species has experienced, in its incessant renovation through the immensity of ages, the course which it has pursued, and the steps which it has advanced toward knowledge and happiness." The French philosopher added that "no bounds have been fixed to the improvement of the human faculties; that the progress of this is perfectibility, henceforth above the control of every power that would impede it, has no other limit than the duration of the globe upon which nature has placed us" (Condorcet 1796: 11). Although progress also seemed to Cordorcet a never-ending asymptotic movement toward the ideal of human happiness and perfection, he nevertheless sketched out the contours of that state of redemption:

> Will not every nation one day arrive at the state of civilization attained by those people who are most enlightened, most free, most exempt from

prejudices, as the French, for instance, and the Anglo-Americans? Will not the slavery of countries subjected to kings, the barbarity of African tribes, and the ignorance of savages gradually vanish? Is there upon the face of the globe a single spot the inhabitants of which are condemned by nature never to enjoy liberty, never to exercise their reason? (Condorcet 1796: 251)

We can therefore confirm that at the center of historical development in eighteenth-century philosophies of history—which were then further developed through the late eighteenth and early nineteenth century by authors such as Fichte, Comte, Hegel, and Marx—there was now the idea of "Man." Furthermore, it was *western* man who was to carry the Olympic torch of progress, and it was the convergence toward *his* condition that provided a measure of progress.

Returning to the initial question raised by Koselleck, we may now wonder whether it is possible to derive a truly paradigmatic change from the humanization of the driving forces behind history. Was this new centrality of man capable of turning the previous sense of time and history upside down? Koselleck deduced from it the founding characteristics of a modernity entirely piled on hopeful expectations regarding the future. He admits that this hope was not new as such, but maintains that in the second half of the eighteenth century it contributed to a fundamental reversal of the conception of history. With secularization, the future was taken away from divine providence. In its place appeared an open temporality that was susceptible only to human intervention, thanks to the "attribution to history of the latent power of human events and suffering, a power that connected and motivated everything in accordance with a secret or evident plan to which one could feel responsible, or in whose name one could believe oneself to be acting." With the removal of creative subjectivity from the hands of God, and of the time of history "from a naturally formed chronology," progress became "the prime category in which the transnatural, historically immanent definition of time first found expression" (Koselleck 2004: 35, 37), depriving history of transcendent sense.

The concept of nature alluded to here by Koselleck belongs to the Enlightenment, depicting a form of existence from which man originates, and from which—in abiding by the lure of his own nature—he must actively attain release through history. He must therefore distinguish himself from a condition lacking creative subjectivity and irreversible time, and is subject to circular resurgences, which mark a continuum that is eternally equal to itself. A nature that is intended thus must no longer set the expiry for a perfectly prefigured destiny along its path, the end of which is prearranged by an omnipotent divine force.

This thoughtful representation nevertheless seems to oversimplify what was in fact a complicated relationship between the freedom, and the responsibility, of choice between Good and Evil that burdens man according to monotheist tradition. If God is omniscient, omnipresent, and omnipotent, how can he not be behind Evil just as he is behind Good? Here a dialectal distinction intrinsic to divinity intervenes, one that allows for a certain degree of human freedom of choice along a path, which is at the same time overall prearranged in its ultimate goal. It is this dialectic between human freedom and divine design that the modern philosophies of history do not overcome, but which, on the contrary, they propose as a major driving force behind historical change. Their concept of "humanity" refers to a transcendent and *not* to an immanent definition of history. The meaning I refer to is camouflaged rather than explained by a terminological creation such as "immanent transcendence" (Tugendhat 2010: 15). In order to reverse the sense of history and sustain an immanent and open temporality it is neither enough to replace God with "that equally elusive figure of humanity" (Gray 2008: 289), nor is it enough for the arrow of time no longer to be aimed at a celestial paradise, as Koselleck and others (e.g., Blumenberg 1983: 29–33) seem to suggest. For philosopher Karl Löwith it is the aiming at a purpose that makes the difference:

> The meaning of all things that are what they are, not by nature, but because they have been created either by God or by man, depends on purpose. . . . History, too, is meaningful only by indicating some transcendent purpose beyond the actual facts. But, since history is a movement in time, the purpose is a goal. Single events as such are not meaningful, nor is a mere succession of events. To venture a statement about the meaning of historical events is possible only when their *telos* becomes apparent.

He adds that the mere fact that we wonder over the meaning of history is a historical derivative, seeing as:

> there would be no search for the meaning of history if its meaning were manifest in historical events. It is the very absence of meaning in the events themselves that motivates the quest. Conversely, it is only within a pre-established horizon of ultimate meaning, however hidden it may be, that actual history seems to be meaningless. This horizon has been established by history, for it is Hebrew and Christian thinking that brought this colossal question into existence. (Löwith 1949: 4–5)

Löwith does not deny the differences between Christian and secular eschatology, indeed he considers the latter as "an indefinite advance toward an unattainable ideal." He also points out that "secular hope for a 'better world' looks forward without fear and trembling," whereas the Christian believer does not due to his fear of the Judgment Day. They

> have in common, nonetheless, the eschatological viewpoint and outlook onto the future as such. The idea of progress could become the leading principle for the understanding of history only within this primary horizon of the future as established by Jewish and Christian faith. (Löwith 1949: 84)

Generally speaking, and taking into consideration the numerous differences which are only briefly mentioned here, we could conclude, if slightly synthetically, that eighteenth- and nineteenth-century philosophies of history replaced the Garden of Eden with the state of nature and substituted the teleology of redemption from savagery and barbarism for the theology of the redemption from sin. Replacing the promise of the heavens, which was represented as an ascent to the kingdom of heaven in order to be reunited with God, was progress toward a society capable of deploying a "humanity almost resembling God" and finally to open the bud that enclosed "the true form of mankind," inherent in its original nature (Herder [1784–91] 1914: 53). The Christian mission—which Löwith saw in continuity with its Jewish foundations (Trüper 2014: 67), but which according to others distinguished itself from biblical Judaism through a "radically dualistic view of the world that goes with apocalyptic beliefs" (Gray 2008: 8)—was therefore translated into a civilizing and humanizing mission, although without the former being completely substituted, but rather only accompanied, by the latter. "The political ideologies of the last two hundred years," John Gray observes, "were vehicles for a myth of salvation in history that is Christianity's most dubious gift to humanity." The same author underlines that an eschatological view on history is also at the basis of the modernity paradigm: "Theories of modernization are not scientific hypotheses but theodicies—narratives of providence and redemption—presented in the jargon of social sciences" (Gray 2008: 105, 260–61).

Regarding the difference between theist and atheist philosophies of history, we can today consider the complete identification of the concept of Enlightenment with the interpretive line prevailing among the eighteenth-century French philosophers to have been overcome. Pocock (1999: 1) observes that the Enlightenment "occurred in too many forms to be comprised within a single definition and history, and that we do better to think of a family of Enlightenments." Belonging to this family are just as much the materialistic yet not necessarily atheist traditions, with their view centered around the human "soul" (Thomson 2008: 13–28), as are the authentically Christian currents, especially Protestant but also Catholic, which in the wake of Newton's philosophy of nature (Jacob 1976: 21–26) and Locke's *Reasonableness of Christianity* of 1695, believed that "Reason and revelation could be reconciled by identifying and emphasizing the moral *essentials* of the Christian faith." In the new spirit of the mid-eighteenth century, they could then turn "to the discourse of sentiment and sensibility." As Helena Rosenblatt (2000: 285, 292) summarizes, "if Enlightened Christians sounded much like Locke in the early part of the century, they sounded more like Rousseau towards the end."

The many forms of the Enlightenment did not in any case scratch the scope of convergence around the assumption of a particular spiritual nature of man, nor around the concept of history as a process aimed at redeeming him of his bestial origins. In this last instance, it was the idea of Man being the bearer of Reason, and therefore the only animal in possession of free judgment and will, which revealed the religious origins of all western philosophies of history. "In taking for granted a categorical difference between humans and other animals these rationalists show their view of the world has been formed by faith" (Gray 2008: 266). So, both the beliefs and the practices of what is called religion ultimately continued to define the space of possibilities of western thinking.

> Atheism, skepticism, and the modern scientific spirit have scarcely enjoyed greater autonomy, for they define themselves only by reference to religion and its claims. An atheist who denies the existence of the soul and of God, and who believes in so doing that he or she possesses sovereign independence of judgment, accepts, often unknowingly, the spirit and terms of a debate (the body/soul dichotomy; a universe governed, or not, by divine providence) that religion has chosen. (Dubuisson 2003: 12)

1.4 A somewhat gloomy utopia

What is the meaning of history? What is its ultimate goal? Renaissance utopias were "constructed as a liminal state, situated somewhere beyond the boundaries of knowledge" (Leslie 1998: 9). It has often been argued that the utopian narrative expelled the past, for it was associated with the hope of transforming society (Liakos 2010: 66). Koselleck also found that

> consistent Enlighteners tolerated no allusion to the past. The declared objective of the *Encyclopédie* was to work through the past as quickly as possible so that a new future could be set free. Once, one knew exempla; today, only rules, said Diderot. "To judge what happens according to what has already happened means, it seems to me, to judge the familiar in terms

of the unfamiliar," deduced Sieyès. One should not lose the nerve to refuse a turn to history for something that might suit us. (Koselleck 2004: 39)

The very same Sieyès ([1789] 2002: 8), however, claimed that the Third Estate should "not be afraid to go back to the past" and that if necessary—as soon it would transpire, more than Sieyès may have wished for—the Third Estate would be even better than the aristocracy at legitimizing its political aspirations through a mythical past.

We should carefully distinguish here the past from history. The very idea that recalling the past might be harmful to the present and worsen the future expectations of happiness would be hardly conceivable without attributing an overall meaning to history. Utopias built upon the relief from history and the end of human suffering are likewise unthinkable without eschatological expectations. Such interpretations depicted history as the path through the Vale of Tears, which in a temporal lapse from eternity leads humankind from Eden to redemption or, in its modernized version, from the state of nature to the state of humanity. Without an idea of redemption or homecoming, or of a steady improvement at least, neither utopian thinking nor the idea of progress would hardly be possible.

One should also distinguish the historical from the mythical past. As redemption has a flavor of homecoming, to be duly awaited it requires the memory of the lost paradise being kept up, like in the words ascribed to the early-eighteenth-century rabbi Yisroel ben Eliezer: "The desire to forget prolongs exile; the secret of redemption is memory" (Haumann 2002: 245). What is meant here to be remembered is not the events of previous exile history, but the being at home before this woebegone history began. It is a mythical past, which recalls that the homeland is elsewhere in place and time. It belongs to the western Platonist "mythic imagination, where origins are considered . . . as the locus of perfection, of initial fullness and simplicity" (Dubuisson 2003: 22). When non-western cosmologies imagine elsewhere-places of perfection, for example, the Tibetan Buddhist "spiritually pure land of Shambala" (Stewart 2011: 459), they rather seem to delineate the possibility of reaching it through personal palingenesis or spiritual perfection in the lifetime, not through history.

In the western tradition, history is humankind's collective place of suffering. "The interpretation of history is, in the last analysis, an attempt to understand the meaning of history as the meaning of suffering by historical action" (Löwith 1949: 3). Although the suffering Löwith refers to is for the promise of a better world, the western view on history cannot be expected to be one-sidedly optimistic. The idea of progress can hardly be associated only with hope and confidence, it also causes fear, melancholy, and sometimes a sense of tragedy based on the assumption that redemption, if any, can be achieved only after history's ending. For Rousseau, since "by its nature society humanized man and by the same process distracted and alienated him again, there was no point in past, present, or future time at which this double effect had not been going on" (Pocock 1975: 504). But even for those who believe that redemption is achievable through and within history, life tends to be all but easy as long as the idea of a West charged with a universal mission makes men and women feel the load of their "responsibility" to history, the final chapter of which is perhaps open, but the meaning of which is already adumbrated.

For this same reason, it is difficult to share an opinion whereby the idea of progress is incompatible with the nostalgia of a lost Golden Age. While the "linear time" of history irreversibly projects humankind toward the future, it also distances it from its origin (Rossi 1997: 76–77). Despite the long path, from which there is no turning back as progress is inscribed in his nature, man gloomily notices the distancing from his happy infancy, lost from his kind, as Rousseau points out. A Utopia which allows the luxury of oblivion cannot be considered one which can release the painful and troubled memory of a lost happiness, and cannot, therefore, do anything other than prefigure the return to a state of happy harmony between man and lost nature, even if it does not mean turning back but going ahead. Not even the Christian kingdom of heaven is described as a return to the earthly paradise of Eden, but is represented as a return to God. Thus, progress does not reinstate the happy yet unconscious animal state, but definitively reconciles the human being with his or her contradictory nature. It therefore signals the return to authentic conditions of being, from which he had been catapulted into the time of history, just as an exile is catapulted into a foreign country.

One original condition that was regrettably lost for Rousseau is freedom, which was indeed possessed but also lost through a consequence of the "nature of man." Freedom was sacrificed to history with the exit from the state of nature and the entrance into a human society based on the social contract: "To alienate is to give or to sell. Now, a man who becomes the slave of another does not give himself; he sells himself, at least for his subsistence" (Rousseau [1762] 1913: 9). From a category of utility and exchange, the concept of alienation, which over time would become increasingly more central to western thinking, was thus transformed into both the religious and psychological conception of the soul as a stranger on earth. Indeed, Plato claimed that souls, given that they conserve the memory of their divine origin, "know that they do not belong to this world, and view their immortality (*athánatos*) as their truth (*aléthia*)" (Galimberti 1999: 505). Accordingly, Rousseau ([1755] 2000: 10) observes that "the human soul modified in society" has so to speak "changed its appearance as to be nearly unrecognizable," becoming different from its original "celestial and majestic simplicity the Creator imprinted on it" (Rousseau [1755] 2000: 14). Similarly, Herder ([1784–91] 1914: 55) highlights the contradiction between divine inspiration and mortality, which reigns over human life. Infinity is a part of it, but "cannot be explicated as it is inhibited by other forces, from the senses and impulses of the beast, and from bonds with earthly life."

Like so, the concept of alienation gives an expression to a dialectal form of the course prefigured by the philosophies of history: the path of humanity is toward salvation, but at the same time is a progressive distancing from the original authenticity the recovery of which will be the only possibility of salvation in the future. With all of the confidence in human progress that an Enlightenment anthropologist may be able to nurture, for Rousseau, on an existential level, it is the "regret of an idealized and unrepairable past, dubbed the state of nature," which stands out (Wolff 2010: 109); a regret from which a strong emotional, nostalgic, and melancholy involvement arises in the historical process. According to Richard Strier (2004: 23), "it is often taken as a basic truth about the whole 'Western Tradition' that the control of 'passion' by 'reason' is its fundamental ethical-psychological ideal." However, Kant ([1781] 1855: 502) himself not only meant that the belief in God is a "rational belief," which "presupposes the existence of moral sentiments," but also shared with Rousseau the idea that the voice of reason is clearly perceivable even to the commonest men, for it is inherent to the nature of humankind. So the commonest man "instinctively" listens to it, as if it were a natural sentiment itself.

In other words, among the most important enlightened philosophers of reason, passions and sentiments were not seen only as bonds of a bestial past and obstacles on the road to happiness and true humanity. In line with previous humanist traditions, these philosophers also attributed to passions and sentiments a critical role for the full revelation of human nature. Feelings gifted rational man with a sense of simplicity and faith, and could be considered a repository of memory of the lost authentic dimension and its utopian value. As Strier (2004: 23) concludes, reducing western tradition only to the control of passion "obscures another strand in 'the tradition': the praise of passion," two strands of one and the same tradition which "exist in opposition and complex interaction."

As has been already mentioned, the sentiment most easily associated with an authentic lost condition is nostalgia. "Nostalgia" is itself another invention that can be placed between humanism and the Enlightenment. It originates in the sixteenth and seventeenth centuries in Switzerland with the diagnosis of *Heimweh*, a derivative illness that encapsulated all physical and mental ailments that mercenaries would suffer with being away from home. The phenomenon was systematically studied by Johannes Hofer (1688) in his medical dissertation as a series of psycho-physical afflictions which could even lead to death. For the first time the term *Heimweh* was used alongside the neologism "nostalgia," invented by Hofer himself for that specific purpose.

Through spreading among all western languages, the concept was to later undergo a sequence of semantic transpositions toward taking on a more marked psychological meaning, eventually becoming a synonym of the soul's suffering, and being sublimated to an existential condition (Boym 2003: 13). This did not happen by chance, given that in western ideology man's place in history resembles the elusive and impenetrable location of what, according to George Herbert Mead, is an "I"-fantasy of the Self. The gaze of the self-conscious cannot help but collect traces of itself in the past or hope to find itself in the future. It is therefore forced each time to refer to the object of observation—the person himself—as an essence that slipped away and is not yet present in both space and time (Mead 1912: 401–06; [1932] 2002: 54–94; [1934] 1974: 178). The spatial–temporal deferral, pertaining to all organisms equipped with a nervous system capable of reacting to stimuli perceived at a distance, is thus transposed as an "unnatural" human condition called estrangement or alienation, a sort of existential "disease of civilization," which sooner or later requires a cure, and, most importantly, can be cured, through the utopian return to a present that will never again pass by.

On the one hand, considering that "the behaviors of memory are always the result of an sometimes conflictual interaction between the individual and the group" (Agazzi, Fortunati 2007: 19), it is comprehensible that the melancholy of loss was then able to be transformed into a powerful fuel for the process of constructing the personal and collective I, interweaving the psychological fabric within the deepest of political clothing. On the other hand, also considering "the potential radical pedagogical authority of memory in that it may make apparent the insufficiency of the present, its (and our own) incompleteness" (Simon 2005: 89), we can understand the potential of such a sentiment for the rebellion of utopian hope, if somewhat vague, and of the pathos of history which derives from it. It is not by chance that, as we shall see, it was the nostalgic poet par excellence, Novalis, who understood before any other how the events of the French Revolution revealed that in the new era of sovereignty of the people it was feelings that would become the indispensable foundation for every power and every consent from that moment onwards.

2

Freedom and sovereignty

> *Bare Virtue can't make nations live*
> *In splendor; they, that would revive*
> *A golden age, must be as free*
> *For acorns, as for honesty*
>
> BERNARD MANDEVILLE,
> THE FABLE OF THE BEES (1714)

Emerging from the debate on the concept of "nature" advocated by philosophers and scientists between the sixteenth and seventeenth centuries, was a world run by mechanical and mathematical laws linked to limitless divine perfection. According to the thinkers already mentioned in the previous chapter, only to the human being the comprehension of such laws was not precluded, given his divinely inherited capacity for reason, of which the very same science was a direct expression. These capacities for reflection were seen as depending on the exceptional possession of a soul, and were not entirely attributable to mechanical laws but rather to divine inspiration, in accordance with the particular religious belief. That is, they were inspired by a faculty of judgment based on the transcendent "purposiveness of nature" according to Kant ([1790] 2002: 274), and were manifest in the faculty of doubt according to Descartes. The vision of nature as a kingdom of objects and perfect repeatability quite clearly descends from classic and Christian sources, similar to the idea of the soul which transforms the individual human into an indivisible subject, and which traces any subjectivity or capacity of free will that is not directly divine to the individual human alone.

The same philosophical discussions were also at the origins of what has been called "liberal thought" since the nineteenth century. Among numerous contrasts and differentiations, this strand of thought is still predominant in western ideology today, especially when speaking in general terms of law, society, and economy. The development of a concept of law and justice compliant with nature, as had been reinterpreted by Grotius, Samuel Pufendorf, Thomas Hobbes, John Locke, and others between the seventeenth and eighteenth centuries, was as fundamental for the vision of human species and society as it was for the philosophy of history, as outlined in the previous chapter. Certain rights were seen as being innate and therefore inalienable, and were mainly understood as rights belonging to the individual. The "social contract" between these individuals was a contract based on the nature of man, which pushed him to interact in social groups in order to form mutual relationships, which were more advantageous than the self-governing solitude. Based on the same methodological individualism, Thomas Hobbes ([1651] 1970: 509) outlined a state of nature in which man was the only judge of himself and was at war with all others, a situation which was inevitably detrimental to survival and justice. In order to reduce the considerable costs and dangers of "all against all," men implement a pact for the common wealth, which supplants their natural rights through imperious and omnipresent laws, necessary so as not to succumb again to instinct. In certain ways at the opposite pole to Hobbes's absolute state or *Leviathan*, in John Locke's *Two Treatises of Government* we find another of the key references for political liberalism. According to Locke ([1690] 1764: 312–48), it is best to restrict the prerogatives of laws to the protection of civil goods such as life, freedom, *habeas corpus*, and property. In Bernard Mandeville's version men form social groups due to an inherent natural drive dictated by a love of oneself, and not by morality or compassion. Still, the end of the poem cited at the beginning of the chapter (Mandeville [1714] 1795: 11) advises us not to misunderstand the methodological individualism of liberal thought: it is not an individualist project, but an interindividual, political or collective ("Nations"), and utopian ("Golden Age") one. Martin Chanock (2000: 23) also points out:

> The long tradition of liberal philosophers of rights, as well as Western-inspired rights declarations, is very clearly about groups. They are about the nature of group life, and how it should ideally work. They endeavour to prescribe the ground rules for associating groups. . . . Furthermore, the attempt to depict Western societies as individualistic misses the point that these very societies, with their powerful cohesive ideologies of nationalism, patriotism, collective action and welfarism, have been and are far more "successful" groups on a larger scale over long periods of time,

with better working consensual traditions of government, than the often fragmented, authoritarian, familial, localistically based societies which invoke their cultural attachment to groupness.

So, while western theory and ideology are based on individualism, western societies are not necessarily individualistic. The originally Christian view of the single person as the indivisible unit of all spiritual commitment and subjectivity contains neither a negation nor a condemnation of collective interest and behavior. With regard to society, individualism rather represents an axiomatic methodological assumption, on the basis of which the mechanisms of group cohesion and group behavior are interpreted and influenced in a certain way. The idea of the social contract is a paradigmatic example of this way of interpreting human beings and action. It does not simply involve an interpretation of the economy and society or of aspects of political power and liberty, but also of nationalism, patriotism, populism, and so on. The socially cohesive power of individualistic ideas can be observed when looking at the American Revolution and the paradigmatic changes that the concept of "people" underwent during the French Revolution. As a first step, however, we should go into further detail regarding the idea of liberty and the reality of liberalism.

2.1 Liberty and liberalism

According to the seventeenth-century discourse on freedom and liberty, all humans are naturally born free and equal and all share equal rights. In the words of John Locke,

> The *natural liberty* of man is to be free from any superior power on earth, and not be under the will or legislative authority of man, but to have only the law of nature for his rule. The *liberty of man*, in society, is to be under no other legislative power, but that established, by consent, in the common-wealth; nor under the dominium of any will, or restraint of any law, but what that legislative shall enact, according to the trust put in it. (Locke [1690] 1764: 212)

These statements lie at the root of western political philosophy, and were established in particular by a strand of political thought that would come to be known as "liberal" in the nineteenth century. As much as the concept "liberty" was central to seventeenth- and eighteenth-century thought, "liberal" as a characterization was only applied retrospectively to philosophical beliefs, such as John Locke's, and to political movements, such as the Whig Party in England to which Locke belonged.

Skinner has highlighted that there was a concept of "liberty before Liberalism" which was markedly diverse from the negative definition according to which "where law ends, liberty begins." Authors like James Harrington who defended that other concept during the constitutional struggle in seventeenth-century England, celebrated the liberty of the commonwealth rather than personal freedom, that is the *civitas libera* or free state. The latter expression implied that the state had to assure the liberty of its citizens not by the goodwill of an absolutist monarch, but by its very law. The main references of these authors were to Roman legal and moral law, Livy's *Ab Urbe Condita* and Renaissance writer Nicolò Machiavelli's *Discorsi*. As they claimed, "it is only possible to enjoy civil liberty to the full if you live as the citizen of a free state," which meant living "as an active citizen under a representative form of government." Some of them were explicit in stating "that only a republic can be a free state" (Skinner [1998] 2012: 5, 57, 68, 77).

Can the neo-Roman notion of the free state in some way be included into the ex-post established "liberal tradition?" We see for example Montesquieu ([1758] 1843: 270) criticizing Harrington's concept of liberty, but also how the latter's insistence on the empire of law and the balance of powers displayed similarities with Montesquieu's own concerns. At any rate, it appears that there was not just one concept of "liberty" before liberalism. Even Locke or Mandeville's ideas entered the liberal line of ancestry only because of an ex-post recruitment. Inclusions and exclusions became logical by the contingency of *later* political developments. Therefore, no clear answer to the above-formulated question can be given. This makes liberalism a changeable and multifaceted phenomenon that never ceased to be debated controversially. "There is no single, unambiguous thing called liberalism," Freeden (2015: 1) notes, but there are liberalisms in the plural, all of which select "certain items from an accumulated and crowded liberal repertoire and leave others out, both because some elements are incompatible with others and because intellectual fashions and practices change."

In fact, the meaning of "liberal" moved away from its common reference to moral and social customs only relatively lately, becoming an adjective with political connotations not before the times of the directorate government and the Napoleonic empire in France. "Liberal," like "conservative," "socialist," and "communist" as a signifier for an ideological orientation or party, was thus a child of the French Revolution (Middell 2016: 25). Over various political stages, one of which was the Spanish *Trienio*—which "loomed large in this imaginary, and its constitution was claimed as a model by liberals elsewhere in Europe" (Simal 2016: 32)—it gradually came to be used by European political forces as a self-referential term, before the noun "liberalism" designated a distinct political movement (Leonhard 2001: 259–61; Kurunmäki 2017: 257–59). Actually, it was a slow confirmation process, which was in fact to become irreversible only in the Revolution of 1848. The English Whigs, however, united with a faction of the Tories to form the Liberal Party only in the second half of the nineteenth century, and the name of the party was not officially determined until Lord Gladstone came to lead the government in 1868, when finally great numbers of people "in all social classes had no hesitation in describing themselves as Liberals" (Douglas 2005: 20). Notwithstanding that almost "all Americans, regardless of class, have shared a common ideology of Lockean or Whig liberalism" (Degler [1959] 1984: 5), in the United States, the adjective "liberal" remained relatively unimportant for even longer in terms of political struggle. Later it was commonly identified as "New Liberalism," a reformist political orientation vaguely leaning to the Left, which was especially present in the Democratic Party from around the 1930s.

For those thinkers of the seventeenth and eighteenth centuries considered among the founders of liberal thought, it was common to underline the "natural" yet specific character of human freedom. Locke ([1690] 1764: 247–48) wrote:

> The *freedom* then of man, and liberty of acting according to his own will, *is grounded* on his having *reason*, which is able to instruct him in that law he is to govern himself by, and make him know how far he is left to the freedom of his own will. To turn him loose to an unrestrained liberty, before he has reason to guide him, is not the allowing him the privilege of his nature to be free; but to thrust him out amongst brutes, and abandon him to a state as wretched, and as much beneath that of a man, as theirs.

Also according to Hobbes, reason is the natural condition and limit of human freedom. Reason is tightly linked to the possession of language, that is, that capability of conceptual thinking and reciprocal understanding, which the other animal species seem to lack. This makes the "free will" of humans differ from instinctive animal behavior. It responds to the nature of man whereby he forms his will according to the possibilities of reciprocal understanding. The private, isolated man may be free to make whatever statements, including meaningless and absurd ones. But in the realm of commonwealth and the political sphere, reason must rule as an expression of natural justice. However, free will is an innate property that cannot be erased, so that for Hobbes—as Skinner ([1998] 2012: 6) remarks—"even the coercive force of law leaves your natural liberty unimpaired." According to this concept of free will, which is rooted in Christian traditions, Hobbes ([1651] 1970: 43, 506), who during his lifetime was accused of "atheism," believed that nobody could take away the individual's innate faculty of decision between good and evil, right or wrong, and obedience or disobedience to the law. Since many subjects decide to behave irrationally, their wrongdoing must be banned and censored, by rough means if necessary. Hobbes maintained that tyranny "signifieth nothing more, nothing less, than the name of sovereignty, be it one, or many men."

In the eighteenth century, Rousseau would claim similarly to Locke that the specificities of human liberty expressed themselves through personal will regimented by reason, whereas collective reasoning expressed itself in the form of consent. At the same time, however, similarly to Hobbes, he underlined the strength of absolute sovereign power, with an emphasis that has generated numerous perplexities. In the early nineteenth century, the liberal Benjamin Constant warned not to transpose "into our modern age an extent of social power, of collective sovereignty, which belonged to other centuries" in mistaking "the authority of the social body for liberty." As individual liberty is "the true modern liberty," Constant continues, political liberty is indispensable as a guarantee of individual liberty. From Locke to Hobbes to Rousseau, all agree that only a government based on consent and "general will" can be considered legitimate: "But the governments which emanate from a legitimate source have even less right than before to exercise an arbitrary supremacy over individuals" (Constant [1819] 2012: 75, 79). For this reason Constant emphasizes how "modern" political freedom must consist in the principle of representation and the rule of law, precisely so as to buffer free will and prevent relapse into tyranny.

The debate around these concepts, which has now continued for three or four centuries, is affected by the abstractness and arbitrariness of the concept of "nature" in as much as its axiomatic and irrefutable character allows any link between "reason" and "free will" to be derived from nature itself. Potentially, this circular argumentation lays the way for any governmental shape or activity to be declared an expression of "general will." On the one hand, "Locke recognized tacit 'consent' as a sufficient indication of the legitimacy of a government" (Freeden 2015: 21), while Destutt de Tracy ([1811] 2012: 37) maintained that it was important that a government made the people happy, considering that "liberty and happiness are the same thing." Benjamin Constant, on the other hand, who more than likely had difficulty in imagining all individuals being happy at the same time, insisted on forms of government that forced the authorities into a continuous negotiation reaching the greatest satisfaction possible. The debate nonetheless indicates that the constitutional forms of government and the level of authoritarianism and libertarian tolerance can vary substantially under the name of liberalism, according to the influence of the historical sources and philosophical interpretations that inspire it. This conceptual variability has also been widely demonstrated within political practice.

Another of Constant's claims, according to which individual liberty is the true modern liberty, is important in further defining the nucleus of liberal thought. As Goodhart (2003: 951) writes: "Lockean natural rights are pre-social and pre-political. This renders rights—and the consensual relationships that flow from them—private. Natural rights are thus de-politicized, protected from government interference, because the limited transfer of right effected through the social contract gives government power only to uphold the law of nature (to protect man's natural rights)." Having a right is tantamount to protection of the personal and familial sphere from interference of political power. Following on were the right to free speech, to the liberty of the press, to freedom of political participation: these rights are in fact connected to each other given that, as Alexis de Tocqueville ([1835] 2012: 91) would point out, the idea that the formation of popular will can be compatible with censorship "is not only dangerous, but it is absurd."

The most basic and most significant setting in which to exercise the right to freedom, however, is the economic sphere, which should be left to private prerogatives given that "communal exploitations are always badly managed," as Pierre-Louis Roederer wrote in the Napoleonic era. The astonishing ease with which "nature" bindingly legitimized property rights can be seen in other passages of the same text. According to the liberal thinkers, private ownership of moveable property is the "natural" result of the work needed for its production. At a later stage, the principle is extended to landed property, since "the right to land ownership is born of the right to moveable property and personal property." In the following stage, this same deduction is then extended to the spontaneous fruits of the land, despite no work being needed for their reproduction, and therefore the "natural" legitimization of property is lost. What might seem to us as a marginal extension actually not only generated a deep rift in the habitual laws of European societies, but also allowed for the "savages" of the colonies who did not cultivate lands to be legally and morally transformed into illegal "intruders" in the environments in which they had lived for centuries and millennia. The institution of inheritance was also declared a "natural" institution, considering that "it was natural that they should pass on as inheritance what they had made for their progeny" and "it was quite natural that these should not, after their demise, become the property of the State or of an interloper" (Roederer [1800] 2012: 12–13, 15). Following the use of the adjective "natural," any objection would have appeared futile. What is "natural" is also "true" in a religious sense, according to the axioms, or beliefs, of the "humanist cult of reason" (Gray 2008: 82).

The Scottish exponent of the Enlightenment, David Hume, explains with exceptional clarity why the right to property is the mother of all rights:

> There are three different species of goods which we are possessed of; the internal satisfaction of our minds; the external advantages of our body; and the enjoyment of such possessions as we have acquired by our industry and good fortune. We are perfectly secure in the enjoyment of the first. The second may be ravished from us, but can be of no advantage to him who deprives us of them. The last only are both exposed to the violence

of others, and may be transferred without suffering any loss or alteration; while at the same time there is not a sufficient quantity of them to supply every one's desires and necessities. As the improvement, therefore, of these goods is the chief advantage of society, so the *instability* of their possession, along with their *scarcity*, is the chief impediment. (Hume [1740] 1994: 9–10)

Property rights, therefore, are at the basis of the social contract, since it is impossible to find a remedy to the instability of possession in the state of nature. The sense of justice is not a natural principle, which forms the basis of the law; on the contrary, it is a derivative of artifices such as the social contract and the establishment of laws, which produces notions of stability in terms of possessions. "There immediately arise the ideas of justice and injustice, as also those of property, right and obligation" (Hume [1740] 1994: 12).

Another interesting aspect is that, according to Hume and other thinkers, property and rights are intimately linked to each other through a dimension of human suffering. Goods acquired through the suffering of labor can be transferred by violence or lawfully and consensually, "without suffering." This is why, according to Asma Abbas (2010: 28–29), the issue of property lies at an important nexus:

It is the paradigm case for conceptualizing injury in Kant and provides the terms in which the notion of *having* rights comes to us. The *having* allows us to imagine injury, property, and rights in a triangular relation. It also allows us to imagine a bearer who embodies the triangulation, tied together in a possessive individualistic ethos that drives the political economy of injury.

The permission to own even our pain, leads "to the core conundrum of representation being whether we can speak for others' suffering or only our own." In the interindividual realm of liberal policies, suffering can be represented only in terms of interest, that is, insofar as it allows a calculable compensation for injury. Interests "are real or potential injuries framed positively or acquisitively in happy liberalisms," while incommensurable dimensions of suffering remain private. This makes a remarkable taxonomy of pain possible: "For instance, hunger and starvation are not considered injuries in the same way as a gunshot wound" (Abbas 2010: 31).

The discourse on suffering, property, and rights can therefore be seen as one of the strands of argumentation in favor of liberty, which "provided an account of rights that dislodged them from their social grounding and represented inegalitarian social relationships as free and equal ones," as Michael Goodhart (2003: 954) states referring to Locke. To begin with, the egalitarian idea could not be extended to "savages," "barbarians," or "semi-civilized" peoples dwelling outside the west (Losurdo 2011: 239). From within the intrinsic logic of a proto-liberal and liberal perspective, based on "nature" and "reason," there was no contradiction between John Stuart Mill's vehement defense of the freedom of speech and of minority opinions as a form of "protection against political despotism" on the one hand, and the defense of despotism as a "legitimate mode of government in dealing with barbarians, provided the end be their improvement," regardless of whether or not they desired improvement, on the other (Mill, J.S. [1859] 1867: 6). The alleged immaturity of the will of the "uncivilized" Other charged Europe and the west with a historical burden. In these self-celebrating representations, the "civilized" nations "were complacently depicted as a tiny island of liberty and civilization in a tempestuous ocean of tyranny, slavery and barbarism" (Losurdo 2011: 165). Since the freedom of man and the liberty of acting according to his own will were seen as grounded in reason, and "savages," "barbarians," and backward peoples, as well as peasants or unlearned workers, were considered anything but "reasonable," what emerged was a sort of "master-race democracy" formed by the worldwide community of the free.

Looking back on the fundamental theoretical elaborations of Grotius, Locke, and others, as well as the Dutch, British, and American practices regarding chattel slavery and the "extirpation/subjugation" of native populations, Domenico Losurdo (2011: 27, 341) observes: "It remains the case that in all three liberal revolutions the demand for liberty and justification of the enslavement, as well as the decimation (or destruction), of barbarians, were closely intertwined. In conclusion, the countries that were the protagonists of three major liberal revolutions were simultaneously the authors of two tragic chapters in modern (and contemporary) history." Losurdo does not mean to deny the "merits and strong points" of the liberal tradition, such as the idea of division of powers, of economic dynamism, or that of freedom of the press, religion, and opinion—however limited these may be to the reasonable mature peoples of the west—but claims that recognizing these merits must not mean removing from our memory either the extraordinary harshness of the British legislation against workers and the poor, or the prevailingly elitist and exclusivist view on political participation, or the prevalently racist worldview on colonialism and slavery which characterized mainstream liberal thought. As Locke ([1669] 2003: 230) stated in *The Fundamental Constitutions of Carolina* of 1669: "Every freeman of Carolina shall have absolute power and authority over his Negro slaves, of what opinion or religion soever." Nor should the merits of liberalism lead us to forget the "similarities to the concentration camp" of the plantation system: that systematic depersonalization which characterized the cruel methods of mass deportation, imprisonment, and punishment, not only rampant in the colonies but in fact widely diffused. Nor should we forget the "one-drop rule" of the racial purity laws of the American

South: the eugenic legal measures such as the prohibition of "interracial marriage" and "miscegenation," which continued well after the end of the Second World War in many American states.

Concerning the destruction of indigenous communities in Australia, Africa, and America, it was not only Benjamin Franklin ([1771] 1903: 185) who ironically wondered whether it was "the design of Providence to extirpate these savages in order to make room for cultivators of the earth." Considering its scale and systematic nature, Tzvetan Todorov (1984: 5) defined the genocide of the Amerindians without any irony as the "greatest genocide in human history." Losurdo (2011: 340) concludes:

> This is not the place to proceed to a comparative history of massacres, decimation and genocides, or to discuss the pertinence of the categories employed to describe them. But one point seems to be settled: it is banally ideological to characterize the catastrophe of the twentieth century as a kind of new barbarian invasion that unexpectedly attacked and overwhelmed a healthy, happy society. The horror of the twentieth century casts a shadow over the liberal world even if we ignore the fate reserved for peoples of colonial origin. . . . The usual hagiography proves unfounded even when, in reconstructing the liberal world, we restrict ourselves to analysing the metropolis and the white community.

The meaning of belittlement can be seen on the internet, where a reviewer of Locke states that in *The Fundamental Constitutions of Carolina* he "set up a system of nobility and serfs, which is so out of character with his philosophy that it seems likely that he was under orders to write as he did" (Stephens n.d.). Intuitively it looks absurd indeed that one could combine the celebration of liberty with a validation of a system of nobility and serfs. In the same text, however, we read nothing on slavery nor on whether it was out of character with Locke's philosophy to validate slavery in its most brutal and totalizing legal form. If this philosophy may seem at odds with the feudal provisions laid down in the never-adopted *Fundamental Constitutions*, the same certainly cannot be said for modern slavery. The "perfect" condition of slavery—Locke ([1690] 1764: 213–14) would state in his philosophical writings—is "nothing else but *the state of war continued, between a lawful conqueror and a captive*." A slave is someone who has "by his fault forfeited his own life, by some act that deserves death." In an epoch in which, for the sake of privatized property, hunters in formerly communal woods were transformed into poachers who deserved death, it is easy to imagine what a savage who stood in the way of a "lawful" conqueror was to deserve. Not only that, but to be philosophically correct the slave owner had to retain unlimited power over the life and death of the slave's body, and this was exactly what the *Fundamental Constitutions* envisaged.

In line with many others, the French moderate liberal Pierre-Victor Malouet also underlined that slavery of barbarous people did not offend the right of nature (Losurdo 2011: 139). More generally, despite speaking of being born free and equal out of God's desire, for the philosophies of nature, history, and the social contract, only a minority part of humanity was defined as "freemen," resulting in the justification of a new and in many ways unprecedented hierarchy among human beings and their ways of living, as we will see in the following chapter. The fact remains that even if reconciling freedom and slavery was made conceptually possible by the philosophical contortions that attributed a transcendent meaning to history, it was not an inescapable logic—also because, "in order to treat a man like a dog, one must first recognise him as a man" (Sartre [1960] 2004:111). Eminent members of the liberal pantheon, from Condorcet to Diderot, from Montesquieu to Kant and Smith, were aware of these paradoxes. They opposed the institution of slavery despite their own prejudices against "barbarians," "negroes," and "savages" in general. At least until the nineteenth century, however, in "no instance did criticism or condemnation of slavery involve exclusion of the beneficiaries or theorists of the institution from the community of the free and the liberal party" (Losurdo 2011: 164).

Liberalism has emerged in various political forms over the last two and a half centuries, and this variety perhaps has been facilitated by the axiomatic character of the underlying philosophical concepts. We should recall once again that the key concept of "nature" is easily adapted to the various themes debated in liberal circles throughout the various eras and circumstances. When something is declared "natural" it takes on an irrefutable truth, given that all things "natural" are held to be "evident" for any human being equipped with "reason," and there is therefore no need for further argument. In this way, numerous combinations of the most diverse themes could come under the name of liberalism, where congruencies did not necessarily exist, and where in fact they were quite often in contrast with each other.

According to Leroux and Hart, the emphasis on political and civil rights was much more marked in the emerging French liberalism than it was in that of the Anglo-Saxons or the Flemish. At the same time, the state's possibility of limiting free competition in the realm of the economy, in favor of reaching collective objectives, was not restricted with the same vigor as it was in Anglo-Saxon liberal thought. In the early stages of French liberalism, eminent figures such as Constant and Tocqueville criticized the British political system for its pronounced aristocracy. Other factors also conditioned the national differences: "France had lost virtually all its colonial empire in 1763. This had imparted to the critique of colonialism and the institution of slavery a diffusion and radicalism hampered, by contrast, in the English and American world by substantial material interests and a national, chauvinistic spirit understandably reinforced by victory" (Losurdo 2011: 141). Economists such as Jean-Baptiste Say and Frédérik Bastiat developed a "strong moral conviction about the justice of property" as a natural right, while in the Anglo-Saxon world, under the influence of Jeremy Bentham and John Stuart Mill, the notions of property "were justified more on the ground of social 'utility' than of natural rights as was the case in France" (Leroux and Hart 2012: 4).

Numerous other variations could be listed. In Germany, with Friedrich List, an economic liberalism would be put into place that was ready to delimit free trade temporarily in favor of increasing the domestic productive capabilities of the nation. In Italy, looking back on the nineteenth century, Benedetto Croce distanced himself from non-"Latin-Catholic" philosophical and national applications of liberalism, refuting both the liberalism influenced by German, Russian, and Nordic romanticism, which longed for a return to paganism, and the abstract utilitarianism which dominated those parts of the world under British influence. Vice versa, "in the language of the ideologues of the British or French Empires, a belief in the duty to defend or export freedom was ambiguously associated with the language of civilization" (Isabella 2016: 80). For Croce (1932: 7–91), all European liberalism, however, was inspired by a "religion of freedom" with which it led Europe along its path to civilization. After 1848, this liberal Europe, seen as a whole, preferred moderation to radicalism, and inter-classist and paternalistic mediation over class struggle. Following the Jacobinism rift and the decades of fierce struggle against the clergy and the reactionary forces, which managed "to exert a strong influence on passive and superstitious populations and to incite them to rise up against the constitutional regime" (Bron 2016: 62), a liberal Europe was now attempting to accept its Christian history. Overall, Croce's accommodating perspective seems to be in tune with the self-representation of a good part of Europe's governing elite during the second half of the nineteenth century. To sum up, the political liberalism of the nineteenth century was a container with assorted contents. "As with cooking, local and regional ingredients and flavours have a considerable impact on the liberal cuisine" (Freeden 2015: 14). Some of if its basic principles nevertheless remained recognizable.

During the twentieth century, the variants of political liberalism came to include other combinations among the basic ingredients. Partially in conflict with the "philosophical liberalism" that had softened liberty in favor of demanding the equality of rights, a "New Liberalism" emerged, which separated individualism as a positive value from self-interest, concentrating particularly on civil and personal rights without precluding solutions on a social and economic level aimed at the collective good and at the welfare state. Following 1945, a "Cold War Liberalism," inspired by intellectuals such as Karl Popper and Isaiah Berlin, also emerged which manifested strongly anti-utopian attitudes. Other branches of liberal thought meanwhile still drifted toward a "realist utopianism," convinced of being able to better the world through reform of institutions and incentives for the individual contribution to the common good (Leopold 2012: 12–21).

The political and social atmosphere of the mid twentieth century was marked not only by the confrontation between socialism and capitalism and by organized mass interest, mass parties with socialist or Christian tones, economic growth, Keynesian policies, as well as a production regime ruled by Fordism, but also by social reforms and new managerial approaches and industrial policies. From within this atmosphere it was much more difficult to defend the theory that justice and rights could be derived completely from the need to safeguard private property. Thus, we find some liberals ready to "clarify" what they claimed to be a misunderstanding. As Dunn (1979: 39–40) underlined, Locke chose to emphasize property in terms of rights and therefore his texts needed a proper translation: "The term which fixes the synonymy onto our own language is 'right', not 'property'." Insofar as Locke was already a liberal, "he was certainly not such *because* of his moral credulity in the market."

With the advancement of globalization and neoliberal policies, and with the implosion of the Soviet system, similar interpretative efforts would become superfluous, if not counterproductive from the point of view of the predominant social interests and political settings. Not only was the "free market" restored in its ideological entirety, it also became the master paradigm for any type of social interaction just as much in common discourse as in the social sciences. Under such circumstances, "Liberal universalism has been replaced with neoliberal globalism; the ethical permeation of individuals has been supplanted by the economic ingestion of territory." As Freeden (2015: 110–11) maintains, thanks to the neoliberals' improper attempts to appropriate the liberal heritage, in the twenty-first century "the complex morphology of liberalism is shattered and becomes barely recognizable." At least initially, this did not hamper the popularity of the liberal "ism." In the twenty years that followed 1989, where on the one hand numerous parties, which had carried liberalism in their name, fell into crisis, on the other, sizable parties with conservative, Christian–democratic or social–democratic backgrounds added the label "liberal–democratic" to their profile identity. Up until at least the financial crisis of 2008, explicitly keeping a distance from liberalism almost bordered on political incorrectness as by then the modern state and the democratic constitution were described as "liberal" in themselves. Liberalism seemed to lack reasonable alternatives: "Our exercise of political power is fully proper only when it is exercised in accordance with a constitution the essentials of which all citizens free and equal may be expected to endorse in the light of principles and ideals acceptable to their common human reason. This is the liberal principle of legitimacy" (Rawls 2005: 137).

On the surface it would seem implicit in these statements to presume that terms such as "humanity," "reason," and "nature" do not define transcendent concepts, but should circumscribe the mandatory and ideologically neutral premise of shaping political consent. In the same way, in the "post-secular age," the "liberal State"—the very same that had secularized sovereignty (Habermas 2012: 98)—was characterized as needing transcendent references that it was unable to provide. In the long run "it needs a mentality which it does not know how to generate through its own resources . . . the religious traditions can still provide a consciousness of what is missing" (Habermas 2009: 9, 13). Rather than "post-secular," however, perhaps in the age of globalization, the "popular" and "national" character that had previously provided a substantial element of sacredness to the liberal project has only been temporarily dimmed along with the welfare state. Before going into detail, however, it is worth looking at the situation in America, where the sacralization of the political sphere took a more direct route than it did in Europe.

2.2 A chosen people in a promised land

The first nuclei of European colonization in northern America were implanted during the early seventeenth century. By 1640, English colonies were established in the areas of Chesapeake (Virginia and Maryland) and the Bay of Massachusetts (New England), French in the future Nova Scotia (Acadia) and Dutch along the Hudson River (New York). English colonization in particular was driven by two principal forces, which resulted in its intentional and organized nature. The first was religion, placed within the context of sixteenth- and seventeenth-century England's post-Reformation political–religious conflicts; the second was business, in as much as even before any ship sailed, the colonization project had been the product of a broad effort of accumulating capital in the hands of a new type of economic association, the joint-stock company. Many of these companies united numerous shareholders and were modeled on the large commercial companies such as the Muscovy Company, the Levant Company, and the East India Company, and they embodied both driving forces, given that the leaders and followers alike were Puritans. In other words, many of the leaders took on the role of entrepreneurs, managers of the colonial companies, political leaders and spiritual guides, all at the same time. They represented "the core protestant belief in individual responsibility for one's own salvation" (Boyer 2012: 10), and were taking on the ocean crossing and the colonization not only in the search of economic fortune, but also as a civilizing mission and utopian quest. The name "New England" was indeed assigned to the northern colony in 1620 in the hopes of rebuilding a "better England" on the other side of the Atlantic.

The Puritan faith that inspired the first English colonization had a long-term impact on American political ideas and institutions. This should be admitted, I believe, as a fact, even if this admission should not give rise to teleological representations of the past. It may be doubted, for example, that "Democracy made her American debut on 30 July 1619, when 22 'burgesses', two from each settled district, elected by vote of all men seventeen and upward, met with the governor's council in the church at Jamestown" (Morison, Commager, and Leuchtenburg 1977: 21). Territorial bodies of elected representatives were not unknown in medieval and early-modern Europe but they did not necessarily anticipate democracy. While religious upheaval and civil wars were devastating the Motherland over the seventeenth century, the self-governance of the North American colonies nevertheless became stronger and stronger, all the while assuming a characteristic shape:

> With both charter and company in America, the [Massachusetts Bay] colony became practically independent of England. The "freemen," as stockholders were then called, became voters; the governor, deputy-governor, and assistants whom the freemen annually elected, and who in England had been president and directors of a colonizing company, were now the executives, upper branch of the legislative assembly, and judicial officers of a Puritan commonwealth. A representative system was devised, as it was inconvenient for the freemen to attend the "general court" or assembly in person, and by 1644 the deputies and assistants had separated into two houses. Neither king nor parliament had any say in the Massachusetts government. (Morison, Commager, and Leuchtenburg 1977: 26)

The system was imitated by the other American colonies wherever the crown allowed it. It still "survives in the Federal Government, and the corporate precedent has given the American system of government a very different complexion from the parliamentary system that was slowly developing in England" (Morison, Commager, and Leuchtenburg 1977: 26). The economic and political motivation of the English colonists went hand in hand with their religious commitment. One of the most prominent political and spiritual leaders of the first English settlements provides us with a clear example:

> In a shipboard lecture en route to America, John Winthrop, Massachusetts' first governor, called the soon-to-be-founded settlement "a city on a hill,"

a model of God's ultimate plan for humanity. Elaborated by a succession of ministers, this sense of divine purpose arose from a particular reading of sacred history. God had chosen the Puritans to create in America a New Zion, as He had once chosen the Jews in ancient times. Sometimes reformulated in secular language, this deep-seated belief in America's unique role in history would long survive. (Boyer 2012: 11)

The Puritan settlers "developed a more or less permanent feeling of being far-flung, of existing on the edge of the civilized world" (Boschman 2009: 36). It implied not only nostalgia and disorientation, and a veritable syndrome of the frontier; it also implied an aggressive confrontation with the wilderness and what it contained, for example, its native human population. The latter did not even systematically oppose the newcomers' settlement. "To native peoples, the land was for use and could be shared" (Boyer 2012: 7). They were rewarded with an unprecedented assault by the self-righteous settlers. Although nowhere "did the colonizers find a truly empty land free for the taking" (Taylor 2011: 9), the Indians were seen and treated as illegitimate dwellers. According to Locke's theory on the origins of landed property, ownership was a remuneration for the cultivation of virgin land. As the natives neither understood nor respected the colonizers' view on property rights, they transformed themselves into "thieves" against whom it was legitimate to wage war. In similar cases, a lawful conqueror had the right to enslave or to kill the defeated enemy. In 1645, a Puritan correspondent to John Winthrop "talked of the desirability of war against the Indians, so that captives may be taken who could be exchanged 'for Moores [Negroes], which will be more gayneful pilladge for us then [sic] wee conceive, for I doe not see how wee can thrive until wee get into a stock of slaves sufficient to doe all our business . . .'" (Degler [1959] 1984: 36).

According to John Cotton, the preeminent theologian of the Massachusetts Bay Colony, the conquest of Indian land was unmistakably justified by the Bible:

That in a vacant soyle, hee that taketh possession of it, and bestoweth culture and husbandry upon it, his Right it is. And the ground of this is from the grand Charter given to *Adam* and his posterity in Paradise, *Gen. 1. 28. Multiply, and replenish the earth, and subdue it*. If therefore any sonne of Adam come and finde a place empty, he hath liberty to come, and fill, and subdue the earth there. This Charter was renewed to *Noah, Gen. 9. 1. Fulfill the earth and multiply*. So that it is free from that common Grant, for any to take possession of vacant Countries. Indeed no Nation is to drive out another without speciall Commission from heaven, such as the *Israelites* had, unlesse the Natives do unjustly wrong them, and will not recompence the wrongs done in peaceable sort, & then they may right themselves by lawfull war, and subdue the Countrey unto themselves. (Cotton 1630: 5–6)

As Arnold Toynbee commented many years ago, the "Bible Christian" of European origin identified himself "with Israel obeying the will of Jehovah and doing the Lord's work by taking possession of the Promised Land, while he has identified the non-Europeans who have crossed his path with the Canaanites whom the Lord has delivered into the hand of his Chosen People to be destroyed or subjugated" (Toynbee 1948: 211–12). No wonder, then, that Indians were sometimes "killed and scalped with veritable religious fervor; they even became targets for shooting practice" (Losurdo 2011: 19). Apparently, to many settlers this seemed to be the only way to confront "that obstinate Disposition in barbarous Nations to continue barbarous," as an anonymous author wrote on August 1, 1763, in the *Boston Gazette*, also observing the extreme "difficulty of introducing Civility and Christianity among them" (Hyneman and Lutz 1983: 35). By 1800 the Indian population had shrunk to about 600,000, "a pathetic remnant of the estimated 2.2 million on the eve of European colonization" (Boyer 2012: 8). Apart from organized and private violence or battlefield casualties, this was mainly the effect of high mortality rates provoked by imported germs and viruses against which the local population's immune system offered no protection.

Compared with Europe, yet other particular aspects characterized the situation in the New World. To begin with, "the availability of land rendered precarious, if not untenable, those European institutions which were dependent upon scarcity of land. Efforts to establish feudal or manorial reproductions in the New World came to nothing." This had a number of important implications. One was the high level of income from free labor, the scarcity of which was at the same time a major stimulus for the import of chattel slaves and indentured servants: "We shall maynteyne 20 Moores cheaper than one English servant," we can read in a source of 1645. Another specificity consisted in the absence of nobility and aristocracy, the social groups which slowed down the unfolding dynamics of capitalist development in agriculture and commerce throughout continental Europe. European visitors to America noted an unknown fluidity of class lines and a comparatively greater social mobility among the white colonists. The widespread distribution of property, especially of land, gave rise to the "middling nature of colonial society" and a comparatively high material standard of living by the average white family. Despite reciprocal tolerance among settlers of different religious beliefs and geographic or linguistic origins, a "fear of the growing number of strangers in [their] midst" had already developed among those born in America (Degler [1959] 1984: 3, 36, 50, 53).

At the beginning of the eighteenth century, preachers and churchmen detected a decline in the religious fervor among the second or third generation of colonial freemen and the new immigrants. As a reaction, the "Great Awakening" movement swept over the British colonies in the 1740s. New evangelical sects such as Methodists and Baptists were founded

(Norton et al. 2012: 110–12). The revivalists "promoted public roles for women, children, African Americans, and Native Americans, and assaulted the established state churches as insufficiently committed to revival. Suddenly, the Great Awakening had become not just the preaching of the new birth, but a popular assault on established power in the colonies" (Harris and Kidd 2012: 8). Regarding the long-term political consequences of the awakening movement, American historiography has elaborated contrasting interpretations. Some scholars assign to the religious rebirth a prominent preparatory function within the Revolution, whereas for others it had no appreciable role in the preparation of American independence. What seems to be agreed upon by the majority of historians is that the consent around religious freedom and the absence of State interference in religious affairs had its roots in the years of the rebirth movement. Harris and Kidd highlight another effect of the Great Awakening:

> It energized the religious culture of the colonies and helped give a spiritual vocabulary to patriots who wished to justify the Revolution in moral and spiritual terms. To most patriots, the Revolution was not simply about taxes and parliamentary power; it was about the sacred cause of liberty. The awakening also gave patriot leaders a new model of popular persuasion. Many of the most famous orators and writers of the revolutionary movement, including Patrick Henry and Thomas Paine, spoke and wrote in evangelical language and cadences, even if they were not evangelicals themselves. (Harris and Kidd 2012: 9)

Following the end of the Seven Years War in 1763, revolutionary upheaval spread far. It would be twenty years of political unrest until the 1783 Treaty of Paris recognized the Declaration of Independence of 1776. What were the catalysts for insurrection?

> Relations worsened as the British government, by the Proclamation of 1763, restricted colonists' westward expansion, reserving the lands between the Appalachian Mountains and the Mississippi to the Indian inhabitants. Religious fears exacerbated the colonists' anger, since Britain granted full religious freedom to the thousands of French Catholics in its newly acquired territories. Further, Parliament sought to pay off its heavy war debt by increasing colonial taxes. The stage was set for a showdown. (Boyer 2012: 14)

Therefore, before the claim for "no taxation without representation" would resonate in the streets and fields of British America, two other major catalysts of the independence movement came to the fore. They consisted of a protest against the regulation of further colonial conquest, and the religious freedom for the Catholic subjects in the annexed former French territories. The protest against the Catholics, who in the eyes of many Protestant leaders represented the "papist" Antichrist, sounds remarkable when compared with the programmatic plea for the "freedom of religion" by the upcoming independence movement. The interdiction of further colonial conquest west of the crest of the Appalachians called forth the protest of influential land speculators. "Opposed to this policy were the promoters of several big speculative companies. Of these the most important was the Vandalia Company, promoted by Benjamin Franklin, George Croghan, and Thomas Wharton of Philadelphia" (Morison, Commager, and Leuchtenburg 1977: 67).

The supporters of the independence movement seemed united under John Locke's motto according to which all persons possess a natural right to life, to liberty, and to property. However, the ideologically driving forces behind it were not only the Puritan millenarianism and the philosophy of natural justice and history, which we have referred to so far. John Pocock maintains that the apocalyptic dimension, "while apparent in the rhetoric of the Revolution, is hardly dominant there. Americans of that generation saw themselves as freemen in arms, manifesting a patriot virtue, rather than as covenant saints." During the years of Revolution and Constitution, the "civic humanism" to which Harrington, Montesquieu, and Thomas Jefferson had given expression became another central element of the Revolution's ideological blend. According to Pocock, the translation of Polybian and Machiavellian ideas into the American context shaped a republican self-understanding that rested "upon a concept of the role of arms in society and in a *vivere civile*." Later, as an effect of the same "Macchiavellian moment," "the *virtù* of the frontier" compensated for the partial "abandonment of virtue" by the Constitution (Pocock 1975: 211, 513, 539).

It cannot be discussed here what it means for Machiavelli's virtue "which one must find in oneself and express in actions" independently from innate rights (Pocock 2003: 561–62) to be inserted into the wider context of the Humanist—that is, basically, Christian—rediscovery of classical concepts (Vasoli 1977: 663). As Pocock (2003: 561) recognizes, pre-Christian concepts of citizenship and virtue were compatible with the Puritan clergy-less commonwealth as well as with natural justice, and even with certain "secularized" apocalyptic expectations. But for Pocock the entanglement between various strands of thought does not invalidate his own emphasis on a particular republican tradition. For analogous reasons, in a book on western ideology like the present the main emphasis has to be laid on the teleological expectation that the American revolutionary process expressed. If it differed in several aspects from the Puritan apocalyptic, the republican ideal of civic virtues also gave voice to teleological and missionary visions (Tricoire 2015: 27).

The American constitutional process lasted for almost a dozen years. On July 4, 1776, the Continental Congress voted on the Declaration of Independence drafted by Thomas Jefferson. Locke's term "property" was substituted with "the pursuit of Happiness," in line with Hobbes's ([1651] 1970: 55) definition of "felicity" as a result of "continual prospering." Nature, mankind, and destiny—a stenographic expression for the western meaning of history—also resonated in Thomas Paine's pamphlet *Common Sense* of 1776, another key text of the American Revolution. According to Paine, reason pleaded for separation, and "the weeping voice of nature cries, 'tis time to part'. . . . The cause of America is in a great measure the cause of all mankind" (Paine 1776: 10, 19).

It remains important nevertheless to underline the multiplicity of ideas that operate in a historical process like the American Revolution. The text of the American Constitution appears to lean less on Puritanism than on the idea of a balance of powers. This was, according to Skinner ([1998] 2012: 35–36), the most remarkable result obtained by the neo-Roman tradition, as "the ideal of a mixed and balanced constitution remained at the heart of the proposals put forward by the so called commonwealthmen in the eighteenth century, and eventually became enshrined (with the monarchical element converted into a presidential one) in the constitution of the United States." In effect, according to what Harrington ([1656] 1992: 8) had written more than hundred years earlier, "government (to define it *de jure*, or according to ancient prudence) is an art whereby a civil society of men is instituted and preserved upon the foundation of common right or interest; or (to follow Aristotle and Livy) it is the empire of laws and not of men."

When voting the American Constitution of 1787, the Convention delegates "certainly did not assume that the electors and the people were the same thing, and most of the delegates did not believe that most individual people could become, or ever should become, electors" (King 2012: 18). Eleven years earlier, Thomas Jefferson had drafted a constitution for Virginia, in which he established that the right to vote was reserved to all

> male persons of full age and sane mind having a freehold estate in [one fourth of an acre] of land in any town, or in [25] acres of land in the country, and all persons resident in the colony who shall have paid scot and lot to government the last [two years] shall have the right to give their vote in the election of their representative. (Jefferson [1776] 1904: 166)

The new Constitution did not change the rule whereby each single state of the Union could define its own electoral law. As a result, the active electorate ranged from 50 percent to 90 percent of all free male citizens. The convention delegates' views differed on "whether or not Negro slaves were human beings (though, in order to avoid rancor and dissension at the convention, they took care not to debate this issue); but, whatever their views, most of them nevertheless took it for granted that chattel slaves, like women and children, should not, or were not in any position to, become electors" (King 2012: 18).

Slavery in American history is sometimes represented as a residual heritage of ancient times, which was overcome in the nineteenth century thanks to a steadily ongoing process of democratization. Carl Degler ([1959] 1984: 30), for example, wrote: "Simply because the Negro differed from the Englishman in a number of ways, it was unlikely that men of the seventeenth century would accord the black man an equal status with Englishmen. Even Irishmen, who were white, Christian, and European, were held to be literally 'beyond the Pale', and some were even referred to as 'slaves.'" In fact, from the seventeenth to the nineteenth century, simultaneously with the affirmation of self-governance in the English/British colonies and the upcoming American Revolution, slavery as an institution was not retreating but expanding. Its practices, rather than becoming milder, were increasingly harsh, and its legitimization became more and more openly racist. It seems that in 1619 the first African workforce arrived as indentured servants who, similarly to their white peers, could hope to be free one day, whereas the first mention of slavery in a legal text seems to be in the 1660 statute books of Virginia. Chattel slavery boomed during the eighteenth century.

Reference to an alleged ancient mentality is also spurious given that it was never intuitive or self-evident that men had the right to enslave other men. Slavery stimulated ongoing philosophical, religious, ethical, and juridical debate. From the mid eighteenth century onwards, the new evangelical sects born from the Great Awakening, for example, the Baptists, organized both free and enslaved members and considered them equal in the view of God (Norton et al. 2012: 110–12). It was hardly due to residual ancient beliefs that only a few decades later many convention delegates would wonder whether "negro slaves" were human beings at all. If we add that on the basis of the 1790 Naturalization Act "only whites could become citizens of the United States," that for "thirty-two of the United States' first thirty-six years of existence, slave-owners from Virginia occupied the post of president," and that in the nineteenth century "the United States reintroduced slavery in Texas, which had previously been taken from Mexico" (Losurdo 2011: 12, 50, 153), it is clear that slavery and racism were anything but mere anachronistic elements in shaping the predominantly Protestant and Whig-liberal political culture of America.

The dominant ideological self-representation of "early America" had been influenced by English, Dutch, and Scottish philosophers, as well as by church reformers and preachers, officers, bureaucrats, and businessmen. America served as a space of utopian expectation for British colonizers, many of whom had already conceived of what "America" was to mean long before setting foot on American soil. In a book on western ideology, similar aspects need to be underlined. This does not mean that American history was nothing but a self-fulfilling European prophecy. Frederick Turner and others stated that "the course of American development owed less to European foundations than to 'American factors'" (Aron 2011: 263). During the one hundred and seventy years from the foundation of the first English colony until American independence, the colonial society had developed differently from that of the Old World, mainly because of the absence of any remnants of feudalism or absolutist ancien régime. "While the speculative philosophers of Europe were laboriously searching their minds in an effort to decide the first principles of liberty, the Americans had come to experience vividly that liberty in their everyday lives" (Wood [1966] 1993: 56). According to Turner's famous frontier thesis, "American social development has been continually beginning over again on the frontier. This perennial rebirth, this fluidity of American life, this expansion westward with its new opportunities, its continuous touch with the simplicity of primitive society, furnish the forces dominating American character." American society, Turner says, constantly rejuvenates expanding the frontier that is "the outer edge of the wave—the meeting point between savagery and civilization" (Turner [1893] 2005: 2).

More recent American scholarly history writing (e.g., Richter 2001; Slaughter 2003; Abbott 2006 and Aron 2006) has challenged interpretations that cast "the colonial period simply as an Anglophone preparation for the United States, defined as a uniquely middle-class society and democracy" (Taylor 2011: 7). While Spanish colonization pushed northwards from Mexico, not only English but also French and Dutch colonies were founded in the St. Lawrence, New England, Hudson, Delaware, and Chesapeake areas. Almost right from the start, colonizers introduced African servants, and later, chattel slaves, and lived in commercial symbiosis not only with their motherlands, but also with each other and the West Indies (Morison, Commager, and Leuchtenburg 1977: 23–31). Until the time of American independence, the world of the native Amerindian population remained a complex geopolitical environment with its own economic institutions, political structure and military power, although weakened by armed conflict and epidemic diseases. Still in the early eighteenth century, Indian leaders hoped to incorporate the European settlers "into a native nexus of diplomacy and trade in the hope that the colonists could learn how to coexist in a shared land." One should not forget that the "Indians also lived in a new world transformed by the intrusion of diverse newcomers bearing alien diseases, livestock, trade goods, weapons, and Christian beliefs." They were however steadfast in rejecting the colonizers' attempts to dispossess them of their land "and convert the survivors into Christian menials" (Taylor 2011: 4–5, 8).

Recent historiography has been attempting a restitution of history and memory to these various, often-"forgotten" realities, in order to highlight how the "colonies mixed diverse European, American, and African traditions into a novel cultural blend" (Norton et al. 2012: 113). Thus recent academic scholarship admits "Indian deaths and the African slaves were fundamental to the success of colonization and the prosperity of the free" (Taylor 2011: 8). Similar statements invert "Turner's triumphant progression into a tragic procession through a land scarred by the legacy of blood-splattering, people-scattering, world-shattering conquests. All of which, its critics contended, left Americans not feeling good, but feeling guilty." (Aron 2011: 262). The latter may be the main reason why the scholarly deconstruction of American historical myths does not easily penetrate the wider public opinion. Turner's frontier paradigm and the idea of the Americans as God's chosen people still remain central to American political self-representation. They also seem to contribute more substantially to western ideology than competing elaborations of American history do.

What is at stake in the present context is neither the matter of whether America is exceptional or different (Shafer 1991), nor whether there can exist at all acceptable ideal types that would allow us to measure the distance of a country from historical "normality." What is of interest here is the role that the very idea of exceptionality had in American history. Deborah Madsen (1998: 1–2) claims that

> American exceptionalism permeates every period of American history and is the single most powerful agent in a series of arguments that have been fought down the centuries concerning the identity of America and the Americans. Though the arguments themselves change over time, the basic assumption and terms of reference do not change, and it is the assumption that derived in important ways from the exceptionalist logic taken to the New World by the first Puritan migrants. . . . In this view, the New World is the last and best chance offered by God to a fallen humanity that has only to look to His exceptional new church for redemption. Thus, America and Americans are special, exceptional, because they are charged with saving the world from itself and, at the same time, America and the Americans must sustain a high level of spiritual, political and moral commitment to this exceptional destiny.

Is American exceptionalism exceptional? This is what Madsen seems to suggest when arguing that the American self-representation reaches a "unique" degree of introspection. Under a critical understanding of western ideology, the exceptionality of American exceptionalism should be challenged. If seen in their global historical context, both America's frontier mentality and its universalistic ambitions look rather like ordinary variants of western ideology. American westward expansion, for example, can well be compared to other episodes of western colonialism. Of course, there are differences related to time and space that distinguish America from all the other cases, but the same can be said for each of the other cases as well. Latinized America, Southern Africa, Australia, Siberia, and so on, also represent unique combinations of contingent circumstances and local ingredients. Peculiarities are therefore not exceptional as such. Consequently, it is not so absurd to believe in a certain parallelism between American history and what happened elsewhere between the fifteenth and nineteenth centuries. The European colonizers, with all their diverging Christian or atheist worldviews and greatly differing political projects, nevertheless shared some basic assumptions about meaning in history. They shared the myths of nature. They were all convinced that the cultivation of wilderness and the civilization of the savages represented a moral duty even more than a political mission or an economic opportunity. They categorized the natives according to stages of civilization. Most of them adopted a self-referential philosophy of law according to which "savages" were unlawfully dwelling in territories in which they had no legitimate claim to property.

In short, the American colonists shared the European eschatological sense of history discussed in the previous chapter. Winthrop and his followers saw "in the pattern of history that their errand was not a mere scouting expedition: it was an essential maneuver in the drama of Christendom." Perry Miller ([1953] 1993: 9) goes on to comment that the Puritan settlers were "performing a job not so much for Jehovah as for history, which was the wisdom of Jehovah expressed through time." A similar confidence in history was true not only for the pious men of the early seventeenth century, but also—in an updated and partially secularized version—for the advocates of liberty of the late eighteenth century. Some years before Condorcet and Herder wrote that Europe was the avant-garde in mankind's march toward full humanity, Thomas Paine ([1792] 1817: 32–33) had already established that America would embody mankind's model to be followed by the rest of the world in the fight for liberty: "What Athens was in miniature, America will be in magnitude. The one was the wonder of the ancient world; the other is becoming the admiration, the model of the present."

According to David Gelernter (2007: 69), the fourth great western religion consists in the "passionate belief in the American community's closeness to God and its obligation to God and the whole world—Americans as a new chosen people, America as a new promised land." On the one hand, we could simply reply that it was this very American sense of election that made America so ordinarily European and so typically western. On the other, and perhaps better, we might also invert the perspective by saying that the pious

Americans were ideologically "European" in the same way the secularized French became "American" when during the Revolution they elected the former British colonies as an example to follow, in particular in the fields of rhetoric and symbols. During the French Revolution and the emergence of new nation-states of Europe, the common belief in the transcendent fate of humanity indeed took the form of another new religion: the religion of the people.

2.3 The religion of the people

To trace a linear path from the inalienable rights of the privileged group of "free men," as was referred to in the *Magna Carta*, to the victory of popular sovereignty, as it was generally understood during the twentieth century, would hardly be realistic. On the one hand the "English myth on how royal power was tamed" draws on an inexistent exceptionality of *Magna Carta* in the European juridical landscape of the twelfth and thirteenth century, in which several "other charters of liberties" were granted to the free subjects by their rulers (Reynolds 2016: 659–60). On the other hand, under nineteenth-century liberal regimes, political participation was in nearly all cases still a privilege restricted to only a minority. Popular sovereignty as we understand it today—that is, as the right of political participation of all citizens of full age, male and female, through voting—was only constitutionally recognized in most western countries after the First World War, in some cases decades later. Even the expansion of English (then British) parliamentarianism, which had begun in the seventeenth century, only very slowly filtered beyond the confines of aristocracy; Henry Parker's phrase, written on the threshold of civil war, according to which "The fountaine and efficient cause [of sovereignty] is the people" (Parker 1642, quoted from Skinner [1998] 2012: 1), still had an elitist background. Not even the American and French Revolutions succeeded in making political rights durably "universal." We could in fact claim that it only came gradually to include the larger part of society between the later nineteenth and the mid twentieth century, when in more and more countries census or property-related restrictions were lifted and female suffrage admitted.

As a direct consequence of the political events in seventeenth-century England, the conditions surrounding the rights of many common people initially worsened. During the same century, Ireland suffered the loss of hundreds and thousands of inhabitants through battlefield casualties, famine, disease, massacres, and the deportation of indentured laborers to the colonies, making the Catholic population suffer "massive expropriation of estates and transplantation of native inhabitants" (Foster 1989: 79) and an "iniquitous deprivation of equal civil rights" (D'Arcy McGee 1869: 216). After the Glorious Revolution, harsh legislation to protect the new concepts of private property also developed in England and Scotland. Forced deportation of workers to the colonies increased because of commutated death penalties. From 1688 to 1820, the number of crimes for which the death penalty was contemplated rose from 50 to over 200, most of which concerned crimes against property. "Thus, what legitimized the pickpocket's killing or execution is the same liberal pathos that had presided over the condemnation of monarchical despotism as the source of political slavery" (Losurdo 2011: 78).

In the United States, equality of civil rights was earlier—and more completely—extended to all free male citizens. The American Constitution of 1787 is introduced by the words "We the people of the United States," but who exactly were "the people," that is, the group owning political rights according to the Convention delegates? For those who voted for the Constitution, "the people" did not refer

> either to the eligible electorate or to the entire American population. This third category was a far more elusive and abstract concept. It was, indeed, a concept, an intellectual tool, a summary phrase. It lacked specific empirical referents. One could talk eloquently—and seemingly meaningfully—about "the people" without referring either to the body of eligible electors or to the whole population. The attraction of the phrase lay in its vagueness. (King 2012: 18)

In continental Europe, and especially during the French Revolution, when national sovereignty became "the keystone for constitutional self-understanding" (Middell 2016: 25), the edges of a social and ideological dispute around the concept of "sovereign people" became more clearly visible because of the tenacious resistance of the nobility and clergy as well as aristocracies and dynasties. During the French Revolution, as well as in 1830 and in 1848, this conflict radicalized as a wider "popular" mobilization was needed to sustain the bourgeoisie's political objectives.

All of these cases raise the following questions: By what principle was the concept "the people" legitimized in its power? And who was included in this concept? Was the concept of "the people" referred to a free association formed between naturally free individuals through a voluntary social contract, or was it a social body already irreducibly collective from the beginning? The German Calvinist Johannes Althusius was convinced of the naturally social character of human beings. Decades prior to the Glorious Revolution he wrote that the "ownership of a realm belongs to the people, and administration of it to the King." He added that such a body, or "universal association," would be a "polity in the fullest sense." The same Althusius ([1603] 1995: 84), however, also underlined that the "members of a realm, or of this universal symbiotic association, are not, I say, individual men, families, or collegia, as in a private or a particular public association." These members in his view were cities, provinces, and other collective bodies, which formed the basic elements of his proto-federalist and proto-corporatist design of statehood. In a way, it seemed not dissimilar to Thomas More's Utopia: "A genuine *res publica*, More suggests, must take the constitutional form of a federated republic" (Skinner [1998] 2012: 31). According to Giuseppe Duso, the widespread recognition of Althusius as the precocious inventor of popular sovereignty is based on an incorrect attribution of modern concepts of power, sovereignty, and people to his thinking. As the author argues, this thinking still lacks "awareness of the particular and decisive nature of modern power that was born with Hobbes and Rousseau, and which . . . implies a foundation and legitimization, which can only come from the will of individuals who find themselves ruled by it" (Duso 2010: 168).

In Hobbes's view, guaranteeing the freedom and equality of rights legitimizes the use of power, the "rationality" of which depends exactly on that guarantee: "For I ground the civil rights of sovereigns, and both the duty and the liberty of subjects, upon the known natural inclinations of mankind, and upon the articles of the law of nature; of which no man, that pretends but reason enough to govern his private family, ought to be ignorant" (Hobbes [1651] 1970: 509). It seems, however, to be a circular argument: if the rational construction of sovereignty is founded on natural freedom and equality, which are self-evident to any reasonable man, then the sovereign power is likewise unquestionable, and the consent of the subjects little more than a power-confirming abstraction. As the sovereign power detains the right to determine what is reasonable, that is, lawful, it also detains full control over the axiomatic preconditions of its own legitimacy. Of course, every man has the natural right to rebel against this power, but he can do it only at the cost of his expulsion from society and on the society's risk of relapsing into the state of nature. Apparently, Locke left more room for mediation between the two alternative solutions. It was clear to him

> that the people at large had certain rights vis-à-vis their rulers, including the right under some circumstance to rebel against them. He did not, however, have much to say about what he meant by 'the people' (though he used the phrase often); he seems simply to have assumed that the people comprised everybody in an organized society other than the rulers of that society. (King 2012: 139)

Hobbes and Locke, therefore, if in different ways, shared the view that it is not the people who govern: they form "the people" precisely in as much as they are not the governors, but the governed. Duso observes that "in this way, the compulsion is established and legitimized through a formal rationality, at the basis of which the consent by those who must obey is established"; he also explains that "according to the natural justice doctrines of the social contract, at the law, and therefore at the command of he or they who have been authorized to represent it, there is no way left to disagree" (Duso 2010: 169). Under this perspective, the people, when they become sovereign themselves, appear in the double role of sovereign and subject. Due to this duplicity, it is the citizen in his role as a subject who has the sole freedom to obey the citizen from whom legitimacy, expressed through an abstract *rational* and *natural* will, emanates. The people's sovereignty did not overcome the circularity in the legitimization of power, but innovated the political method of dealing with it.

If we adopt a benevolent interpretation, even the roots of the rule of law can be glimpsed within this reasoning, as it envisages the sovereign to be obligatorily subjected to the principle of sovereignty that he emanates. Actually, the legitimization of sovereignty by two speculative axiomatic constructs such as "nature" and "reason" left room for a wide range of solutions ultimately determined by power relations. Intellectually we *can* believe in these constructs or not, but politically, we *must* believe in them, due to the taxing strength of an interpretative power which postulates that each subject is able to grasp its substance. What can the man who "pretends but reason enough to govern his private family" actually understand of Hobbes's fantasies? What is he willing to understand? How can these understandings of "nature" and "reason" be instilled in him, the responsible citizen, as if they were his own? In various respects, German conceptual history, on the one hand, and Michel Foucault, on the other, may exaggerate the breaches carried out by the Enlightenment and revolutionary period. They nevertheless grasp an important discontinuity, which occurred in the context of the establishment of the people's sovereignty during the late eighteenth century. Foucault ([1978] 2007: 41–81) describes the innovative "techniques of power" in terms of "rationalization." I would describe them in terms of sacralization, which I understand to be a matter of specification of, rather than juxtaposition to, Foucault's "rationalization."

One of the most perceptive observers of the French Revolution and of the period in which popular sovereignty was established in Europe was the Romantic poet Novalis. His 1799 pamphlet *Christianity or Europe* is not wrongly considered a founding manifesto of modern conservatism, even if probably less influential than Edmund Burke's essay against the French Revolution. It is without doubt a concise critique of the revolutionary project. Yet, read against the light, the text also reveals, in some sense, significant passages of appreciation. Indeed, for Novalis, the French Revolution is not—as it claims to be—the political realization of the Enlightenment, but rather marks its end.

The hideous *philosophes* had disparaged "fantasy and feeling, morality and the love of art, the future and past"; their work was "purging poetry from nature, the earth, the human soul and the sciences. Every trace of the sacred was to be destroyed, all memory of noble events and people was to be spoiled by satire, and the world stripped of colourful ornament. Their favorite theme, on account of its mathematical obedience and impudence, was light." From this point of view, the French Revolution instead sent signals of regeneration. This was not merely an indirect stimulus for the reevaluation of religion from the perspective of conservative or reactionary resistance, as could be observed in the Vendée and elsewhere. It was also because these same revolutionaries restored faith, passion, feeling, sacredness, veneration: the Pantheon, funeral rites, deified Reason, sacralized Nature, the existence of the Supreme Being decreed by parliament, and so on. "The attempt of that great iron mask, which went by the name of Robespierre, to make religion the middle point and heart of the republic remains historically remarkable" (Novalis [1799] 1999: 70, 73).

Although the French revolutionaries were far from the Puritan bigotry of certain American revolutionaries, a colossal sacralization of the political sphere was also taking place in France. Even if certain revolutionary priests like Claude Fauchet may have claimed that Jesus was "the popular God who died for democracy of the universe" (Hesmivy d'Auribeau 1795: 835), the sacralization was not necessarily religious in its usual meaning of the word. Sacredness is not in fact an exclusively religious prerogative in terms of traditional religions. Under these circumstances, it manifested itself in particular through philosophical concepts, such as "nature," "reason," "humanity," and "the people." These were concepts that permeated revolutionary political rhetoric in an attempt to translate the eschatology discussed in the previous chapter within the political dimension. Novalis, as the anti-Enlightenment poet par excellence who probably underestimated the sentimental elements of the Enlightenment philosophies of history, had nonetheless good reason for pointing out this fundamental change in the political sphere.

What exactly did it entail? When thrown into the turbulent reality of revolutionary upheaval in the aim of politicizing the masses, the Enlightenment, which up until 1789 had mostly been the intellectual disposition of powerful elite, was propagated by means of idealization, sacralization, and the stimulation of sentiment. The actors of the intellectual life "who resorted to the metaphor of light and the social role of the *philosophe* staged themselves as the champions of reason and progress who would dissolve the darkness of barbarism"; this habit was functional for asserting their "own leadership over the great majority of the population" (Tricoire 2015: 26). According to Jonathan Israel (2014), in the revolutionary process the "radical strand" of the Enlightenment, inspired by *philosphes* such as Diderot, Helvétius, and d'Holbach, and represented in the ranks of the political leadership by Brissot,

Condorcet, Sieyès, and others, actually took the lead of the revolution. According to the same author, the revolutionary policies made a more selective borrowing of the ideas of "moderate thinkers" like Voltaire and Montesquieu. Israel explains that Rousseau—or more precisely Robespierre's post-1793 institutionalized Rousseauism—was contrary to true Enlightenment and thus counterrevolutionary. The author's conclusions are based on the analysis of intellectual and political controversies regarding, for example, theist and atheist ideas, and the choice between constitutional monarchy, republic, and authoritarian populism. As we shall see, "the allies of the first stages of the revolution became the most hostile opponents at a later stage to the point where they were fighting against each other to the death" (Middell 2016: 25). No doubt, for these conflicts philosophical controversies mattered. At the base of the missionary political endeavor for intellectual leadership there was, however, a common philosophical conviction, which in the present context has to be underlined. In Tricoire's opinion, the civilizing and "self-colonizing" mission that all Enlightenment philosophers shared, and which consisted of bringing Roman virtues to the barbarian majority of the French and European people, makes "the differentiation between 'true' and 'false', 'radical' and 'moderate' Enlighteners obsolete" (Tricoire 2015: 28).

Along with enlightened universalism, the protagonists of the French Revolution were convinced that they were "fighting for the liberation from despotism not only of the French people, but of the entire human race" (Middell 2016: 24). In 1790, an official ceremony "was attended in Paris by British, German, Dutch, Italian, American, Persian, Arabian and Turkish representatives." The "world delegation" was organized by the democratic Prussian Baron "Anacharsis" de Clootz, a major figure of the Revolution who would advocate that France should "liberate" the rest of Europe. On the occasion of the ceremony, he declared that the present "foreigners from all the countries of the world" were committed to "the imminent liberation of their unhappy fellow citizens" (Serna 2016: 44).

One can observe how at each stage of the revolutionary process, and even when social exchanges occurred at the highest levels of power, the elites' strategy toward the inclusion of "the people" seemed to follow the principle outlined by Alfred Fried, according to whom, given "the insufficient development of a capacity for reason among the subordinate classes," the dominant classes endeavor to transmit their patriotism "by stimulating a series of sensorial perceptions" (Fried 1908: 8). Thus the sovereign people, in its making and constituting itself as the nation, was promoted to the status of a historical individual, surrounded by a naturalistic and quasi-religious mystique that was supposed to establish the new legitimacy of power derived from the "eternal laws of reason, justice, and nature" (Robespierre ([1791] 2009). Robespierre ([1792] 2009) also claimed "the King is sacred pursuant to a fiction, the people are sacred through the sacred law of nature." Even among revolutionaries, several were shocked by the political–religious implications of sacralization. Condorcet (1796: 180), himself a prominent victim of the Jacobin repressive regime, wrote of the alliance between superstition—his word for all religion—and despotism and its revenge over the French Revolution:

> One nation only escaped for a while this double influence. In that happy land, where liberty had kindled the torch of genius, the human mind, freed from the trammels of infancy, advanced towards truth with a firm and undaunted step. But conquest soon introduced tyranny, sure to be followed by superstition, its inseparable companion.

Considering the surprise for Condorcet and Novalis, equally great although caused by opposite expectations, we should wonder whether the need for the people's sovereign power to prove it possessed myth, sacredness, and whether sentiment is simply contingent on the revolutionary mobilization or typical only for the authoritarian populism of Robespierre, or whether it is not, in fact, structural. In order to establish this new power that was anchored to the rising class (perhaps galaxy) of the bourgeoisie, it was first necessary to demonstrate that the nation-people did in fact exist and, following this, that it was more legitimate as a sovereign than the alternatives, a demonstration which did not prove to be easy to carry out. Although the dogmas of law of nature and social contract, and the philosophy of history, had been ready, the vagueness of the word "people" still needed some work to adapt it to the new requirements of political power.

Due to the political manifestation of the idea of popular sovereignty during the French Revolution, in addition to the concept of "sovereignty," the concept of "people" was also rearranged. During the ancien régime the word was used for common people, that is, the majority group of people excluded from political decisions. According to Abbot Emmanuel Joseph Sieyès's 1789 pamphlet, *Qu'est-ce que le tiers-état?*, "the people" corresponded to the Third Estate. Sieyès claimed that these were the people, the common people, therefore those without power in the old regime, who formed the true nation. What does all this mean?

After the Nazi era and the Second World War, another debate formed around the concept of "people." In particular, Hannah Arendt was

> struggling with a distinction between *ethnos* and *demos*. The *demos* signifies the nation as a self-governing democratic body of citizens who may or may not be ethnically homogeneous while the *ethnos* means the nation as an entity that is ethnically, linguistically, or religiously homogeneous. The conflict between the *ethnos* and the *demos* had been playing itself out in

European political history since the French revolution, and to the detriment of the idea of the *demos*, of the sovereign people. (Benhabib 2000: 43)

The theory is that, in the case of the French, the principles of the social contract were constructed around the concept of *demos*, that is, those who were excluded from power overturned the system in order to take control, whereas the transition in Germany occurred through ethnic, authoritarian, and potentially totalitarian input. This model—which hinges on undeniable historical differences between the French and German paths to nation-states—was later in an underhand manner applied to the entire "civilization gap" that runs between West and East, and North and South: the more backward the nations, the higher their rates of ethnicity, political savagery, and intolerance. The Balkans is a popular example in "demonstrating" the validity of this thesis (Petri 2017: 1–22). However, other curious "demonstrations" emerge, which are also in favor of the "good" type of people's sovereignty: "the term 'nation' in this context must be understood as denoting not a natural phenomenon but, on the contrary, an entity *constituted* by the logic of the social contract" (Higuchi 1998: 147). In order to make this ideology work, the most evident meaning of the word "nation," as derived from the Latin term for "birth," is denied, as is, therefore, its reference to biological descent. Saime Tugrul provides another version, according to which

> The idea of nation is directly related to ethnicity—*ethnos*—whereas people are connected with *demos*—common people—(which is one of the etymological elements for the word *democracy*). Especially in modernity, when the term *nation* replaces the term *people*, the two different notions of *demos* and *ethnos* are confused, and the major ethnic group claims to embody the characteristics of organic unity and people. (Tugrul 2013: 77)

In this case, etymology is better respected; it is history that is rearranged to make the ideology work. It would actually be difficult to agree that the word "nation" was a neologism that replaced the allegedly older word "people." Both terms preexisted and emerged as prominent concepts during the revolutionary period, and both were semantically adapted to the needs of the people's sovereignty, practically becoming synonymous as Abbot Sieyès explicitly claimed.

It has often been alleged also that the Enlightenment inspired the concept of *demos*, whereas *ethnos* belonged to the realm of romanticism. John Gray (2008: 79) observes that the "belief that society should be an organic whole is far from being only a Romantic idea, however. The fantasy of seamless community is as much a feature of Enlightenment thinking as of Counter-Enlightenment." Gray's statement indicates that this widely ruminated-upon schoolbook myth, according to which romanticism actually was what it claimed to be, that is, a counter-Enlightenment movement with its own ideology, would eventually deserve revision. Nostalgic mood and the praise of sentiment, transcendence, spontaneity, and beauty, which are considered among the "essentials" of romanticism, were already forceful during the Enlightenment. What made of this cultural movement a major agent of nation building was its timely awareness of the new poetic, symbolic, and artistic needs of communication, which would allow to popularize such formerly elitist contents among the emerging bourgeoisie and the wider society. The Romanticists did not invent the idea that society "should be an organic whole," they were better at selling it.

However, the whole debate on *ethnos* and *demos* seems to miss another fundamental point: even when "nation" is referring to a self-governing democratic body of citizens who are considered not to be ethnically homogenous, such as, for example, colonial and immigrant societies, the question still remains as to which criteria are used to decide that only a fraction of humankind is considered to be citizens of that democratic state, rather than all members of humankind. Already Aristotle ([~ 350 BC; 1885] 2000: 102) had pointed out the logical incoherencies of the inclusion/exclusion mechanisms of citizenship: "He who has the power to take part in the deliberative or juridical administration of any state is said by us to be a citizen of that state; ... But in practice a citizen is defined to be one of whom both the parents are citizens." The Greek philosopher's theoretical concept implied a disenchanted acknowledgment of power in contrast to a right of descent that would transform any foundation of a new state into an illegitimate act. Since violent power is enough to found a state but hardly to run and transform it into a durable social setting, it needs mythical transcendence to legitimize itself against the violent arbitrariness of its own origins. Modern democracy thought of resolving this contradiction by referring to "the people," which is conceived of as a subject that is supposed to have existed long before the nation-state, and could therefore deliver it a transcendent legitimacy. However, as modern democracy claims to interpret universal human values, whether or not *ethnos*, or *demos*, or any other of the invented categories determine exclusion from citizenship is far less interesting than the very fact that democracy operates such a discrimination at all.

The standard interpretation, however, is as follows: "In contrast to the German model, in the French model, the nation is built upon the *demos* with the *ethnos* receding to the point of becoming almost invisible" (Rosenfeld 2010: 156). It is simple to prove that the idea of *citoyen* in France is also based on bonds of blood and soil. Moreover, it was precisely the French and continental European version of popular sovereignty which invented what later was to be called *ethnos* as a way of distinguishing inclusion and exclusion.

Talking of belonging to a community of subjects as defined by language or blood was basically unheard of in the dynastic and imperial Europe of the previous period. Only the ruling nobility drew legitimacy from descent and distinction. What we would today call an ethnographic discussion in fact took hold within intellectual circles not before the mid eighteenth century. As far as the link between cause and effect is concerned, considered in its entirety, it is blatantly clear that the myth of descent from ancient European tribes (from the Celts and Germanics to the Etruscans), which were publicized by these circles, formed a counterprogram of culture and politics, that is, one that was "popular," against the ancien régime. Functionally it was the social capsizing of a noble proposition, for which the bloodline, which was sometimes considered under the term "nation," underpinned feudal and dynastic legitimacy. In conclusion, with the French Revolution, legitimacy inferred from biological lineage was not overcome, but was democratized.

In the German-speaking area, the uses of *Volk*, understood as a linguistic and tribal community, and *jus sanguinis*, in legally determining citizenship and state affiliation, only came about as a result of the disintegration of the *Heiligen Römischen Reiches Deutscher Nation*, or, better, of all factors which contributed to such disintegration, from the French Revolution, and the socioeconomic transformations taking place at the time, onwards. The states that emerged from the disintegration in order to restore the dynasties in 1815 by that point were forced to legitimize their sovereignty on the basis of the *Volk*, which was now tacitly recognized, if not yet as the sovereign, at least as one of the sources of the sovereign's legitimacy. The new states introduced the inclusive criterion for the status of subjects or citizens by family lineage with few exceptions, whereas this status under the ancien régime was defined by territorial residence. With this, the concepts of *Fremder* (stranger) and *Ausländer* (foreigner) acquired new meanings. It was not yet a matter of being "non-German," but in any case of not belonging to the "host" state in light of different blood and land ancestry. There was one significant exception, however; the nobility still enjoyed full German national status, that is, they held the prerogative to maintain their rights and privileges throughout the Germanic Confederation. Therefore, it was later and more gradually with respect to France, but not dissimilarly, that what was understood to be the principle of legitimacy, the *Deutsche Nation*, was to pass from the Second to the Third Estate, from the nobility to the "common" people.

Thus, emerging as a replacement for noble lineage (at times mythical in origin), which was supposed to sustain the dynastic legitimacy of power through a divine grace, which had expressed itself through the concession of conquest by the original class of warriors, was now the myth of ancestry from an anonymous blood chain formed by humble common people rooted in their home land "since the dawn of time." This change was the result of a revolution, which Anne-Marie Thiesse (1999: 23–66) has acutely called "aesthetic." It is very clear in the text of *Qu'est-ce que le tiers-état?* how Sieyès hoped that "the nation might well recover from the belief that thence forward it would be reduced to the descendants of mere Gauls and Romans" and that "the blood of the Franks" now should better mingle "with the blood of the Gauls." However, he addressed his conciliatory invitation to the nobility only after reminding them that should they try to oppose the people's sovereignty and it would be better they "turn home to the Franconian forests" where they had come from. According to Sieyès, noblemen were internal strangers to the nation "because of their origin, since they do not owe their assignment to the people," while the Third Estate "contains everything that pertains to the nation while nobody outside the Third Estate can be seen as part of the nation" (Sieyès [1789] 2002: 5, 8–9).

Rather than being denied, the theory of the two populations therefore underwent an inversion. Where it was born as a legitimization of French aristocracy, whose members represented themselves as the direct descendants of the Frankish conquerors, it was now being thrown back against those who had invented it. The "true people" came from the Celtic tribe of Gaul, with occasional grafting received from the ancient civilization of Rome and—why not?—minor admixtures also of some drops of blood from "the Sicambrians, Welches and other savages from the woods and swamps of ancient Germany" (Sieyès [1789] 2002: 9). The primitive and binomial population-land cult was in fact visible both during the revolution phase and later, for example, in Michelet (1846). Blood and soil were combined to produce the mixture for the unchangeable "original character," also known as spirit, of the people-nation, and to corroborate the "natural" right of that people to be the sovereign over its own land. This was one of the reasons for the success of the neo-pagan and anti-Latin theories which rampantly spread through the continent between the eighteenth and nineteenth centuries.

Declaring the people's sovereignty did not, however, merely occur as a result of overthrowing the legitimizing myths of the old regime. Alexander Pushkin's rhetorical question "Be subject to a king, be subject to a people—Is it not all the same to us?" (Boym 2010: 82) can be answered in the negative, at least if we refer the "king" to old-style monarchy, because there is a new aspect, which deeply affects social living and the daily uses of power. This aspect concerns "popular consent," that is, a widespread sharing of judgment, meaning, and feeling (on which, it must be conceded to Pushkin, even the autocratic and neo-absolutistic regimes of the nineteenth century became increasingly, if reluctantly, dependent). In the political process, practical consent is an essential element that no type of political power can do without—not even one based on the axiomatic principles of reason and nature, according to which it is a self-evident contradiction of common sense to be "irrational" or "unnatural" in the public sphere (it would thus theoretically be simply a matter of repressing, marginalizing, or "curing" those who are). Given that also under the conditions of people's sovereignty neither the divergences of opinion nor the difference between governors and governed disappear, while the audience to which the political discourse has to be addressed simultaneously comprises the major part of society, the modern conception of nation introduces radical changes into this field.

In slightly more schematic terms, we could say that for the ancien régime, political power did not need the consensus of that muddled mass called "the people." On the contrary, this was precisely one of the names given to distinguish that irregular humanity whose consent did not count at all and whose members were only supposed to show reverence toward power, without necessarily believing in it or being emotionally committed to it (Rahn 1998: 129–48). From the moment in which that irregular humanity was to represent a collective subject capable of becoming a sovereign nation, the matter of consent assumed a completely different character. Within this, Foucault's observation gains particular relevance, where power "always has to be considered in relation to a field of interactions, contemplated in a relationship which cannot be dissociated from forms of knowledge" (Foucault [1978] 2007: 66)—or from forms of belief and feeling, we might add.

As Benedict Anderson (1991: 5–8) pointed out, the chances that a national community can constitute itself depend on the possibilities it offers to individuals to imagine themselves as a part of it. In other words, it depends on the quality of the discourse, its imaginary force and emotional attractiveness. According to Ernest Renan, even when a nation has established itself, its continual existence then depends on "a daily plebiscite, just as the existence of an individual is a perpetual declaration of life" (Renan 1882: 27). When a nation constitutes itself in a state configuration of power, its conditioning of the individual and its being conditioned by him is no longer symmetrical. It is a power constellation which makes it difficult for the average individual to pronounce a yes today, a no tomorrow, and then who knows the day after. The daily voting of "yes!" in the national plebiscite of Renan becomes almost compulsory. It is similar to the Christian creed with which the faithful reaffirm a pact closed way back in time, and which is symbolically renewed to exorcise their hidden doubts and fears of temptation.

From the sacred, to the myth, to the rituals of self-ascertainment, analogies between the national community and the religious community are overwhelming. It is not surprising, therefore, that the central role as the vehicle of any message in modern political communication is assigned to emotions. From the French Revolution onwards—and here Novalis had understood very clearly—politics in Europe had become a matter of mass communication and could not be uttered any longer without exciting the senses, evoking emotions, regenerating the sacred, and assigning transcendent meaning to power. In the nineteenth century it was especially the nation, to which all history was apparently destined to converge, which was thought to be incapable of erecting itself based on the remnants of the "cold" political calculations of the Enlightenment and the absolutist state. As Giuseppe Mazzini deplored, the division between reality and poetry was still very much visible, too visible, even half a century after the French Revolution. He therefore still saw his own time as the result of an era "of decadence, when Art lost its religious and prophetic nature. From this comes poetry's merely meager influence on the masses today, on life." A "notably national" poem, however, should "ooze with the tears of mothers and the blood of martyrs, be sad as is suffering, strong as is faith," and encapsulate within itself "the intimate life of the entire race" (Mazzini [1847] 1939: 61, 64). Thus, after Christianity the idea of nation in the west seemed to have become the main object of worship, of sacredness, of extreme sacrifice, involved in rituals and in proclaiming one's faith, and therefore, in many ways, a religion in a full-fledged sense of the word. Mazzini also in *Giovine Italia* of 1832 summarized the concept by pointing out how "the people" represent "our entire religion compacted into one single principle" (quoted from Levis Sullam 2010: 9).

In the rhetoric of the French Revolution, words such as catechism, apostolate, sacred flame of liberty, laws of nature, purity and duty were not uttered randomly either. A new, political, modern religion had been born, which was just as fanatically consecrated as that ancient one with a universal apostolate. Meanwhile, the Christian religion—as traditionally understood—did not abdicate its role of power endorsement. It also proved to be compatible with the reviewed terms of people and nation, the philosophical arrangement of which had emerged from the secularization of its own traditional eschatological narrative.

The fratricidal conflict between progressives and conservatives, clerics and anti-clerics, bigots and atheists, which despite becoming so resentful that it frequently ended in bloodshed, must not mislead us when it comes to the idea of nation. Nor is it completely convincing to claim with Carl Schmitt (1923) that the Christian faith, still influenced as it was by the heritage of the embodiment of tolerance typical for medieval society, was now the innocent victim of anticlerical, anti-Catholic and even anti-Christian nationalism (Cardini 1997: 9, 30). Throughout the nineteenth century and beyond, the main churches of Christianity, that is, Catholicism, Protestantism, and Orthodoxy, each differently carried out a role that was all but secondary in nation building. This is not just the case for Catholic countries such as Poland, Ireland, or Croatia, where this was unmistakable, but also in Protestant contexts ever since Oliver Cromwell and the Puritans depicted England and its inhabitants as "a new Israel, a chosen people" (Barker 1937: 82), or Denmark, where

Nicolai Frederik Severin Grundtvig's Christian inspiration had great influence (Grundtvig 1808, 1844). To quote another example, of Orthodox national commitment, we could recall that in 1821, "as legend would have it, Bishop Germanos, the Metropolitan of Patras, raised the flag of [Greek] revolution" (Gallant 2016: 41).

However, it was not just leaders of the various churches or intellectuals close to them who raised the banners of national struggle with Christian spiritual impetus. The revolutionary republicanism characteristic of the Polish Maurycy Mochnacki (Mochnatzki 1833: 73–84), for example, and even the Mazzinian anticlericalism, also made free use of emotional Romantic intuitions, Christian spirituality, and even the utopian conjectures voiced by Novalis. For Giuseppe Mazzini, the people's Europe that he so yearned for was clearly borrowed from the Christian Europe. He wrote that Christianity, "considering its substance and not its shapes, . . . cast the bases for a universal justice, and created that passion for teaching, that predication of the Truth, that proselyte spirit which later procured many guardians of the holy cause of humanity and rights" (Mazzini [1829] 1939: 101–02). Notwithstanding the peaceful and ecumenical image that it preferred to show of itself, Christianity was not inferior with respect to the other ideological tendencies in backing the competition of all nationalisms against all others. The First World War, for example, delivers clear examples for this. The very same Catholic faith, so European and so universal, and so vertically integrated in its supranational hierarchies, did not hesitate in bestowing divine legitimacy and moral absolution upon believers who fought each other from both sides of, for example, the Austrian–Italian frontline, shooting to kill one another, each in the name of a divine investiture for the defense of his own sacred nation (Gemelli 1917: 137; Achleitner 1997: 14–16).

The conceptual horizon had in any case been like this from the beginning. During the Parisian debut of the Declaration of Human Rights at the National Assembly, biblical allegories and parables were incessantly cited and mixed with the references to Enlightenment visionaries whose philosophical concepts were destined to be brought to revolutionary glorification. The Declaration "attests the Supreme Being, the guarantor of human morality. It breathes the sentiment of *duty*," as the historian Jules Michelet (1847: 202) was to summarize half a century later. In order to consolidate this result, the nation then set out with full awareness to weave the concepts of nature, people, and nation into the fabric of society from childhood, seeing as the political edifice rested on the loyalty and faith of each individual.

The dogmas of faith and the sentiments of the sacred are not born spontaneously, just as the relative "logical-dogmatic relationships" are rarely spontaneously assembled in the "psychic constitution" (Amadori Virgilj 1906: 110). They are the product of constant indoctrination imparted during childhood and adolescence, generation after generation. These were also the hopes of Robespierre ([1792] 2009), who was expecting that "the emerging, purer generation, who are more faithful to the sacred laws of nature, will start to cleanse this land defiled by crime." It was therefore the time for pedagogy as a national educational priesthood. This pedagogy was determined to link the development of personality with its immersion into a sympathetic, patriotic, and compact community. According to the Swiss pedagogue Johann Heinrich Pestalozzi, an honorary citizen of the revolutionary French Republic, this education was to begin with the "observation and understanding of the geographical conditions included within the field of vision" of the infant. As Adolph Diesterweg would add, "we can only come to understand things which are unknown and foreign to our sensorial perception through the comparison of similar and familiar objects." For that reason, "for each pupil the most important and irrevocable aspect is the knowledge of the space in which he lives as well as the combination of civic and political factors which affect him, and which he is destined to affect" (quoted from Tromnau 1889: 6–9). In the first half of the nineteenth century, Friedrich Fröbel accordingly dedicated himself to the "education of the spirit and the preparation of sound and valid knowledge of nature, so that industry may grow, and esteem and authentic appreciation of the fatherland may be instilled." Like Diesterweg, Fröbel also intended on starting from the landscape, from the river that flowed behind the school, from the family of the pupils, in order to explain the world to them. The "correct understanding of all objects from the outside world" can be traced "from the observation to the concept, from the particular to the general, which from there returns again in a different relationship, from the general to the particular" (Fröbel [1821] 1862: 246–47, 259).

A similar pedagogical strategy in some ways aimed to make the national appearance of existence physically possible to experiment on through the appropriation of the objects belonging to the surrounding space. It treasured the spatiality and corporealness contained in some of the concepts linked to the representation of the "outside" world (to understand, to remember, etc.). Rising from the particular to the general, however, and then returning to the particular through this, eluded the immediateness of experience postulated by Fröbel. What was being depicted as essential, and transmitted from appropriate objects, could be interpreted as "typical" and "characteristic" of national particularities only because the objects had already been transformed into metaphors by previous indoctrination. The sentimental connotations of small communitarian spaces which were thought to allow such immediate experiences, such as homeland, *heimat*, *pays*, *terruño*, *paese*, *родина*, *szülőföld*, *domovina*, *hemland*, and so on, were crucially important in achieving such a result. They were reinterpreted as local or regional reservoirs of mythical origin—Vico ([1744] 1816: 62) had written "heroic origins stored in reduced forms within vulgar language" about dialects—and were rewritten as spaces of childhood experience and as metaphors of the nation (Núñez Seixas 2006: 11–17; Confino 2006: 19–31; Thiesse 2006: 33–64). In this way, a nostalgic feeling of loss was associated with the homeland metaphor of nation, one that sparked a sentiment of belonging and a desire for repossession, and so commanded the acceptance of destiny and the "natural" duty to commitment and sacrifice, which this included.

This educational strategy was then widely adopted in schoolbooks, and in the ethnographic, geographic, and historical textbook literature of the nineteenth and twentieth centuries, aiming to weave systematically the psychological plan into the fabric of politics, constantly reminding the individual of his responsibilities toward the collective. One of the innumerable examples is Augustin Scherer's geography schoolbook, used in the education of generations of Tyrolese students up until the First World War. In this book the word *Hoamatl*—little homeland—which in Tyrolese dialect was merely a technical term for a farmstead or paternal estate, in as much as it was linked "to the deep affection that good children have for their parents and the paternal home," became a metaphor for the greater homeland. "We have another, greater *Heimat*, and it is the beloved homeland of the Tyrol. Here we are all at home; many good friends and acquaintances live here, and our forefathers have lived here for many generations." And it is not simply a home from which to come and go, but an entity that dwells in the soul: "And now observe the thick line that traces the outer borders of the Tyrol on the geographical map. You will immediately see the shape of the Tyrol: is it not true? It almost resembles a heart!" (Scherer 1860: 3, 8). As Amadaori Virgilj (1906: 59, 79) wrote, "as patriotism followed its trajectory, its rising evolutionary line: first restricted to the town, then to the community, then to the principality, and finally to the political State and nation," wrapping it "in its affection." The idea of nation, "formed with representations, is in itself able to reproduce, it can renew itself without any external stimulus, fostered by the pleasing sentiment that it evokes." Through the education and social practice of language, it can therefore become the cement of power—in accordance with a dynamic that has received ample, if varied, acknowledgment in the theories of eminent nineteenth- and twentieth-century social science scholars, by Michel Foucault and many others.

Approving the ultimate truths regarding the Supreme Being and the sacred, the Parisian assembly representatives of the revolutionary bourgeoisie deleted the most un-empowering, sacrilegious, disillusioned, and skeptical, expressions of the Enlightenment tradition, and replaced them with ones that were empowering, morally compelling, and psychologically conditioning. In the previous system of power the moral obligations which the "people" had internalized were integrated on the social level in a more indirect and ambiguous manner, being mainly relegated to the functions of social and ideological control allocated to the religious institutions, which certainly sustained the secular powers but which also enjoyed a certain independence. It is already possible to find episodes of patriotic appeals addressed to the people during exceptional situations when mass mobilization was needed, especially by the absolutistic regimes and empires of the seventeenth and eighteenth century. Normally, however, the rulers expected factual obedience and ritual loyalty from their subjects, but had little time to waste with shaping and monitoring the sincerity of the common person's inner beliefs and emotional commitments. All of this, for the sake of the people's sovereignty, needed to change. The myth and sentiment of the nation were supposed to shape the psychological disposition of each individual. It was about instilling a strong sense of duty in the population, one that was so strong as to compel them to sacrifice their lives if necessary. Thus, following the French Revolution, the space of individual freedom theoretically prefigured by the Enlightenment was immediately restricted, if not quashed, in favor of forms of a psychologically compelling personal accountability.

Is all of this still significant today? After 1945, the "era of extreme nationalism" was considered to have been overcome in most of Europe. It was the welfare state and economic growth rather than national pathos that "rescued" (Milward 1992) the nation-state and reinforced its capacity of social integration as well as political participation and consent. After 1989 the nationalist resurgence in the ex-socialist countries was explained by their political backwardness, their having been "badly accustomed" to democratic practices, and their weakly developed "civil society." In a "mature" democratic society, "reasonable decisions are preferable to unreasoned ones: considered thought leads to the former, emotions to the latter, therefore deliberating is preferable to visceral reaction as a basis for democratic decision making" (Kuklinski et al. 1991: 1). This is, or was until recently, more or less the recurring self-representation of western political modernity: the rational government, step by step, frees itself from the influence of emotion and instinct. In fact, rather than disappear, the practices and symbols dedicated to emotional mobilization change ground, wherein the same transcendent and "irrational" motivations for being a nation, despite being submerged in the processes of integration, globalization, and reinforcement of localism, bunk down in the background. Stored but not extinct, they are ready to emerge, and not only on symbolic–recreational occasions such as sporting events. In situations of serious political or military conflict, they are ready to return to the fore, together with viscerally felt stereotypes regarding the "other," which seemed to have been forgotten for generations.

The other interesting aspect is that, even after two and a half centuries of popular sovereignty in the west, the *ethnos* never ceased functioning not only as a separator between citizens of each nation-state and the rest of humankind but also as a marker for minority groups as "internal strangers" and as a generator of hierarchy in colonial and immigrant societies. Nor has the *demos* of "the people" who lack almost any power ceased to make them feel different from "them," that is, from the mighty who govern from high up in the people's name. The constitution, which regulates the temporality of the government mandate, has not overcome—or shown interest in overcoming—the distinction between the governors and the governed. The substance of that difference called "power" has therefore not been extinguished or fundamentally changed. Power etymologically means "capability of doing or accomplishing something." While in the most elementary meaning this "something" means taking lives away (Canetti [1960] 1985: 529), in the numerous attenuated and institutionalized forms of power, it typically means that the governors are capable of conditioning the lives of others, because fear does not disappear. "It is reduced but doesn't recede. Fear *is never forgotten*" (Esposito 2010: 23). Even though it sways between various representations, some of which are similar while others are miles apart, the twofold meaning of the "people," in the name of which the governors govern and the governed protest, remains. The difference between the powerful and the impotent therefore remains also, and the concept of the people appears ever more abstract and transcendent.

Therefore, the concept represents a "real relation between social agents" and simultaneously a discursive construct that contains totalizing claims of social representation. As Laclau (2005: 73–74) argues, it requires continual back-and-forth movements of division and recombination in order to envision ever and again the reestablishment of the people in the power from which it was separated by a previously traced "antagonistic frontier." An efficiently working welfare state, for example,

> would be unable to differentiate itself from anything else, that society could not totalize itself, could not create a "people." What actually happens is that the obstacles identified during the establishment of that society—private entrepreneurial greed, entrenched interests, and so on—force their very proponents to identify enemies and to reintroduce a discourse of social division grounded in equivalential logics. In that way, collective subjects constituted around the defense of the welfare state can emerge. The same can be said about neo-liberalism: it also presents itself as a panacea for a fissureless society—with the difference that in this case, the trick is performed by the market, not by the state. (Laclau 2005: 78–79)

Democracy therefore does not cause the ritualistic and symbolic elaborations of the relationships between "us" and "them" to become obsolete. On the contrary, it possibly needs them even more, as the impotent are no longer supposed to exist, but are—according to the theory—*demos* and thus fully armed with rights such as free opinion, active participation, association, information, and most of all, their ballot card. Yet it remains impossible to represent symbolically any form of power without pointing out the potentiality of an arbitrary or violent imposition, especially today when "politics and government are increasingly slipping back into the control of privileged elites in the manner characteristic of pre-democratic times," while, however, "the forms of democracy remain fully in place" (Crouch 2004: 6).

Against the backdrop of social power relations which are increasingly asymmetric, national cohesion is nonetheless capable of regenerating itself through the excitement and manifestation of collective sentiment. The discursive recreation of "the people" never was only intellectual and verbal; it always drew also on other aesthetic codes. Following the emotional excitement of the French Revolution and its flood of symbols, the discursive recreation of "the people" was "entrenched with the development of modern mass-entertainment forms in the nineteenth and twentieth centuries" (Sutherland 2012: 333). As Guy Debord ([1967] 1994: 5) noted, the spectacle appears increasingly "at once as society itself, as a part of society and as a means of unification." It is against this background that Meghan Sutherland (2012: 334) identifies in the present media world aesthetic conventions of spectacular entertainment that "automatically stage their audience as a generalized figure of 'the people'" and subject the spectator to movements of affection and disaffection.

On the one hand, we can interpret these ways of modern mass communication as an expression of the people's sovereign–subject duality that already had been foreshadowed by "the Hobbesian anamorph, a figure of double vision, a performer and spectator at once" (Boym 2010: 21); on the other, we should be aware of how the developments in media and communications technology alter the aesthetical and emotional appearance of that duality. Today, television and other mass media "serve as ceremonial techniques which integrate the nation in so far as they keep both true and hyped crises alive in the consciousness of all, and demonstrate the discursive power of a collective subject." At first sight, political discourse material, called information, supplants the emotional staging of mass meetings. However, the "function of sensation is maintained seeing as information is often *revelation*, and the act of revealing a *performance*. Quite differently to the ceremonies of the past, this performance no longer generates adoration, but indignation." The *demos*, the indignant spectator, can do nothing but take notice of the "gap between the sovereignty of holding information and the un-sovereign inability to act." (Jahn, Rahn, and Schnitzer 1998: 14–15). Each time they leave the polling booth the ranks of power turn far away:

> Their sentiment of democratic power still requires the mystery of an alienated and distant power, which they now believe to be personified by

the political caste. However, they no longer need it in order to adore that alien power, but to *experience* their own power as citizens through the act of revelation. So, democratic power *appears* through public possession of information. The media transmit and generate a virtual society that comes into "existence" by way of a synchronization of excitement and representation of opinions. (Jahn, Rahn, and Schnitzer 1998: 14–15)

Indignez-vous! (Hessel 2010) is thus the most functional exhortation for an appropriate political cohesion in the present times. It may also become the trigger for a "populist" rearrangement of power structures when the reciprocal estrangement between the powerful elites, on the one hand, and the powerless "sovereign people," on the other, reaches levels that in the perception of one or even of both sides appear to be unbearable.

2.4 Democracy and the rule of law

It seems that for all political powers based on the principle of territory it is essential to delimit or suppress the freedom that in other circumstances is understood to be elementary and intuitive: discretional movement of bodies through space. When we open the door of a bird's cage, we claim to have set it free, even if it is heading toward an unknown or insidious destiny. Strangely enough, presenting our passport and then being perhaps denied entry by a sovereign state to which we do not belong, does not necessarily damage our feeling of personal freedom. This suggests that the concept of freedom is not absolute but relative. In eighteenth- and nineteenth-century Europe, increasing control over movement and settlement, not only at the hands of the empires but by the aristocratic republics and absolute monarchies as well, was tied to the introduction of new forms of taxation and proscription. It brought about the introduction of permits of stay and expatriation, of passports and systematic border controls, of civil registries, compulsory repatriation, punitive deportation, and so on. Whereas civil liberties enjoyed greater legal recognition than ever before, the control of residence and movement was even more elementary for popular-sovereignty states, for which the term "democracy" gradually took hold as a positive value in the political sphere of the nineteenth century.

Democracy as a concept assumed various connotations since the discussions on forms of state in Plato and Aristotle, which was then discussed by Scholastic, Humanist, and Enlightenment theory. It was often coupled with dubious and negative meanings, and warnings against the danger of a tyrannical regression of the majority government dominated by the destitute *polloi*. It was only from the end of the eighteenth century that the concept of democracy was occasionally superimposed over "republic" and "popular sovereignty," and it was only "by the mid-19th century that liberalism and democracy began to consolidate what now seems to be an inseparable relationship" (Freeden 2015: 27). Nevertheless, there was still much room left for diverging political, legal, and social emphases. The need to establish clearly where the people begin and end thus becomes urgent for a democracy. Who and under what conditions can be included and can therefore expect to be able to enjoy political and social rights? As the debates regarding migration of the early twenty-first century show, only the practical denial of the theoretical universality of such rights and the definition of exclusion mechanisms are able to protect the cohesion of the sovereign people of a nation-state (Petri 2012b: 32–51).

As we have already seen in Hume, the definition of the concept of "freedom" has proved to depend on interpretations that are not based on intuition, but on philosophical axioms assigned to cleansing the semantics of undesirable meanings. In considering Kant, the metaphor of the bird in a cage is not relevant, given that the freedom derived from natural justice is not the same as that which is found in the state of nature, but is one that is driven by reason. "The attachment of savages to their lawless liberty, the fact that they would rather be at hopeless variance with one another than submit themselves to a legal authority constituted by themselves, that they therefore prefer their senseless freedom to a reason-governed liberty, is regarded by us with profound contempt as barbarism and uncivilisation and the brutal degradation of humanity" (Kant [1795] 1903: 130). Also following Svetlana Boym's thoughtful reflections, the bird's escape from the cage might perhaps be considered a case of "liberation," but has little to do with "freedom," a concept that can be exclusively related to "the realm of human artifice where the plurality of humanity manifests itself in its distinctiveness and multidimensionality" (Boym 2010: 11).

We can conclude that in the western, especially Kantian, tradition, freedom belongs exclusively to the de-bodied dimension of the masks in the social play or, otherwise said, is basically *personal* freedom. For this motive, the bird's freedom is different from man's, as man should delight in remaining free in the cage represented by his theoretical conjectures and abstract will as dictated by reason and aesthetic judgment. The bodily dimension of freedom, although remaining central to punishment and coercion, and the most intimidating menace that power can exercise after the threat of death, appears to be below the dignity of political consideration. Yet, it remains crucial to the definition of the political body itself, which unavoidably originates from an arbitrary act of power. In feudal law, the *libertates* were privileges granted by the sovereign. In the modern commonwealth too, the freedom to move in space at one's discretion is a freedom among those who continue to represent a privilege based on concession, because it is "rational." Here Kant's theory echoes the tradition of social contract theory according to which human will in society cannot be allowed to free itself from reason. However, the philosopher from Konigsberg could not impose his concepts in all matters.

The democratic states, which evolved following the American and French Revolutions, attempt to incorporate the republicanism outlined by Kant. The latter, however, in fact distinguished the form of state from the form of government. The form of state—monarchy, aristocracy, or democracy—defined who was sovereign. The form of government could be republican or despotic in all three cases. The category into which the form of state would fall was a matter of separation of power: "Republicanism is the political principle of severing the executive power of the government from the legislature." Of the three, Kant clearly indicated that the form of state most inclined toward despotism was democracy or popular sovereignty: "Democracy, in the proper sense of the word, is of necessity despotism, because it establishes an executive power, since all decree regarding—and, if need be, against—any individual who dissents from them" (Kant [1795] 1903: 125). In the case of "democracy" his warnings remained unheard.

Political theory has of course long since cleared up Kant's alleged misunderstanding. In responding to his skepticism, it adduces that the states he was thinking of were of a permanent, direct, populist democracy, and not a wise combination of rule of law and representative democracy based on a balance of powers and the constitution. It was not populist but representative and constitutional systems that widely spread the English, American, and French examples to all western democracies and beyond. It is, however, a given that even despite this they have frequently proven to be compatible with the delimitation or abolition of the very same rights they deem to be essential, and which are counted as fundamental values. The most well-known example is *habeas corpus*, the right to not be imprisoned longer than a limited period without an accusation formulated following the consideration of the judicial authority. Although *habeas corpus* as defined by article 39 of *Magna Carta* belongs to liberalism only in terms of an invented tradition, it remains that it was incorporated into the English Bill of Rights in 1688–9, into the US Constitution in 1787, and into practically all other constitutions until becoming a part of the United Nations Universal Declaration of Human Rights in 1948. Yet even in democratic or liberal constitutional regimes there are a multitude of examples of violation or denial of this right, from the administrative detentions, or those of the police, which strike marginal sections of society and immigrants, to the "emergency" policies which suspend constitutional obligations, to the extrajudicial detentions, or to those that are based on convenient judicial figures in the "fight against terrorism." It is also worth pointing out that the system of concentration camps implemented by the Fascist and Nazi regimes was not based on new norms but had in fact extensively adopted previous norms. These were confinement institutions created by the Italian liberal regime, and the preventative detentions in prisons and concentration camps already in use in the Republic of Weimar, which in both cases were not set up in order to punish crimes that had been committed, but to prevent crimes which had "not yet" been committed at all, in clear violation of *habeas corpus* (Poesio 9–16, 102). More recently it has been stated that

> the US remains a functioning democracy, and it may be that legislation enabling torture and removing *habeas corpus* will be reversed under future administrations. The fact remains that it has ceased to be a regime in which the power of government is limited under the rule of law. The checks and balances of the constitution have failed to prevent an unprecedented expansion of arbitrary power. (Gray 2008: 237)

There are also numerous violations of the private sphere in democratic regimes, as well as conditioning of the circulation of information and ideas. As Noam Chomsky wrote,

> It has long been recognized that state power is not the only form of interference with the fundamental right to "receive and impart information and ideas" . . . [and that in 1946] the prestigious Hutchins Commission on Freedom of the Press warned that "private agencies controlling the great mass media" constitute a fundamental threat to freedom of the press with their ability to impose "an environment of vested beliefs" and "bias as a commercial enterprise" under the influence of advertisers and owners. (Chomsky 2003: 76–77)

Against today's powerful editorial oligopolies in the printing sector and in radio and television networks, the reference to press agencies almost sounds touching.

It is obvious that these structures condition the development of a majority conviction on which governmental action is based through free elections. They therefore intervene in the relationships between majority and minority, increasing the risks of a majority dictatorship (Horwitz 1966), a danger dreaded—keeping an eye on the "social issue"—by the same champions of liberal thought. "In our time," wrote Tocqueville ([1835] 2010: 307), "freedom of association has become a necessary guarantee against the tyranny of the majority. . . . There are no countries where associations are more necessary, to prevent the despotism of parties or the arbitrariness of the prince, than those where the social state is democratic." In a dictatorship, anyone who freely manifests a differing opinion must expect to be hurt by an act of repression. But what can someone in a democracy who freely expresses a minority opinion expect? What is the relationship between repression and the majority consent? It would be naïve to think that every repressive policy must go against majority approval. Repression causes indignation, resentment for injustice and solidarity only in certain conditions, whereas it finds approval or lack of concern in many others. In an environment of vested beliefs created by the dominating media, and controlled by the large concentrations of power, following extensive hate campaigns and the diffusion of hysterical fears, even ferocious repression does not produce repugnance in the majority of people who see it, or who look away.

If democracy was therefore reduced to a mere method of exercising power pro tempore through the simultaneous mandate of free elections, motions for individual and collective freedom would risk being emptied from the inside out. An analogous consideration can be applied to motions of justice and equality. Colin Couch (2004: 3) criticized reductionism within the dominant interpretation of the concept of democracy, which "stresses electoral participation as the main type of mass participation" and "has little interest in widespread citizen involvement or the role of organizations outside the business sector." Analogously with the promise of equality and participation, we could say that the promise of freedom cannot be satisfied by the majority/minority game alone.

We cannot say, however, that the American and French revolutionaries had not considered all of these aspects. Even though many of them were not at all fearful that the people's religion would gain an advantage over the law, they designed their institutions with numerous safety measures. Perhaps it was not so much a mistrust in the absolute transcendent legitimacy of popular sovereignty as the experience of the monarchy that propelled them toward constitutionalism and the rule of law. It needs to be recalled that the protagonists of "the civil war with outside intervention known now as the American Revolution" (Chomsky 2003: 75) were dealing with their king as a political and military opponent, and that elements of a controlled, pro tempore monarchy could be traced within their constitution. Furthermore, at the beginning, the French absolute monarch was seen to be an insurmountable part of the transformation process itself, and an ally against the nobility's privileges. Safety measures were therefore included in the constitution to prevent the intrusion of ever-present absolutist and autocratic prerogatives tied to the old regime, the same prerogatives that would, however, ultimately become essential in the defense against the most peremptory pretensions of popular sovereignty.

We once again return to France in 1789, where Montesquieu's idea was highly regarded among revolutionaries, although it is worth highlighting that it had been conceived of before the occurrence of popular sovereignty, and independently from it. Montesquieu had ruled that an indivisible and unlimited sovereignty will always be tyrannical, and that there were two types of tyranny: "An actual tyranny, which consists of governmental violence, and a tyranny of opinion, which is made known when those who govern establish things which upset the nation's way of thinking" (Montesquieu [1758] 1843: 337). In his eyes, separation of powers was an essential requirement for an effectual rule of law, whether a monarchy or a republic, and this rule of law—a monarchy or a republic—could potentially be besieged by the repressive arbitrary violence of the government, or equally, by a sort of dictatorship of hegemonic opinions.

Montesquieu's reasoning was similar to Kant's, although referring to different concepts: Kant's "republic" looked similar to the rule of law in Montesquieu's thinking, while for the latter "republic" was easier to couple with "democracy." Democracy was in any case only one of the forms of state where the rule of law could be considered, and Kant was in fact skeptical whether they could be united. Nonetheless, the prevision whereby whoever the sovereign subject may be, they must become so through a fundamental written or habitual constitution or law, would appear to be a consequence of the reasoning laid out by Montesquieu. The same reasoning mandatorily establishes a set of binding rules for the legislative institutions, which become effectual prerogatives for the surveillance over the respect of constitutional norms.

Kant and Montesquieu are essential reference points for liberal political philosophy and for constitutionalism, yet the distinction made by both between the sovereign, on the one hand, and either despotism or rule of law on the other, is today considered to be a distinction that can be attributed to the fact that they were "men of the times." What is meant by this is to suggest that they could not yet understand that democracy was in fact the premise for any true rule of law. The German constitutionalist Dieter Grimm, for example, claims that in order to configure a rule of law in its most comprehensive meaning, it must necessarily take the shape of a democratic political system:

> Neither can the two elements of constitutionalism, democracy and the rule of law, be separated without diminishing the achievements of both. It is universally acknowledged that a document which does not aspire to place political power under the rule of law does not deserve the title "constitution." The same recognition cannot not be taken for granted when talking of democracy as a legitimizing principle of public power. In fact, whichever other legitimizing principle that is different from democracy would undermine the function of the constitution. When the right to exercise power is instead based on absolute truth, whether it be religious

or secular, this truth will always prevail in a conflict with positive rights. (Grimm 2012: 325)

The same author furthermore claims that through the American and French Revolutions every right "became obligatorily positive. This was also true for that part of the law which had the task of regulating institutions and power" (Grimm 2012: 323). Sieyès ([1789] 2002: 53), too, had previously maintained that the "nation is above all, it is the source of everything. It's will is always legal, it is the law itself. Prior to and above the nation, there is only natural justice." Grimm (2012: 324) continues stating that the "modern constitution is a set of juridical norms and not a political philosophy. These norms are based on a political decision and not on a preexisting truth." He then adds, however, that the "constitution originates with the people, which is the only legitimate source of public power." This means that sovereignty is a principle that founds, and for this reason transcends, the established political power. In a monarchy, divine investiture and a legitimacy derived from conquest and lineage are axiomatic and obligatory truths that no concrete manifestation of political power is allowed to put into question. The truth of the people is certainly no less mythical, "absolute," or "preexisting." Neither are the people who are "sacred due to the sacred law of nature" (Robespierre) less axiomatic.

From 1789 until 1814 when France frequently went through political turmoil, it quickly and quintessentially condensed the potential for future developments, beginning with popular sovereignty. In those few years, within the frame of those same "sacred values" of people and nation, a wide range of political forms was tested, from elective and pluralist representation to universal male suffrage, to the crude dictatorship of terror and the charismatic plebiscitary regressions defined as "liberal" by Napoleon. Even later, in the political systems based on the people's sovereignty, the transformations which led to abandoning the principles of the rule of law constantly lurked in the background. Between the two world wars, only a few European countries maintained their full capacity for exercising parliamentarian and constitutional rights. The European dictatorships of the twentieth century incorporated both instances of degeneration dreaded by Montesquieu, realizing a tyranny of violence and a tyranny of majority thought at the same time. Indeed, Grimm is certainly correct in pointing out the connection between the two elements of constitutionalism: abandoning the rule of law generally means abandoning the democratic system also. However, this does not imply that the presence of one guarantees the presence of the other.

We should furthermore ask why plebiscites so often marked the beginning of modern despotic regression, and why they were generally accompanied by calls upon "the people" which simultaneously referred to various historical meanings of the word: *ethnos, demos*, crowd, common people, man of the street, middle class, lower class, and the marginalized. The first point of slipping from democracy to Caesarism in fact seems to be this idea of the people as an absolute and exclusive source of political legitimacy. The "preexisting truth" of the people can in certain circumstances cause the rule of law to deteriorate rapidly. This happens when the people's representatives emphasize that "its will is always legal," weakening and abolishing the distinction between sovereignty and political power introduced by the constitution, and with this, its balance, at the hands of other powers. It in fact happens when such an emphasis is supported by the assumption that the people are an exceptional sovereign due to natural justice, and are therefore superior above all others: more good, more correct, more equal, more sacred, more authentic. This happens when, in the name of this natural superiority, the conclusion is reached that the people less than a king or an emperor must accept the inevitability of being controlled by counter-powers. As Rousseau ([1762] 1913: 90) claimed, when the people rule, "all the springs of the State are vigorous and simple and its rules clear and luminous; there are no embroilments or conflicts of interests; the common good is everywhere clearly apparent, and only good sense is needed to perceive it." Succumbing to "the power of mythological suggestion" that Rousseau's abstract "community of the heart" (Esposito 2010:142) exerted over them, French revolutionaries would claim at the National Assembly that the legislative body of the people is entitled to an "absolute and unlimited sovereign power" because it is "the result of the general will" (Marat 1789: 47).

This radical rhetoric also certainly needs to be contextualized, in as much as it was heading against the already predictable destiny of moderate constitutionalism, which became increasingly polemical over the dangers of a tyranny of the majority also because of its elitist worries that the lower and destitute classes would gain political influence, would support anti-bourgeoisie stances, and would eventually put into practice some sort of legalized social revolution. According to Skinner ([1998] 2012: 77–78), at the time of the American and French Revolutions the attack on "the suggestion that an equal right to participate in government is indispensable to the maintenance of civil liberty," as promoted, for example, by the British philosopher William Paley, made "the classical liberal case." On the other side, republicanism was also aware of the "dangers" of mass participation, as reactionary popular mobilization against the constitution and the republic on several occasions proved to be more successful than the mobilization in favor, causing some radical liberals to claim that "the majority of the population [is] unsuited to the exercise of political rights" (Bron 2016: 62). This makes us understand why early liberalism would "refer to democracy with coldness, hostility and sometimes frank contempt" (Losurdo 2011: 341).

Liberals such as Charles Comte and Charles Dunoyer avoided similar dilemmas by turning to the classics which had also highlighted that in practical terms the theoretical link between freedom and reason implied a principle of delegation and professional government of the *res publica*. "If the people are to be free, it is not enough that they should have a constitution and laws; they must have in their midst men who understand them, and others who are willing to implement them, and still others who know how to respect them" (Comte and Dunoyer [1817] 2012: 51). Hume had already provided useful arguments in favor of the restriction of political participation that would be typical of most nineteenth-century constitutional regimes, starting from the principle of property as the nucleus of the social contract. The "lower sort of people and small proprietors," he wrote, may be good enough to participate in the political affairs of their municipality or district, but "they are wholly unfit for county-meetings, and for electing into the higher offices of the republic. Their ignorance gives the grandees an opportunity of deceiving them" (Hume [1754] 1987: 522). Similarly, Germaine de Staël ([1818] 2012: 62) had intended limiting republicanism to small states, leaving monarchies to the larger ones. Feeling the growing pressure from social and political demands from the subaltern classes, many liberal regimes would actually end up severely restricting the right to political participation. In 1789, the revolutionary pathos of the most radical factions was also motivated by the fear of a similarly distressing result.

Beyond this, decidedly relevant political diatribe, the philosophical foundations on which the sacralization of the sovereign people was based were nevertheless not so far from those of the moderate liberals. In 1811 Destutt de Tracy ([1811] 2012: 40) felt it necessary to restate them in the context also of the limitations that he saw in Montesquieu's approach:

> There is by right, only one power in the society, and that is the will of the nation or society, from which all authority flows; . . . Montesquieu does not deny this, he is only unmindful of it; he is entirely taken up with his triple powers, his legislative, executive, and judiciary, considering them as rivals, and as powers independent of each other; and that it is only necessary to reconcile or restrain them, each by the other, in order to make every other thing make go on well, without taking any notice, whatever, of the natural power from which they are derived, and upon which they depend.

It was not only in the rise of Napoleon Bonaparte—defended here by Destutt de Tracy—that the world was able to comprehend the irresistible "natural power" behind the people's sovereignty. There would be numerous other examples to list. Neither the charismatic leaders nor the European dictators of the twentieth century wanted to do anything other than interpret this absolute sovereignty of the people in its entirety. It seems that the very idea of the people and the philosophy of history it references manifest a desire for wholeness and totality, which leaves it open to similar involutions. The rule of law and the ideas of constitution and separation of powers are similarly derived from the history of western political thought, but they appear much less burdened down in historical mysticism, at least in their juridical and procedural aspects.

Montesquieu asked that the sovereign should be beneath the law independently from the social and philosophical connotation of his sovereignty. In Montesquieu's time, the concrete integration of sovereignty and political power usually coincided. The emergence of popular sovereignty and the constitution divided them, subjecting political power to the control of counterpowers, and contextually causing the sovereign people to become more absolute and mythical, but also more theoretical and abstract. Whenever the desire is expressed to integrate them again in order to obtain a more authentically popular political form, a foul smell of tyranny begins to spread. On the one hand, every time the distinction between democracy and rule of law is even slightly blurred, as if the first was indicative of, or guaranteed, the second, this rule begins to run risks. The same risk holds, on the other hand, when major concentrations of power succeed in establishing a "tyranny of opinion" that is able to shape "the nation's way of thinking." Then the political struggle easily polarizes between those forces who pretend to fight for the re-appropriation of sovereign power by the "true people," and powerful perception-shaping and mind-controlling elites who pretend to defend "true democracy" against the populist and demagogic assault. Under such conditions, the rule of law and all it implies for political freedoms and individual rights is destined to be seriously called into question.

3

Hierarchy among equals

> *When the Beast emerged from the western sea*
> *as a fictitious ghost who was an actual ghost*
> *to the niggers He carried in his pouch of filth*
> *his Moby Dick ship called Jesus . . .*
>
> AMIRI BARAKA,
> BEGINNINGS: MALCOLM (2003)

As humanist ideals gradually condensed into Enlightenment philosophies, western universalism began to coexist with the conceptual and practical establishment of a growing number of hierarchies between groups and places. The coexistence between an ideal of universal equality among all human beings and the obsessive practice of partition, discrimination, and bordering is not sufficiently explained in claiming it to be a historical paradox. Partition and discrimination represented more than just the logical opposite to universalism, and more than removable obstacles that stood in the way of progression toward universal "brotherhood." The representation of the coexistence between equality and hierarchy in terms of a dialectical contradiction is perhaps a more appropriate one. According to that representation, both universalism and hierarchical partition each contain the other as a necessary condition of their own discursive construction (Balibar 1994: 198). Alana Lentin, for example, states that "it is because of the possibility of egalitarianism, proffered by the revolutionary ideal of universalism, that racialization becomes a viable political tool" (Lentin 2004: 37).

While from an inside perspective of the western worldview it is important to understand the dialectical discursive nexus between universality and particularity as well as between equality and hierarchy, one might wonder whether the terms of such a contradiction can be likewise perceived from external viewpoints. Seen from the outside, western universalism does not necessarily appear to be universal to begin with, but may in fact seem to be a rather straightforward, partisan claim for hegemony and power that is not at all contradictory. What non-westerners think is, of course, of little value to enlightened westerners. As a result of their self-referential thinking the latter claim that the hegemony of moral goodness is theirs, that is, it belongs to those who accept the universality of universalism (with all of its inner contradictions, as some writers thoughtfully add), over the evil others who do not. Furthermore, seeing as humanity is declared to be the final goal of history, no matter whether in narrow utopian terms, or as the moving target of everlasting perfection, the same distinction takes the shape of multiple temporal and spatial disparities between the advanced and the backward. It may be hard to believe but these are the astonishingly simple basic parameters of all western ideological partition practices, from the shooting of wild Indians who refuse to become civilized, to the sophisticated theoretical confutation of critics who dare to doubt the universality of natural and hence inalienable human rights.

3.1 European spaces

In Europe—the historical homeland of the idea of the west—partitioning and bordering were frenetic during the era in which the nation-states were established. Beginning in the eighteenth century it carried on throughout the nineteenth and twentieth centuries and still today does not appear to be over. At the basis of such development, there were initially other profound structural social and economic changes, which increasingly demanded a territorial organization of political power. For seventeenth- and eighteenth-century Europe, this was undoubtedly an innovation. However, the tight relation between socioeconomic change and the emergence of the territorial state is not a universal rule. The complex territorial presence of both secular and religious powers (also called the "dualism of powers"), which was typical of medieval Western Europe (Le Goff 2001: 9), was due to historical contingencies that did not apply to all world regions. China, for example, operated under territorial state logic for millennia (Duara 1995: 35–58, 186), but there were indeed numerous other large states, which established a vertically integrated formation of state power in managing their territory and boundaries. Among these, there were both ancient and more recent states, from the Romans to the Incas. They manifested rather varied technological, economic, and social conditions that differed greatly from each other. Therefore, the tight bond between socioeconomic "stages of development" and forms of political power, which has been postulated by a historiography that was accustomed to transforming European events into universal rules, is actually difficult to confirm.

However, this should not prevent the acknowledgment that in the European case important socioeconomic factors were driving the new territorial organization of power. In the early modern era, this was expressed through absolute monarchies as well as through more or less traditional parliamentary participative forms, from England to Switzerland, and from the provincial states to the noble parliamentarianism of Poland. From at least the eighteenth century, also within the great European empires—Hapsburg, Tsarist, Ottoman—never-before-seen forms of territorial government sprung from socioeconomic, technological, and military transformations. During the nineteenth century, these political and administrative reforms overlapped with a creeping process of political nationalization, enhancing centrifugal forces to the detriment of the empires' formerly efficient integrative organization and ideology.

The socioeconomic factors, which pushed in favor of such transformations, were mostly the same as those that provided the reasons for "overturning" the traditional concepts of *nationes*. As we discussed in the previous chapter, the derivation of these concepts can refer to nobility, either directly, when used in reference to the link between lineage and legitimacy, or indirectly, when applied to the identification of territory and its subjects through dynastic reference. This was the case, for example, in the classifications of "native" and "national" origins of merchants or students within the system of estate (Schulze 1999: 112–13, 168–69). These concepts were "overturned" by a concept of popular sovereignty, which legitimized itself by way of a sort of naturalization that considered anonymous and collective ancestry to be entrenched in the territory. Under these circumstances, the connection with the concept of Europe came about through ethnographic, mythological, and poetic worship of the pre-Christian and pre-Latin "Old Europe." Great writers of the era, like Herder, Scott, and Fauriel, received these ideas from earlier thinkers such as Macpherson, Gray, Muralt, Haller, and Mallet, and circulated them. These ideas eventually passed into common use in nineteenth-century history and folklore, and became outstanding features of invented tradition and public memory (Thiesse 1999). Folkloristic and ethnographic investigation, the "rediscovery" of allegedly old chants, dances, tales, customs, rites, and so on, sustained the mythology of the origins and the idea of legitimacy and authenticity of the sovereign people. It was of little importance if the investigated phenomena were effectively "original" or, rather, as they were most of the time, simply posthumous inventions or reinterpretations of their former meaning. Overall, the principle of people inhabiting a territory contributed to establishing a kind of natural right of the popular sovereignty.

Yet another principle, also derived from nobility, seems to have been "overturned" during the era of popular sovereignty in order to grant legitimacy to power: the right, if not obligation, to conquer. Theoretically, for the nobility, a former cast of warriors, it might have been an unmistakable privilege in itself, descending directly from the strength of the weapons, without needing transcendent justification. In fact, however, if for no other reason than the power of weapons needing to then be translated into a durable government, a divine investiture was in any case invoked. Particularly in the crusades, and the colonial, anti-Turk, or confessional wars, this missionary consignment would be invoked. Thus, the overturning: with the French Revolution in full force, the nation-people also mobilized to conquer due to the universal historical mission that the revolutionary community insisted on incorporating, a mission to be put forward and to be defended from the subversion by the "princes" who were ruling the surrounding lands. It was "the nation, the community of the entire population, which made possible an unprecedented mobilization in the war against the monarchies of Europe" (Schulze 1999: 169). In this way, the sovereign people, from the moment in which they claim the right and obligation to conquer, substitute the previous transcendent sense with one of civilization and progress. For example, when speaking of freeing another people from the domination of a despotic and anachronistic power.

Civilization and progress are two concepts that are intimately linked to the name of Europe, and one could wonder how two nations were able to go to war against each other in the name of the same principles. Is this just an example of the selfishness of the nation-states that has been impeding the effective unification of Europe for centuries? This recurring question postulates the existence of a clear-cut opposition, which, however, does not encompass the dialectal dimension of the relationship between Europe and nation. As Gerard Delanty (1999: 272) points out, "the national identity, from the age of the Enlightenment, represents a universalist ideology which, paradoxically, requires appealing to Europe to legitimize its national particularism." In other words, the European nations do not claim to reunite in egotistic self-satisfaction with the aim of fulfilling their own needs. In order to legitimize their individual existence they claim to have a special mission to achieve, that is, to uphold the cause of human progress. As the Marquis of Condorcet, in fact, said, given that European history preceded the history of mankind, the European nations' universal mission was a European mission.

Similar theories were able to assign a historical hierarchy to the geography of the entire globe, classifying its parts according to parameters of progress. The driving desire to trace a boundary between Europe and Asia, even against the geophysical objectivity otherwise invoked, was proof of such. Accordingly, those theories enabled the reaffirmation, even if in a modified, secularized version, of the legitimacy of colonial occupation. If Europeans crossed the boundaries of Europe, conquering "empty," exotic, and "backward" territories, where time stood still et cetera, once again they did not do so (only) out of selfish will for dominion or exploitation, but (also) because of the weight of the universal and humanitarian mission that burdened their shoulders.

However, among European spaces also, geography described new downward slopes along the mental axes of progress and civilization. Moreover, these tendencies did not wait for the arrival of the modern nations in order to emerge and manifest. In the sixteenth and seventeenth centuries the attributed inability of the "Levantine" areas under Ottoman or ex-Byzantine rule to accomplish a more "rational" economic and administrative organization was already being increasingly matched with the "savage" and "uncivil" nature of the inhabitants. For example, the Venetians testified poor institutions, and a lack of social cohesion and sense of civility within the *Morlach* peoples on the Dalmatian border. Whereas according to George Sandys (1621), who was traveling in the Ottoman Empire in the early sixteenth century, the Ottomans had erased former ancient Greek and Christian *civilitie*; for Sir Henry Blount, who traveled to the Turkish Balkans, the Turks were "the only moderne people" of the area, whereas the savages were the peoples under their rule. As he maintained, "to our *North-West* parts of the world, no people should be more averse, and strange of behavior, than those of the *South-East*." He added that especially in the most remote places "there are many *Mountainers* or *Outlawes*, like the wild *Irish*" (Blount 1636: 2, 13). The latter observation demonstrates that spatial axes, such as northwest and southeast, assumed a metaphorical value. They stood for the position of the inhabitants on the time axis of progress.

If these seventeenth-century recompositions of the European mental maps visibly reflected the debate in humanist and natural-law philosophy, then the birth, the mutation, the expansion, the breakup, and ultimately the reunion of new nation-states within the European expanse produced a further leap in quality from the eighteenth century onward. With the new political and military boundaries, new mental and symbolic maps also emerged in Europe, generalizing the idea of a hierarchy among geographic areas in need of being reorganized according to their level of civilization. In order to transform a bordering state, or in any case an adversary, into a target of controversy and possible assault, even in Europe it was necessary to launch accusations of religious or despotic obscurantism. This observation holds, first, for the Grande Nation. In addition to believing it had the right to expand the national territory in accordance with the principle of the "natural frontiers," following the revolution it believed it had the historical responsibility to bring "liberty, equality, and fraternity to the European continent" (Forrest 1989: 120–22). The French meant to "deliver messages to the rest of the universe and France's message was necessarily the best European message (that is, 'civilized message') delivered to the rest of the world." Europe was therefore naturally supposed to become a "sphere of French influence" (Frank 2002: 311–12).

It would in any case be difficult, in fact almost impossible, to identify in the continent one single national narrative that had not followed the French example and had decided not to ascribe a European leadership or at least a particular European authenticity to its own community, especially with respect to its direct neighbors. A prevalent spatial–temporal development, which meant a reducing rate of "European-ness," can be observed from west to east. The French believed themselves to be more European indeed than the Germans, the Germans considered themselves more European than the Polish and the Czechs, the Czechs in turn more than the Slovaks, who believed themselves more European than the Ruthenians, the Ruthenians more than the Russians, the Russians more than the Turks and the Chechens, and so forth. According to Larry Wolff (2010: 114), the ideology of civilization "related to the Enlightenment's intellectual differentiation of Europe into a presumptively civilized western Europe alongside a supposedly backward Eastern Europe."

The west–east divide became the principal European space metaphor of civilization, progress, modernity, history. Europeans who were unfortunate enough to dwell east to someone else, would unfailingly try to divert the discourse, such as the English who underlined the savagery of the Irish; or the Germans, who claimed the superiority of their *Kultur* over the French *civilisation*. Another such example is the reaction against Tocqueville's comparison of America and Russia, the former combating wilderness with the weapon of freedom, the latter combating civilization with the weapon of serfdom. Pushkin opposed this hierarchy by praising Russia's other, better, freedom, which in Svetlana Boym's (2010: 94) words proved to be "an object of a nostalgic or futuristic desire, not a set of rules for everyday behavior in the present." That nostalgia and utopia were the motives of intellectual estrangement from political affairs should be proof enough that the Russian version was driven by western eschatological visions of history. The defiant Russian Slavophil grudge "against Europe," as interpreted by "one of the great anti-Occidentalists in the Occidental tradition" (Boym 2010: 107), Dostoyevsky, was also fed by the offense felt in not having the Russian civilizing—European—mission among the barbarians of Asia recognized (Dostoyevsky [1877] 1917: 461–71). The Russian mission in Asia had been expressly encouraged by Mazzini ([1866] 1939: 101), provided Russia left the "western westerners" to run the western Slavs, who the Italian republican considered more civilized than the Russians themselves.

The axis between west and east, however, did not remain the only leader of this geographical hierarchy. Others were added later on: one between north and south, as well as other infinite variants in more directions, including a myriad of regional diversities and contingencies. The civilizing trend between Great Britain and Ireland, as we have seen, ran from east to west. Overall, however, even at the end of the twentieth century, Western Europe still was considered more European than Central Europe, the latter being more European than Eastern or Southeastern Europe (Pomian 1993: 47–60). We only need to look at the negotiations and criteria, as well as the discourses, that have been created around the inclusion or exclusion of this or the other country in the expansion of the European Union ("Serbia on its way to Europe," and the like), and at the tone of comments regarding the political and cultural life in Russia.

The idea of progress thus induced, and continues to induce, the imagination, inclusion or exclusion of, and therefore the organization and delimitation of, European expanses. In the nineteenth century, the civilizing and cultivating efforts gave legitimacy to both territorial occupation and cultural homogenization of the territory, including the new extended borders. Examples of such are numerous; I can cite only a few. For Prussia, Polish presumed backwardness was legitimization enough of German sovereignty over the territories of the former Kingdom of Poland. They boasted efficient work, the propagation of *Bildung* and cultural advancement: all German imports in Prussian eyes. The *deutsche Kulturarbeit* ("German cultural effort") legitimized, or better, ennobled and required what was originally a foreign presence, but which was now the way of realizing an Eastern Europe that was otherwise condemned to lethargy and backwardness (Serrier 2004: 27–48). Provoked by such German self-admiration, Polish patriotism responded with analogous forms of civil organization and rhetoric, involving economic cooperation and mutual assistance (Schattkowsky 2002: 45–51). Not so paradoxically, for these Prussian Polish the usurping foreigner became a reason to not only protest, but also to proudly distinguish themselves from the poor conationals forced to live in underdeveloped conditions under the rule of the "anachronistic" Tsarist regime. And further, in the imagination of the German nationalists, the Bavarian warrior, who had traveled south of Brenner during the early Middle Ages to become a Tyrolese peasant, was seen to have achieved a Germanic *Kulturboden* through the incessant "German effort" of reclaiming valleys and conquering mountains for the rural economy (Wopfner 1921: 5–38). Whereas in the imagination of his counterpart, the Italians, who identified themselves with the ancient Romans, following an inadvertent thousand-year long break, after 1918 returned to bring the "pride and glory of the Italian endeavor" (Vacante 1963: 186) to the backward Tyrolese tribe, that is, industrialization, urbanity, and progress. The cultural action that was adopted to justify border repositioning can also be found in so-called Slavia Veneta incorporated into the Kingdom of Italy (Wörsdörfer 2004: 49–78).

Present in all of these discourses, which, again, are merely a random selection of examples, was a type of "historical right" to occupy, civilize, and "cultivate" territories, which the nation was under obligation to remove from dark, despotic, reactionary, anachronistic forces. From this it is clear how the more recent "humanitarian interventions" and the "responsibility to protect," sometimes promoted with the backing of the United Nations (Kennedy 2006: 204), other times pursued beyond international law provisions—seen, for example, in the breakup of Yugoslavia—is not far removed from these previous practices of bordering and re-bordering in the interests of a nation's "European-ness."

If the final purpose of history was presumed to be of universal value, the principle legitimizing occupation needed to be universal also. In 1861 the German economist Johann Karl Rodbertus-Jagetzow ([1861] 1890: 280–81), after writing "We are a colonizing people. But our colonies are not overseas, they are grafted directly onto the trunk of our race: east of Elba they reach Lake Peipus and the most southeastern corner of the Carpathian mountains," and after emphasizing that the Germans could not have achieved their conquering efforts "were they not charged with the duty of colonization by history, along the same lines as their neighbors," observed a humanitarian superiority even with respect to those neighbors: "In our conquered dominions we have not 'improved the indigenous,' wiping them off the face of the earth with brandy and smallpox, neither have we bled them dry through our proconsuls, nor have we tortured them in twenty-two ways in order to extort taxes from them. Centuries ago in Lusatia, Silesia and Pomerania we freed them from that serfdom within which Russia still flounders today."

This passage, also merely one episode of many in the rhetorical race of civilization, which distinctly marked the European nations' practices of dividing and sharing, shows us how there was no substantial difference in the method of classification of European and extra-European territories. Even in the bitterness of economic exploitation, voices among the Spanish colonizers declared that a more respectful treatment would be reserved for the Aztecs and the Native Americans—with respect to, in particular, the African slaves—given the "level of civilization," although modest, that they seemed to have achieved. Moreover, notable differences within European colonialist policies emerged through a further classification of "civilization" and "barbarity" that placed Native Americans at a lower stage in comparison with the ancient Asian civilizations. However, despite recognizing that "the Amerindians had legitimate political authority and ownership of their lands under natural law," the Iberian legal doctrine concluded that the Spanish crown, in their efforts of having to "defend" travelers, missionaries, and gold diggers, was motivated by a rightful cause in its occupational efforts (Kochi 2009: 37). While vast lands of America were perceived as "virgin lands" and "empty" for conquering and exploiting, attempts at expansive territorial occupation and establishment of colonies in Asia were being abandoned, at least in part (Reinhard 2008: 11–64).

Additional differences obviously existed between the first colonialism of the Spanish and Portuguese kingdoms, the second phase of Dutch-, British-, and French-dominated colonization, and the imperialist race for the almost complete splitting up of Africa between the mid nineteenth century and the First World War, which saw the involvement of other powers such as Belgium, Germany, and Italy. There were also differences between France and Great Britain in their approach to nineteenth-century territorial occupation. France applied a policy of assimilation and compliance with the institutional norms of the motherland in its colonies, rife with faith in the universal value of its systems. Great Britain was dedicated to an imperial pragmatism shaped by a more "anthropological" view, and gave more space to native cultural tradition by forming unequal pacts with the indigenous authorities and by leaving them with certain functions of command and government, according, also, to a *divide et impera* logic.

However, no matter what the approach was, the underlying classification did not diverge. Where civil and advanced countries broadened their sovereignty to lands in which "primitive" forms of community and education were practiced, exercising this sovereignty was not simply a right, but a moral obligation to history itself to educate the natives and waken them to progress. They, of course, had no right to resist. The null value of their social, legal, and political institutions was ascertained by western conceptions of the law. Tully (1993: 4) underlines the role that "Locke's theory of property played in the justification of English settlement in America and the dispossession of the Amerindian First Nations of their property and sovereignty." Another good example of the self-referential reasoning of the western civilizers was delivered by the liberal politician and philanthropist Leopoldo Franchetti, who strongly supported Italian peasant colonization in the Eritrean Highlands. The jurist brilliantly contested the Eritrean natives' protest against land confiscation by arguing "it would be futile to discuss the juridical implications of the indigenous rights to land. Speaking about property in a sense conferred to by the Roman Law would only disseminate confusion. . . . In barbarian and semi-barbarian societies, the rights upon land are generally malleable and not well defined" (Franchetti 1891: 32). No Roman law, not even a land registry: this was no-man's land! The colonizers' approach to the problem of property was also at the same time the expression of an educational effort: "European colonizers took possessive individualism to be the foundation of civilized society; the corollary was that private property was unknown in 'savage' Africa. These colonizers encouraged the idea of individual rights in the name of modernity and to effect the evolution of human societies from status to contract" (Ibhawoh 2007: 91). At the beginning of the nineteenth century, Europe's African colonies were mainly based around the coastal areas with a few significant exceptions. One of these was South Africa, where colonization had been heading north since the late seventeenth century.

> In 1671 the first purchase of land from the Hottentots beyond the limits of the fort built by Riebeek marked the beginning of the Colony proper. . . . Advancing north and east from their base at Cape Town the colonists gradually acquired—partly by so-called contracts, partly by force—all the land of the Hottentots, large numbers of whom they slew. Besides those who died in warfare, whole tribes of Hottentots were destroyed by epidemics of smallpox in 1713 and in 1755. Straggling remnants still maintained their independence, but the mass of the Hottentots took service with the colonists as herdsmen, while others became hangers-on about the company's posts and grazing-farms or roamed about the country. In 1787 the Dutch government passed a law subjecting these wanderers to certain restrictions. The effect of this law was to place the Hottentots in more immediate dependence upon the farmers, or to compel them to migrate northward beyond the colonial border. Those who chose the latter alternative had to encounter the hostility of their old foes, the Bushmen, who were widely spread over the plains from the Nieuwveld and Sneeuwberg mountains to the Orange river. The colonists also, pressing forward to those territories, came into contact with these Ishmaelites—the farmers' cattle and sheep, guarded only by a Hottentot herdsman, offering the strongest temptation to the Bushman. Reprisals followed; and the position became so desperate that the extermination of the Bushmen appeared to the government the only safe alternative. "Commandoes" or war-bands were sent out against them, and they were hunted down like wild beasts. (Cana 1911: 237)

European expansion from the coasts toward inner Africa intensified during the late nineteenth century, heading into the "heart of darkness," through first appealing to the merchant companies, and later to the state military forces. The United States was also involved: following 1820, with the help of the American Colonization Society and other "philanthropists" and politicians a number of notionally emancipated Afro-American ex-slaves, instead of enjoying full political rights, were increasingly "perceived as an anomaly that would sooner or later have to be rectified" (Losurdo 2011: 50). They migrated more or less voluntarily from the United States to what would become the Republic of Liberia. This action was supported by President James Monroe, who, in 1823, would author the interdict against any European intervention in the ex-colonies of the Americas. Was his position shaped by "anti-colonialism," as we would claim? As has already appeared from Condorcet's quotations, what we today call "anti-colonialism" was in fact made up of two different faces. On one side, there was a certain philanthropic scandal due to the vileness and brutality in what was inflicted on the indigenous people and the imported slaves, perpetrated more by the European colonizers than by the armies. On the other, there was full support of the independence of these same

European colonizers from the "burdensome domination" by the motherland. As can be gathered from the American Declaration of Independence (1776), these two types of anticolonialism did not always go together. Among the grievances brought against the king of Great Britain, the independent colonies claimed that he "has excited domestic insurrections amongst us, and has endeavoured to bring on the inhabitants of our frontiers, the merciless Indian Savages, whose known rule of warfare, is an undistinguished destruction of all ages, sexes and conditions." Starting with the thirteen eastern states, the United States rapidly expanded its civilizing efforts to the west, where the "merciless Indian savages" lived and died. The Indian Removal Act was established, determining the deportation of Native Americans to reserves which were assigned to them on a permanent basis, but not without stating that "such lands shall revert to the United States, if the Indians become extinct, or abandon the same" (US Congress [1830] 1846: 412). Following hundreds of years of settlement, the European colonial settlers in South Africa and the Americas slowly Africanized and Americanized their national group mythologies, but they did so in typically European terms and therefore their approach to mapping out the frontiers also remained European.

3.2 Human races

At the end of the fifteenth century, the Inquisition demanded the expulsion from Spain of all Jews who would not convert, probably inaugurating the most significant among the "processes of stigmatization and exclusion of Jews between the end of the Middle Ages and the Renaissance" (Schaub 2015: 79). Following 1492, between 150,000 and 200,000 Jews were expelled, while around 50,000 chose to be baptized so they could stay. These *conversos* often returned to their previous religious practices, or in any case were suspected of such. From the sixteenth to the seventeenth century, an almost permanent persecution in the pursuit of *limpieza de sangre* fell on the community of *conversos*, who were eternally suspected of undermining the Holy Faith. Similarly, and more or less in the same era, the *moriscos*, Muslims who had converted or "reconverted" to the Christian faith, were also suspected of secretly plotting against the one true and sacred faith, of undermining the church and the monarchy, and of infecting the community of believers with secret practices from their previous faith. A century after the abovementioned events, Miguel de Cervantes had one of his characters, the dog Berganza, say:

> O what curious things I could tell you, friend Scipio, about that half Paynim rabble. . . . Hardly will you find among the whole race one man who is a

sincere believer in the holy law of Christianity. Their only thought is how to scrape up money and keep it; and to this end they toil incessantly and spend nothing. The moment a real falls into their clutches, they condemn it to perpetual imprisonment; so that by dint of perpetually accumulating and never spending, they have got the greater part of the money of Spain into their hands. They are the grubs, the magpies, the weasels of the nation. Consider how numerous they are, and that every day they add much or little to their hoards, and that as they increase in number so the amount of their hoarded wealth must increase without end. None of them of either sex make monastic vows, but all marry and multiply, for thrifty living is a great promoter of fecundity. They are not wasted by war or excessive toil; they plunder us in a quiet way, and enrich themselves with the fruits of our patrimonies which they sell back to us. They have no servants, for they all wait upon themselves. They are at no expense for the education of their sons, for all their lore is but how to rob us. (Cervantes [1613] 2014: 211)

At the beginning of the seventeenth century, the last remaining 300,000 *moriscos* withdrew toward North Africa and into the Ottoman territories in search of respite from the repressive fury. In another novel Cervantes directed his gaze toward the gypsies, "born of parents who are thieves, reared among thieves, and educated as thieves, they finally go forth perfected in their vocation, accomplished at all points, and ready for every species of roguery. In them the love of thieving, and the ability to exercise it, are qualities inseparable from their existence, and never lost until the hour of their death" (Cervantes [1613] 2014: 223).

The underlying motive for the discrimination and persecution in sixteenth-century Spain can more than likely be attributed to religious reasons, which in turn constituted the principal ideological pillar of the monarchy and the community bonds on various levels, especially political, in as much as the principal source of the Kingdom of Spain's legitimacy was the renewed Christianization of the territory. In this context, the Other and the Diverse, or whomever was presumed to be such, served to reaffirm the solidity of the community. The Other and the Diverse were collectively attributed with certain negative characteristics, such as not being Christian and infecting the community of the faithful and their honest customs with evil habits they had acquired not only through birth and blood, that is, congenitally through natural inheritance, but also because of tradition, unbelieving, and bad upbringing. These are forms of classification, which see no need to accurately separate genetic heredity, the color of skin, or other features of the body, from beliefs, religions, practices, customs, and languages. Similar stereotypes and forms of discrimination have presumably existed and indeed still exist in various moments of history in all four corners of the earth. Yet, it makes sense to look at modern western racism as a specific case (Schaub 2015: 49). In the west, groups characterized in such a classificatory way began to be referred to as "races," a term which would go on to become a characteristic marker of western stereotypes and discrimination—taking on all the risks of a marker, the absence of which can sometimes be misleading in understanding the pathology's true development.

Prior to the anonymous publication of François Bernier's essay in 1684 on the division of the earth into various settlements based on "species or race," there does not seem to have been any theory on race that systematically focused on physiognomy. Previously, physical features or skin color were not overly dwelled upon, and neither was there a clear distinction in designating the Other between what would go on to become the distinction between nature and nurture, the biological and the cultural dimension. Historically it was colonialism and slavery that created a "notion of 'epidermilisation' as the means by which racial identities are entrapped within the skin" (Lentin 2004: 27). However, also Cervantes's descriptions of Jews, (converted) Muslims, and Gypsies are indirectly contaminated by the colonial atmosphere. His novels referred to a period between the end of the fifteenth and the beginning of the sixteenth centuries, but his own language already belonged to a later period, when the construction of "tables of human races or frames of classification" that prelude to modern racism (Schaub 2015: 245), was in full swing. Pope Pius II had given the concept of Europe a renewed political meaning time earlier, and the Iberian, then European, transoceanic colonialism had become a well-established reality which was used to employing some of the cruelest methods to "eradicate and cancel from the face of the earth those miserable nations": the Native Americans (de las Casas [1552] 1821: 17). After this "encounter" with those exotic worlds to colonize, European explorers and anthropologists developed a holistic point of view with the aim of explaining the "customs," "character," and "mentality" of peoples who were previously unknown. "There are three things that constantly influence the minds of men, climate, government, and religion," Voltaire (1764: 95) would state.

In conceiving of a mapping of human geography according to physical features, Bernier in fact borrowed from this holistic view, having deduced these features from the millennia-long interaction between populations and the environmental factors of the territory they inhabited, such as climate, water quality, and so forth. The theory on race thus also fits into place, right from the beginning, in the interaction between "natural" and "cultural" factors, drawing upon one of the cornerstones of the western vision of humankind. According to this vision, human beings in all their historical forms of existence intrinsically carry as much of a trace of their bestial origin as they do a cultural and spiritual predestination to achieve full humanity. It is a vision that incorporates man's original and prospective equality as much as the differences on the scale of progress, which distinguish human groups by their passage from their origins to the finish line. The concept of race lies within this field of meaning.

Within this vision, however, plantation slavery in the "new world" nevertheless represented a certain problem for the standard-bearers of liberty. It was one of the pillars of western economic development if we consider, for example, the role of cotton in the incipient British industrialization. It was essentially for racist reasons that, as Gibbon ([1776–89] 1907: 253) observed, "even Grotius himself (*de Jure Belli et Pacis*, 1. iii. c. 7), as well as his commentator Barbeyrac, have laboured to reconcile [slavery] with the laws of nature and reason." The pronouncedly racist character of plantation slavery was accentuated after American independence, as "the American colonists were led to identify the boundary line principally in ethnic identity and skin colour" (Losurdo 2011: 50). Earlier, Voltaire (1761: 147) did not hesitate to attribute at least domestic slavery to a severe civil shortcoming of the Africans themselves, in as much as "we purchase household-slaves only from the negroes; we are severely reproached for this kind of traffic, but the people who make a trade of selling their children, are certainly more blameable than those who purchase them, and this traffic is only a proof of our superiority."

Through historical commonalities and cultural transfers, and due to a mythological sense of affiliation, the civil, political, and cultural backwardness attributed to the "oriental races" was less daunting. At least some—for example, the Huns, Saracens, Tartars, Turks, and Persians—were attributed with having an equal capacity for military force, even if motivated by innate cruelty, deceitfulness, and wickedness. The western view on peoples of Africa and other populations considered negro, was instead characterized by boundless arrogance. These populations tended to be disdainfully compared to the animal kingdom so much so as to be excluded, at least by some authors, from any possibility of ever reaching full humanity. It was in this way that black skin in its blackness became an inescapable condition of inferiority, something that needed to be explained separately. According to Bernier, the cause of blackness in Africans "must be sought for in the peculiar texture of their bodies, or in the seed, or in the blood." Their hair "is not properly hair, but rather a species of wool, which comes near the hairs of some of our dogs" (Bernier [1684] 2000: 2). Almost a century later, the respected father of cosmopolitism, Immanuel Kant ([1777] 2000: 17), after explaining scientifically "why all Negroes stink," underlined that "besides all this, humid warmth generally promotes the strong growth of animals. In short, all of these factors account for the origin of the Negro, who is well-suited to his climate, namely, strong, fleshy, and agile. However, because he is so amply supplied by his motherland, he is also lazy, indolent, and dawdling." David Hume ([1777] 1987: 198, 207–08) remarked that

> Different reasons are assigned for . . . *national characters*; while some account for them from *moral*, others from *physical* causes. By *moral* causes, I mean all circumstances, which are fitted to work on the mind as motives or reasons, and which render a peculiar set of manners habitual to us. Of this kind are, the nature of the government, the revolutions of public affairs, the plenty or penury in which the people live, the situation of the nation with regard to its neighbours, and such like circumstances. By *physical* causes I mean those qualities of the air and climate, which are supposed to work insensibly on the temper, by altering the tone and habit of the body, and giving a particular complexion. . . . And indeed there is some reason to think, that all the nations, which live beyond the polar circles or between the tropics, are inferior to the rest of the species, and are incapable of all the higher attainments of the human mind. . . . I am apt to suspect the negroes to be naturally inferior to the whites. There scarcely ever was a civilized nation of that complexion, nor even any individual eminent either in action or speculation. No ingenious manufactures amongst them, no arts, no sciences.

So, even in those who theoretically abhorred the legal institution of slavery, it is difficult not to grasp their desire to "explain" or diminish the condemnation of the capture, exploitation, commercialization, humiliation, and extermination, of the central and western African populations so as to make it more understandable. Following Bernier's writings, race theory drew upon physical features, for the most part skin and hair color, then the shape of the face and cranium, the stature and posture of the body, degenerative illnesses and longevity, then progeny and blood, as well as—and here the author was most insistent—the beauty or ugliness of the women. The theory explained such features in terms of physiological and hereditary adaptation to the natural environment, even well before Mendel. Was racism therefore a biological proto-Darwinian theory in its origin? The quotes of Hume and Kant cited here condense the dominant western idea of race, and despite their continual references to the body, what is actually revealed is how this idea was not at all biological or "based on natural inferiority" (Schaub 2015: 167). They did not deem "negroes" to be biologically inferior given they were strong, fleshy, and agile; they in fact considered them to be superior to white people in any respect in which their savage animal-like condition was advantageous. At the same time, they were considered lazy, indolent, and dawdling, making them unsuitable for the industrious life with which the white avant-garde enabled humanity to progress in the tempered hemisphere. Johann Friedrich

Blumenbach refused the idea of more than one human species for reasons of scientific rigorousness: "We are with great probability right in referring all and singular as many varieties of man as are at present known to one and the same species" (Blumenbach [1795] 2000: 37); he was nonetheless unable to resist the temptation to compare physical features to stages of development: "The orang-outangs at first sight afford . . . a little probability to the opinion of a close connection between apes and the human race. Uncivilized men, too, make a slight approach in many corporeal particulars . . . to the structure of other animals" (Blumenbach 1828: 544–45).

The racism does not lie in the parallels drawn between certain men's and certain apes' bodies, but is instead encompassed in the expression "uncivilized man." As Fanon pointed out,

> not only must the black man be black; he must be black in relation to the white man . . . Black Magic, primitive mentality, animism, animal eroticism, it all floods over me. All of it is typical of peoples that have not kept pace with the evolution of the human race. Or, if one prefers, this is humanity at its lowest. (Fanon [1952] 1986: 110, 126)

Fanon felt that if you wear a black skin, whatever you do or whoever you may be, you look uncivilized. The independent variable in virtually all formulas of western racism is not complexion, but the ladder of civilization, or *Kulturstufe* as the Germans say. And what does this ladder of civilization refer to? It refers to the western philosophical fantasies regarding humanity and the meaning of history. Lazy, stinking, not yet civilized negroes make "the human being" in Kant's, and in other western eyes, a less-convincing "final end of creation."

Also at the climax of positivist racist thinking, at the turn of the twentieth century, it was not biological theory but the metaphor of progress and backwardness that reigned over racist theory. This was the most general principle of hierarchical differentiation between human bodies; not just between colonizers and the colonized, but also among Europeans, and not just between whites and blacks or otherwise "colored," but also where the "black" was just a darker shade of white. Take, for example, the thesis of southern otherness developed by the Italian Alfredo Niceforo, which, like other positivist racist theories, was only "biological" in a very superficial sense. In *L'Italia barbara* (1898) and other writings, Niceforo adduced evidence of population migrations as well as cranium types and forms, additionally relying on biometric and medical data. He also stated, however, that social environments interact with physical and psychological human characteristics, and avoided establishing a clear-cut dichotomy between cultural and biological factors. On that basis, the Sicilian-born author supported a theory according to which

> the Northern and the Southern Italians belong ... to two different races. ... In the North of the Tiber valley settled the *Aryan* element, in the South the *Mediterranean* one, creating in Central Italy a blend of the two. ... Still at the present day Italy is more or less divided into the same two zones of settlement, with the *Aryans* (*Celts* and *Slavs*) predominant from the North down to Tuscany, and the *Mediterraneans* in the South. (Niceforo 1901: 9, 20, 22)

Again, the latter were not considered biologically inferior; on the contrary, their bodies were better proportioned than those of the northern Aryans were. Why then should the southern, if compared to the northern, be an inferior race? Their inferiority was due to the effects that physical differences, facilitated by ongoing influences of the social and natural environment, exerted on psychology. The ego of southern individuals was restless, whereas the northern was quiet. The southern were intelligent, had vivid imaginations and plenty of fantasy, but suffered from a deficit of attention, a variable will, an excess of banal emotions and impulsivity, and lacked practical sense. Contrarily, the northerners were slower but more rational and practical thinkers. They controlled their emotions and were more persevering and concentrated. Whereas the southerners were unable to adapt to collective organization, "in the Aryan tribe the individual merges easily with the aggregate. ... This is why amongst the Aryans prevail collective phenomena such as industry, political association, and a compact organization of social endeavor." Which of the two races, Niceforo rhetorically asked, held better requirements for "modern progress"? In modern mass societies the most important terms in the formula of progress were civil sense and collective organization capabilities. Thus, the psychology of the southern race was "inferior if compared to that of the northern one. It is much less prepared to win the modern fight for progress" (Niceforo 1901: 124–25, 137, 149). Similar theories are enjoying a recent revival under the brand of sociobiology, which pretends to comparatively measure the "intelligence quotient" and other factors of "human progress" displayed by different races (Schaub 2015: 21–48).

To speak of mapping and hierarchy means speaking of relationships of power, of command over those and others, of one group of human beings over other human beings. Even if the those and the others are "races," "civilizations," "peoples," "cultures" rather than "ranks," "classes," or "orders," it is in any case a social hierarchy. According to Stuart Hall (1992: 255), "the central issues of race always appear historically in articulation, in a formation, with other categories and divisions and are constantly crossed and recrossed by the categories of class, of gender and ethnicity." If nothing else, it is for this reason that a strict boundary between "colonial racism" and "social racism" does not exist, the differentiation runs wild and often uninterrupted in an open field. It is not only the "negroes" who smell bad, but also the poor peasants, the workers, and especially the "anti-socials," the marginalized, the homeless, and the "born criminals," or whoever it happens to be in that moment in time.

This differentiation along the vertical axis of the same society also traces back to the dawning of scientific racism. Indeed, Bernier ([1684] 2000: 2) observed that

> although the Egyptians, for instance, and the Indians are very black, or rather copper-coloured, that colour is only an accident in them, and comes because they are constantly exposed to the sun; for those individuals who take care of themselves, and who are not obliged to expose themselves so often as the lower class, are not darker than many Spaniards.

The highlighting of the physical differences between high and low classes was even more remarkable in that the author was at the same time emphasizing that among Arabs, Persians, and Indians there were indeed differences, but not really in terms of "species." For Bernier, an Arab gentleman manifested more racial similarity with an Indian gentleman than with a peasant of his own country. Just as it does not seem to be appropriate to dwell too much on the differences between "biological racism" and "cultural racism," the same applies to the ideological differences between "colonial racism" and "social racism." This holds in particular for the peak period of positivist scientific racism, the champion of which, Cesare Lombroso (1871: 223), not only detailed the physical and physiognomic features of "born criminals" so that they could be repressed before they could commit a crime, but also outlined the differences between the white man and man of color. Not long before Lombroso, toward the mid nineteenth century, in his subdivision of humanity into races, Joseph-Arthur de Gobineau matched the Hobbesian framework of transition from the state of nature to a social contract with the concept of nation that dominated the teleology of the time. Not all human families, he wrote, manage to leave behind the state of nature;

> but it is a step that every tribe must take to rank one day as a nation. Even if a certain number of races, themselves perhaps not very far advanced on the ladder of civilization, have passed through this stage, we cannot properly regard this as a general rule . . . especially the Polynesian negroes, the Samoyedes and others in the far north, and the majority of the African races, have never been able to shake themselves free from their impotence; they live side by side in complete independence of each other. (Gobineau [1855] 2000: 47)

These two dimensions, the social hierarchization and the matching of race to nation transformed racism into a formidable biopolitical tool of the western nation-state, right at the peak moment of scientific objectification of the concept of race. In this way, racism became a "*supplement internal to nationalism*, always in excess of it, but always indispensable to its constitution and yet always still insufficient to achieve its project, just as nationalism is both indispensable and always insufficient to achieve the formation of the *nation*" (Balibar 1991: 54). It was in the same environment that the modern European anti-Semitism could prosper:

> The malleability of the racist theory enables its use both as an underpinning of the nation's superiority and as a legitimate excuse for any failure which, it could be argued, remained inevitable as long as the "race" was threatened by internal impurity. Undoubtedly, it is on the basis of such logic that modern political antisemitism evolved . . . following 1870. The efficiency of the amalgamation of science and politics epitomised by Social Darwinism, indeed the infusion of politics with a language of (scientific) "race," laid the foundations for a reworking of the old religious scapegoating of the Jews into a scientifically grounded theory that ultimately justified their extermination. (Lentin 2004: 48)

If we find numerous confirmations for rampant political anti-Semitism in Eastern Europe, Germany, Austria, and the France of the *affaire Dreyfus*, starting with the pogrom of Odessa in 1871, it is also true that the first signs of a union between anti-Semitism and nationalism emerged further back. Suffice to mention that Ernst Moritz Arndt (1814: 180–201), German patriot of the *Freiheitskriege*, wrote that the Jews were ruining the German man's customs and were degrading the race, just as they had already ruined Poland and subverted French culture. When more than a century later the political practice of anti-Semitic persecution, and then extermination, led by Adolf Hitler's Nazi Party, was able to take root, it could draw upon an ideology of anti-Semitism which had already been well instated. Above all else, it was the fruit of the theory and practice of racism as such. It would be mistaken indeed to believe that the "philo-Semitism" of a Gobineau or a Nietzsche ([1886] 1921: 219)—according to whom, "the Jews are without a doubt the strongest, purest and most resilient race living today in Europe"—was less racist and less a valid source of inspiration for the Nazi leaders than the unbridled anti-Jewish hatred of an Arndt.

The immensity of the extermination of around six million Jews—systematic and serialized from 1942 until 1945—for reasons, which beyond any other concurrent factor, were dictated by an irrepressible racist hatred, caused Nazi anti-Semitism to be suspected of being of a different kind to that of other racisms. According to some suppositions, this was because of an extraordinary diabolical characteristic of Nazism; according to others, it was, conversely, because of an exceptional intrinsic characteristic of the "Jewish people," whose prophetic destiny would thus be further carried out at the hand of the Nazis. These, I believe, are misleading equations. Was there, behind the extraordinary crime, really an extraordinary ideology? A racism conceptually different from that which legitimized the abuses perpetrated against the "negroes," the Indians, the "wild Irish"?

To answer this question, it is interesting to understand how Hitler himself explains why he became an anti-Semite. When living in Linz as a boy and adolescent, he mentions in *Mein Kampf*, he knew Jewish compatriots. Young Adolf felt slightly uneasy on hearing that their ancestors had been persecuted for confessional reasons, and even "looked on them as Germans." As a young man, after moving to the multicultural metropolis of the Empire, Vienna, he became aware of the Jews as a "problem" thanks to the anti-Semitic campaigns conducted by the charismatic burgomaster Karl Lueger from the Christian Social Party. It was then that he had his personal moment of awakening: "Once when I was walking through the inner city, I suddenly came across a man with black curls dressed in a long caftan. My first thought was: is that a Jew? At Linz they did not look like that." Hitler explains how simply seeing, hearing, and smelling the *Kaftanjude* ("The smell of these caftan wearers later often made me feel nauseous"), that is, the oriental Jew, opened his eyes to the true nature of that "race": an oriental race which, often camouflaged as a westernized middle-class citizen, a banker, stockbroker, artist (of "degenerate art"), or especially a Social Democrat or Bolshevik party leader, was plotting to undermine the ethical, aesthetic, national, and cultural order with the purpose of bringing down the west. "It was terrible to realize, and yet at the same time it was impossible not to, that the Jews seemed especially destined by Nature to play this shameful role. Is it for this reason that they can be called the chosen people?" (Hitler 1936: 59, 61–62)

The orientalist motivation also emerges in Hitler's opinion of Russia, which, as he claims in 1937, had already fallen victim to the Jews and had therefore become "the greatest threat to culture and human civilization," as "the Russia of today is fundamentally the Russia of 200–300 years ago." According to Hitler, "our European states" needed to react to the fact that the power had been taken away from "the true Russian people," who were oppressed by a "terrorist formation" and a "brutal dictatorship" at the hands of an "alien race" (Hitler 1937: 84–89). It used to be the Mongols or the Tartars, but was now "the Jew" and therefore in any case an oriental despotism, the dark Steppes, that was preventing the Slavs from being able to be free as Herder had asked, or from escaping from the backwardness of their lethargy in order to enter into an authentically western—human— dimension. It was with similar arguments to this that the most well-known anti-Semite in the world placed his theory of race within the most traditional orientalist hierarchies.

We also come across an accusation against the Jews of a pact with the forces of Evil, aimed at destroying human culture and civilization; an occultist and animist insinuation, while at the same time a contraposition between nature and spirit, with a religious trace of Christianity, all welded together in the defense of the final destiny of humankind, jeopardized by the Jews.

> Should the Jew, through the aid of his Marxian creed, triumph over the peoples of the world, his crown will be the funeral wreath of mankind, and the planet will drive through the ether once again empty of human life, just as it did millions of years ago. Eternal Nature takes inexorable revenge for the violation of her order. And so I believe that I act today in accordance with the will of the Almighty Creator: in standing guard against the Jew I am defending the Lord's work. (Hitler 1936: 69–70)

According to Gray, while the Nazis' eschatology "was a debased imitation of pagan traditions," their demonology "came from Christian sources (not least the Lutheran tradition). The world was threatened by demonic forces, which were embodied in Jews." Hitler's millennial prophecy derived "from Joachitic speculation, mediated in Germany through the Anabaptist wing of Reformation and through the Johannine Christianity of Fichte, Hegel and Schelling" (Gray 2008: 94, 96). On the whole, the exaltation of nature and an almighty god, guardians of the ultimate destiny of humanity, prefigured by the philosophies of history and the Christian journey toward redemption, as well as the orientalist connotation of the "revelation" inserted into the autobiographical narrative, demonstrate how any attempt at de-westernizing Hitler's anti-Semitic ideology is unacceptable. De-westernizing Hitler, as Robert Young (1992: 249) points out, is equal to a "refusal to come to terms with the violence intrinsic to western culture."

3.3 World cultures

If "western culture" is an acceptable expression, it is so analogously with Dubuisson's reasoning concerning the term "religion." Similarly to "world religions," the expression "world cultures" manifests the idea that the distinction between "nature" and "culture" must hold universal value, and perhaps with this, the spatial–temporal mappings and distinctions provided by the philosophies of history. In fact, the dichotomy between nature and culture is the typical product of regional tradition—western, not universal. Within it are a great number of differing definitions of the term, not all of which have the same ideological value. For example, in biology "culture" is not limited to human beings, but applies to the "passage of information from one generation to the next by non-genetic means" also in other animal species (McFarland 1999: 515). However, in most of the modern era's conceptualizations of "culture"—and it is to these that we refer to here—the concept indicates an exclusively human dimension:

> The first end of nature would be happiness, the second the culture of the human being. . . . Thus among all his ends in nature there remains only the formal, subjective condition, namely the aptitude for setting himself ends at all and (independent from nature in his determination of ends) using nature as a means appropriate to the maxims of his free ends in general, as that which nature can accomplish with a view to the final end that lies outside of it and which can therefore be regarded as its ultimate end. The production of the aptitude of a rational being for any ends in general (thus those of his freedom) is culture. (Kant [1790] 2002: 297, 298–99)

This is culture according to Kant, where science and experience are seen to be instrumental in preserving the existence of humanity and metaphysics as "the completion of the *culture* of human reason" (Kant [1781] 1855: 514). Throughout the modern and contemporary age a similar concept of culture has been progressively transposed from having a meaning predominantly based around customs, beliefs, rituals, and the so-called material culture, to having more abstract spiritual, moral, aesthetic, and symbolic connotations, as well as incorporating aspects of psycho-pedagogy, language, art, and processes of memory. In particular, between the nineteenth and twentieth centuries a concept of symbolic orders shared by human subgroups emerged from the new cultural anthropology debate, that is, a concept of "cultures" in the plural form. Furthermore, given that within this debate "culture outlines a level (the superior level) of that complex and composite biosocial reality that is Man" (Remotti 1992: 646), it is possible to see how the nature–culture dichotomy remained alive and well under the blanket of theoretical and methodological sophistication, and also remained compatible with the hierarchical orders in terms of eschatological temporality.

Clifford Geertz (1973: 5) wrote that it is far more difficult to explain scientifically the realm of imagination than environmental data or even economic and social factors. More difficult still is to grasp an underdeveloped realm of imagination that has not been so clearly elaborated on a theoretical or aesthetic level, such as that which we can find in western intellectuals or artists. However, even an everyday imagination that has not been reflected on, or uncritically acquired through tradition, or even an exotic one, can be interpreted by the social scientist, as the needs and desires are of an existential nature and as such are universal. They are therefore entirely recognizable, describable, and interpretable, even in their infinite variations, by an observing anthropologist. "Believing, with Max Weber, that man is an animal suspended in webs of significance he himself has spun, I take culture to be those webs." We can therefore say that the irrepressible desire of the western anthropologist tribe to decode the social expressions of others, which otherwise remain enigmatical "on their surface," is caught in a web of typically western meanings, which are not at all universal.

This debate, which continues up until, and partly coincides with, the second half of the twentieth century, should be kept in mind when we look back to the end of the Second World War, during which the hierarchical mapping of human beings was at its worst. The "uncovering of the crimes of the Holocaust" initiated a process of rethinking which led to "the scientific discrediting of biological theories of race; an often grudging recognition of the crimes of colonialism; and the end of apartheid." Since then "it has become taboo to refer to race in an openly discriminatory way" (Lentin and Titley 2010: 4). Integrated into this rethinking process of public and political discourse were the marginalization of positivist anthropology and the development of cultural anthropology.

After 1945, after Auschwitz, and after discriminatory partitioning had taken serial extermination to the extreme, nobody wanted to hear about "races," at least not in Europe. People preferred to talk about "cultures"—a "high"-sounding word in Kantian meaning—or at least about "civilizations." However, in order to be able to settle humans on the *Kulturstufen* ladder to progress in politically correct terms, a doubly mystifying operation was needed. The first part consisted in sidelining racist theory entirely to the field of science concerning "nature," as if it had emerged from the gibberish of biologistic ranting. This was an attempt at making the world forget that racism in fact originates from culturalist ranting, and that only later did it find an auxiliary support in biological positivism. As such, the critique concentrated on "racial Darwinism" and allowed for the classification of humans to be saved, returning it almost completely to its original place within "culture" and "civilization."

In order to exemplify the transition from positivist anthropology to cultural anthropology we can return our attention to Italy and consider a piece of writing by physician and painter Carlo Levi, an anti-fascist opponent from Turin detained by the Mussolini regime in the south of Italy. The description of his experience written between 1943 and 1945, *Christ Stopped at Eboli*, when compared with Niceforo's racist theories, seems to indicate the transition to a different type of description of the "southern man," at least at first glance. The text later had particular influence on the anthropological image of the

"Mediterranean man." Levi's "southern civilization" is even more abysmally far from the "modern struggle for progress" than Niceforo's "southern race." Levi, who grew up in an industrial region, admitted to having visited and described

> a country unknown to him, and unknown languages, labor, toil, suffering, misery, and customs as well. There he came to know not only animals and magic, and ancient problems still unsolved, and the potency that withstands power, but also the pride that is ever present, a contemporaneousness that is inexhaustible . . .; a motionless world of possibilities at once infinite and closed, the dark adolescence of centuries poised to stir and emerge. (Levi [1945] 1982: 6–7)

The standing still of time, an eternal return, and magic rites place this different civilization "beyond history and progressive reason," as the cover text of the original edition (Levi 1945) reads. Although drawing on "culture," the text was published in the immediate aftermath of the Second World War, when biological markers of difference were not yet fully taboo. While Niceforo did not disdain cultural features of "race," Levi did not disdain physical features of "civilization." Whereas the few indigenous people equipped with a feeble glimpse of civilization in his description tend to be blond with light eyes, the others, especially the peasants, are described as having "opaque black eyes," with their women living "in a world ruled by magic" and dominated by an "animal-like submissiveness." Their children, "pale and thin with big, sad, black eyes," feature a "mixture of young animal spirits and precocious maturity." In this "desolate land" the "race is weakened" by poverty and disease, vegetating in a condition that "amounts to slavery without hope of emancipation" (Levi [1945] 1982: 43, 150–51, 171, 204–05).

It was not merely terms such as "culture" and "civilization" which gradually replaced "race" within the task of revealing various diversities assigned to different stages of progress. In order to represent the distinctive and characteristic features of the various human collectives, the term "ethnicity" was officially instated by UNESCO in 1950 as a replacement of the compromised term "race":

> National, religious, geographic, linguistic and cultural groups do not necessarily coincide with racial groups: and the cultural traits of such groups have no demonstrated genetic connection with racial traits. Because serious errors of this kind are habitually committed when the term "race" is used in popular parlance, it would be better when speaking of human races to drop the term "race" altogether and speak of *ethnic groups*. (UNESCO 1950: 6)

Essentially races still existed for the UNESCO of 1950, but it was better not to speak about it, in order to "replace biological theories of human difference with a culturalist definition of diversity" (Lentin 2004: 76). This approach was also favorably seen by minority groups, which in the following decades relied upon a nonessentialist concept of ethnicity. "The term ethnicity acknowledges the place of history, language and culture in the construction of subjectivity and identity" (Hall 1992: 257). On the whole, however, one is forced to conclude that the "historical anti-racist project to replace 'race' with 'ethnicity' as a non-hierarchical means of describing difference" (Lentin 2004: 27) was also a failure. Replacing the word "difference" with the word "diversity," or turning "consciousness" black, does not suffice in preventing frequent biologist contaminations of "ethnicity" in the use of the word, or in crushing the essentialism of the ethnic subdivisions in hegemonic discourses. Even the best "ethnicity" that claims its grassroots diversity with pride ultimately remains in a cage of stereotypes, the bars of which are not necessarily wider than those belonging to a cage of "races."

In the first phase, during the period from around 1945 to 1980, that we might call "anthropological" or "ethnographical," the advanced westerners tended not to define themselves as ethnicities. They lived in a complex society, filled with a democratic and cosmopolitan culture, unlike the simpler and amorphous societies—or communities? big debate!—of the "underdeveloped peoples." They thus believed that the term "ethnicity" was well suited to these people, and signaled an opportunity to keep them under "participant observation," to monitor their way of thinking, something that was, of course, in their best interests. If the western man tends to have already achieved his full Kantian faculties of self-determination, or in other words, is a free man, the non-western man must be understood and interpreted in his ways of being conditioned by beliefs, rites, customs, and traditions, and in his being constantly tormented by the provocations of western freedom and modernity that contradict his conditioning. Approximately, this is what the western ethnographic and sociological fantasies were saying and indeed still say regarding themselves and others.

In the second phase, which we could call globalization, we have become witness to numerous neocolonial wars and mass migration from the less-rich or peaceful areas of the former Third World to the west, where neoliberal policies simultaneously reduce and partly dismantle the post-war welfare state. Faced with an "invasion" of immigrants of a "different culture and ethnicity," many of these same westerners have started to reevaluate themselves as "ethnicities"—an ethnicity threatened by alien forces intent on attacking their "identity." Stuart Hall (1992: 256) claims that beyond any semantic taboo this way of conceiving of ethnic differences has become one of the core characteristics of contemporary European racism. As Paul Gilroy (1992: 52–58) points out, there are still many more bitter fruits of these dominant cultural concepts of ethnicity and identity ready for harvest in the season of globalization. The apparently benevolent conceptualization of immigrant cultures in terms of ethnicity produced ambiguities in anti-racist and multicultural movements, which has contributed to the evaporation of traditional left and right distinctions regarding immigrants or potential immigrants. We could cite among its many outcomes the increasing acceptance of the western anti-Muslim racialization by feminist and gay organizations. This was a consequence of the post 9/11 publicist drumfire regarding headscarves, homophobia, and honor crimes, which represent purported elements of Muslim culture juxtaposed to the allegedly genuine western values of gender equality and sexual emancipation (Petzen 2012: 97–114).

Is post-9/11 Islamophobia racist? We turn here to the core question of race and culture after the Second World War. Whenever the term is defined in the narrow and misleading terms of biologistic concepts, anti-racism can be conveniently reduced to the resistance against extreme right-wing movements. According to Gilroy, this would, however, exclude what he calls the ordinary racism of immigration laws from criticism and resistance, as well as the unequal opportunities in the economic, social, and juridical spheres. According to the author, these are new forms of racism camouflaged by discourses on culture and ethnicity.

> Apart from the way that racial meanings are inferred rather than stated openly, these new forms are distinguished by the extent to which they identify race with the terms "culture" and "identity," terms which have their own resonance in anti-racist orthodoxy. The new racism has a third important feature . . . . We increasingly face a racism which avoids being recognized as such because it is able to link "race" with nationhood, patriotism and nationalism, a racism which has taken a necessary distance from crude ideas of biological inferiority and superiority and now seeks to present an imaginary definition of the nation as a unified *cultural* community. (Gilroy 1992: 53)

It seems fairly predictable that some readers will object to Gilroy dismissing the connection between "race" and the idea of physiognomy too easily, in actually speaking of other forms of discrimination that have nothing to do with racism. The author is aware of and preempts this criticism by developing a theory of racism as the external surface of various social relationships. I also believe that this criticism should be rejected, for two reasons.

The first, as I have attempted to point out, is that pure biological racism is a chimera in as much as theories, which condense physical differences, become racist for the fact that they classify the differences according to "cultural" considerations. If the term "race," "rather than a color-coded fact, ignored by some and accepted by others, is an imposition born of domination" (Lentin 2004: 26), then the converse conclusion is that Gilroy has some right in branding ideas of ethnicity and national *Leitkultur* ("leading culture") as racism. In the western view on former colonies a similar substitution occurred.

> The African case illustrates specifically how the evolving relationship between using race as the way to describe difference, and using culture to perform the same task, is part of the intellectual history of empire. Even while the earlier social sciences were freeing themselves from racially determined explanations of difference, they remained within a broad narrative of cultural evolution in which there were backward cultures (which could, if guided, move forward). (Chanock 2000: 18)

Chanock's observation alludes to a second reason: the substitution of "race" with "culture" for the same purposes. One should, however, stress that the very term "culture" already implies evolutionary stages and thus constitutes a hierarchical and discriminatory differentiation in its own right. This at least applies when "culture" is understood, along with Kant's definition, as the means through which nature accomplishes its final purpose that lies beyond its own reach. Said differently, one does not necessarily need there to be a physical aspect behind "race" in order to trap human groups into stereotypes that can place them on the ladder of progress. The idea of there being "reason" behind "culture" is sufficient to divide them into ignorant and enlightened, inferior and superior, backward and advanced, intolerant and tolerant, un-free and free, irrational and rational, bad and good, inhuman and human. Any reference to the "natural" or "biological" dimension is only to provide evidence, but is not sufficient for interpreting the presumed differences between human beings in evaluative terms. The distances that separate them are a derivative of the very idea of culture.

The concept of "multiculturalism" is also for this very same reason a term to be considered "slippery and fluid" in addition to being highly ambiguous. More than anything, it seems to have emerged from a paternalistic neocolonial resistance to "their cultures." Indeed, the integration policies directed toward "other cultures," despite more than likely being advanced with the best of intentions, were often unable to dismiss the sticky paternalism of their own stereotypes. However, before positively defining this reality the term became a famous target of criticism because of its presumed failure:

> since 11 September 2001 commentators, politicians and media coverage in a range of Europe and Western contexts have increasingly drawn on

narratives of the "crisis of multi-culturalism".... Blamed for everything from parallel societies to gendered horror to the incubation of terrorism ... it provides a mobilizing metaphor for a spectrum of political aversion and racism that has become pronounced in western Europe.... In an era where the concept of race is taboo and the charge of racism diluted, contested and inverted, multiculturalism provides a discursive space for debating questions of race, culture, legitimacy and belonging. Presenting it as "failed experiment," and inserting it into a causal historical narrative, allows anxieties concerning migration, globalization and the socio-political transformations wrought out by neoliberal governance to be ordered and explained. (Lentin and Titley 2010: 2–3)

Overall, in the postcolonial era the western global view remained firmly humanist and universalistic, even if it set its former racist mappings to one side for the time being. Western political, cultural, and economic hegemony remained uncontested and was destined to be reinforced after Soviet implosion. The hopes of those western intellectuals with sympathies for the Third World that the newly independent peoples, who had previously been kept in artificial underdevelopment by colonialism, would now "make it" to development turned out to be an illusion in many cases. This was not, as many of the "miffed" progressive observers complained, solely caused by the corrupt local elites, the corruption of which has been favored in fact by the overall context surrounding the end of colonial power. In JanMohamed's view, the "moment of 'independence'—with the natives' obligatory, ritualized acceptance of Western forms of parliamentary government—marks the formal transition to hegemonic colonialism" (JanMohamed 1985: 62). Ideology played a major part in this transition. According to Gilroy (2004: 21), it is important to understand how "the postmodern geopolitics of today's new imperium can be mapped on to the breakdown of the colonial order and how those interrelated categories, race and humanity, have been pivotal in the transition from one to the other."

3.4 Global rights

In the early 1980s, economist Theodore Levitt (1983: 92–102) argued that new communication, transport, and travel technologies were dramatically lowering the cost structure of production and distribution, giving rise to a commercial reality that was new at least in the unprecedented dimension of a global market for standardized consumer goods. Although not new in itself, it was from that period that the term "globalization" became popularized in its present meaning. At the basis of what is perceived as a recent phenomenon there are, however, also long-term trends. The words written by Marx and Engels in 1848 still seem to apply: "The need of a constantly expanding market for its products chases the bourgeoisie over the whole surface of the globe. It must nestle everywhere, settle everywhere, establish connections everywhere. The bourgeoisie has through its exploitation of the world market given a cosmopolitan character to production and consumption in every country" (Marx and Engels [1848] 2010: 16). The tendency for world markets to converge was attributed by Marx and Engels to the intrinsic dynamics of "the capital," a term with which they labeled a specific mode of production seen in its entirety of economic and social relations. The economic mechanisms at the basis of interpenetration between world markets, as described by the authors, still resonate in current times.

Marx and Engels went on to write that the bourgeoisie "has resolved personal worth into exchange value, and in place of the numberless indefeasible chartered freedoms, has set up that single, unconscionable freedom—Free Trade. In one word, for exploitation, veiled by religious and political illusions, it has substituted naked, shameless, direct, brutal exploitation" (Marx and Engels [1848] 2010: 16). How then can we evaluate the British Prime Minister Lord Palmerston's comment in 1841? Following the victory of British India over China in a war fought to open up China to free British opium shipments, he said, "there is no doubt that this event, which will form an epoch in the progress of the civilization of the human races, must be attended with the most important advantages to the commercial interests of England"? (Nazemroaya 2012: 121). This was truly a farsighted evaluation, inasmuch as drug trafficking today holds a prominent place among worldwide trade of tangible goods; the 2005 value of the drug trade, for example, was estimated at 320 billion US dollars (Haken 2011: 3). Drugs not only move huge volumes of capital, they also help to blackmail rural populations in wide-ranging regions of the world, from Afghanistan (where opium production increased again after the western occupation of the country) and Southeast Asia to Latin America. Morally, Marx and Engels blamed the attitude of English colonialism, but if it had thrown "the veils," why did it continue to invoke "the progress of the civilization of human races"? Where did the moral scandal come from? Perhaps from the fact that Marx and Engels themselves upheld this same progress? The authors attribute the ruling class with a historical mission: "The bourgeoisie, by the rapid improvement of all instruments of production, by the immensely facilitated means of communication, draws all, even the most barbarian, nations into civilization" (Marx and Engels [1848] 2010: 16). Moreover, on the civilizing mission of the British bourgeoisie, Marx commented:

> England has broken down the entire framework of Indian society, without any symptoms of reconstitution yet appearing. This loss of his old world, with

no gain of a new one, imparts a particular kind of melancholy to the present misery of the Hindoo, and separates Hindostan, ruled by Britain, from all its ancient traditions, and from the whole of its past history. . . . we must not forget that these idyllic village-communities, inoffensive though they may appear, had always been the solid foundation of Oriental despotism, that they restrained the human mind within the smallest possible compass, making it the unresisting tool of superstition, enslaving it beneath traditional rules, depriving it of all grandeur and historical energies. . . . England, it is true, in causing a social revolution in Hindostan, was actuated only by the vilest interests, and was stupid in her manner of enforcing them. But that is not the question. The question is, can mankind fulfill its destiny without a fundamental revolution in the social state of Asia? If not, whatever may have been the crimes of England she was the unconscious tool of history in bringing about that revolution. (Marx [1853] 2005)

These are sentences which express a full awareness of the brutality of enforced free-trade practices, but which at the same time lay out strict adherence to the western philosophy of history, to its orientalist constructs (Ahmad 2000), and to the idea apparently shared with Lord Palmerston that mankind has a destiny to fulfill in progressing from savagery to barbarism and finally to a true humanity. In dealing with this same social and economic change, Karl Polanyi preferred to place more emphasis on the social contingencies rather than historical "laws," and to further highlight the creative contribution of the ideology. According to the author, before the "great transformation" to capitalist market economy, "the economic system was submerged in general social relations; markets were merely an accessory feature of an institutional setting controlled and regulated more than ever by social authority." It was the findings of Humanism and Enlightenment, such as the emergence of Locke's new concept of law within human affairs, "that of the laws of Nature," which alongside technological development, pushed the great transformation ahead: "The discovery of economics was an astounding revelation which hastened greatly the transformation of society and the establishment of a market system, while the decisive machines had been the inventions of uneducated artisans some of whom could hardly read or write" (Polanyi 1957: 67, 119).

Thus, when in the early 1980s the word globalization was popularized, it was not only an older word but it in fact also referred to long-term tendencies of social and economic development. Some distinctions between several "waves" of this process should, however, be made. Although "technical change has been driving the costs of interactions steadily downward for many centuries" (Crafts and Venables 2003: 323), markets became global to a more comprehensive extent during the second half of the nineteenth century, when new information and transportation technologies, such as telegraph, telephone and steam shipping led to increasing worldwide price convergence of capital, raw materials, and agricultural products. After the First World War and the 1929 crisis had broken up the drift toward increasing market integration, the dynamic was more forcefully resumed around 1970. While both waves of globalization were similar in the reduction of transaction costs, "the uniqueness of recent globalization is heavily shaped by the dramatic reduction in communications cost, what is sometimes referred to as 'the death of distance.'" Baldwin and Martin (1999: 1–2) add a second peculiarity: the higher level of inequality in the worldwide economy that already existed at the start of the second wave, and which today has reached unparalleled levels.

In the meantime, the economy of the two world wars, the world economic crisis, the Korean War, the labor movement and the bloc confrontation had all hampered, then disciplined, commercial trade and capital flow. Contradicting the theoretical prescriptions of neoclassical economics, after 1950, these measures proved to be functional for sustained economic growth, social welfare, mass consumption, and a modest top–down redistribution of income and wealth.

> One basic principle of the Bretton Woods system was regulation of finance, motivated in large part by the understanding that liberalization could serve as a powerful weapon against democracy and the welfare state, allowing financial capital to become a "virtual Senate" that can impose its own social policies and punish those who deviate by capital flight. The system was dismantled by the Nixon Administration with the cooperation of Britain and other financial centres. The results would not have surprised its designers. (Chomsky 2003: 61–62)

Among these results we witness the shift from what Zygmunt Bauman called "solid modernity" to "liquid modernity," meaning that capital's almost unconditional freedom of movement works heavily to the detriment of the much more settled labor force, and increasingly worsens the laborers' bargaining power worldwide (Bauman 2000: 130–67).

At the beginning of the new millennium, David Harvey pointed out what he saw as a relational nexus between the social and economic conditions of the globalization process, neoliberal ideological hegemony, and the territorial logics of power, referring specifically to Europe:

> Ultra-imperialism of the kind now favoured in Europe has, however, its own negative connotations and consequences. If Robert Cooper, a Blair adviser, is to be believed, it favours the resurrection of nineteenth-century distinctions between civilized, barbarian, and savage states in the guise

of postmodern, modern, and premodern states, with the postmoderns, as guardians of civilized collaborative behaviour, expected to induce by direct or indirect means obeisance to universal (read "Western" and "bourgeois") norms, and humanistic (read "capitalistic") practices across the globe. The postmodern, mainly European, states are, from this perspective, not an "old Europe" at all but way out ahead of the United States, which seems to have some difficulty shedding its modernist ways. (Harvey 2003: 209–10)

In the early years of the new millennium, the author expected that in "the absence of any strong revival of sustained accumulation through expanded reproduction, this European version of liberal imperialism can only move ever deeper into the neo-liberal quagmire of a politics of accumulation by dispossession throughout the world in order to keep the motor of accumulation from stalling." He also expected that this would "hardly be acceptable to wide swaths of the world's population who have lived through, and in some instances begun to fight back against, accumulation by dispossession and the predatory forms of capitalism associated with it" (Harvey 2003: 210). Following the 2008 crisis, while the predatory forms of capitalism became even more pronounced, they also further eroded the capacity for resistance of "wide swaths of the world's population." An unorganized, flexible, and atomized workforce, weakened by the apparent absence of alternative solutions, this population had few margins for fighting back.

The greatest misunderstanding, in my opinion, regarding the reasons why those who suffer from globalization have so far abstained from fighting back is that they stem not only from economic and social weakness, but also from the power of ideology. While it is more than likely that nobody would think that imperial ideology and sentiment can be restricted to the small world oligarchy of bankers, industrialists, politicians, technocrats, and military leaders who "run" great parts of the planet today, the ideological and quasi-religious pervasiveness of hegemonic mental dispositions may still, however, be underestimated. Especially the French term *mondialisation* incorporates the missionary and altruistic self-understanding of western societies, which generously are the performers "of symbolic investiture and of *donation-of-meaning* to the world" (Marramao 2012: 7). At the same time, one should not underestimate the great variety and ambiguity of subaltern ideological elaborations of the globalization process. Another result of the uneven global battle of ideas is that what at first glance may indeed look like a "backfiring," quite often takes the shape of a war among the poor, which ends up further easing exploitation or geopolitical predominance. This is the case, in particular, of "clashes" that the west labels as ethnic or religious, and which can easily be instigated from the outside.

Bauman (2000: 170), among others, highlighted the nexus between the global hegemony of liberal economics and the increasing desire for identity and community. He stated that "communitarianism is an all-too-expectable reaction to the accelerating 'liquefaction' of modern life, a reaction first and foremost to the one aspect of life felt perhaps as the most vexing and annoying among its numerous painful consequences—the deepening imbalance between individual freedom and security." Not only in the west did the desire to maintain a regional authenticity as a form of refuge and security make itself known, for example, through the fight against the fast-food chain McDonald's (representing *mondialisation*) by the producer of genuine cheese, José Bové. The same "rediscovery" of the authentic and of traditions in language, culture, and religious practices that had been menaced with extinction by neocolonialism and globalization was seen elsewhere as well, from the Andes to Greenland and the Pacific Islands. Contrasting with the expectations of globalization and its protagonists—the superpowers, the multinationals, the central banks, the finance sector—is the presumed return to the origins, to that harmony between destiny, community, and nature that had been lost. In actual fact the triumph is another, if not the most complete one. Martin Chanock (2000: 22) argues that the authenticity discourses of non-western elites "draw consciously on the major dichotomy of the grand narrative of Western history—that of *gemeinschaft* and *gesellschaft*—but allocate cohesive Community to the non-West, and atomised Society to the West." This representation in itself reproduces western thinking and confirms the "profound symbiotic relationship between the discursive and the material practices of imperialism" (JanMohamed 1985: 64).

This can be shown here by looking briefly at some examples. The reflections of the Singaporean poet and scholar Edwin Thumboo show how difficult it is to escape the semiotic hegemony of the west when it comes to the defining of a postcolonial Self in the language of the colonizers:

> Freedom from colonial rule is its repossession as national space. For an ex-colony it is only the beginning of the challenge to re-create or create a nation. Because the colonial powers created—often ignoring traditional boundaries—and exploited such space according to the economic structure best suited to the prosperity, wealth, welfare and the global and strategic vision of the colonizers. (Thumboo 1996: 16)

The author is worried that the former colonizers, by turning the experience of the formerly colonized into mere abstractions "dissolve their uniqueness, mute their counter-reformation and invent/introduce new, distracting interests" (Thumboo 1996: 14). Is it deceptive to wonder whether the reference to the western idea of "nation" in fact represents a "distracting interest" as well?

The fear of regional uniqueness being dissolved, because of advancing globalization, spread widely among scholars, in particular, those from what time ago was called the Third World. Their difficulty lies in positively describing in noncolonial terms what this uniqueness consisted of before colonial destruction. This problem becomes evident, for example, in the subaltern studies approach of Ranajit Guha, who attempts to define the Indian culture's precolonial authenticity following the condemnation of western teleological historicism. Guha sketches out his proposition against historicist "becoming," in favor of an *Eigentlichkeit* in line with Martin Heidegger's thought. According to this interpretation, existence can strive for approaching authenticity by accepting the solitude of the human being thrown into history. It was through his younger self in his autobiographical remarks that the poet Rabindranath Tagore realized this: "But in the history of that day there was no one more other than myself who saw those clouds in quite the same way as I did or was similarly thrilled. Rabindranath happened to be all by himself in that instance" (Tagore [1941] 2002: 97). Guha interprets this scene as a sort of poetic translation of the philosophy developed by Heidegger in *Being and Time*. For the young Rabindranath it is the moment in which Man wakes up to his being in the world so as to better understand himself. He can only reach utmost recognition of himself within his existence if he accepts the situation assigned to him by destiny, and this acceptance can only come about through the experience of a historicity of daily life that is ritual and prosaic yet not teleological: "That monotony speaks of the recurrence of something that has been there in all your yesterdays. Everydayness is thus necessarily informed, like historicality itself, by a sense of the past." Guha must surely be right when in supporting the Indian historian of philosophy Surendranath Dasgupta, he also sees a feature of Indian thought in this search for an "immediacy of that primal sense of grasping the world as one's own" (Guha 2002: 82, 92–93). I am certainly not qualified to doubt this. However, from the "privileged position" with which western scholars "can afford to ignore non-western research without hampering their reputation," I perceive that Guha's argument makes western scholarship here again "primarily an exporter but not an importer of theory" (Sachsenmaier 2007: 472). When the controversy over the historicism, which caused Marx to observe that India was a country that oriental despotism had deprived of history, turns into a criticism of a temporality that alienates the Indians from their authentic being, then we can say at least that the line of reasoning is in harmony with another important strand of western philosophy. According to Heidegger, the greatest possible proximity of existence to being lays in *Lebensvollzug*, that is the acquiescent performance of daily life.

That the teleology of the *Weltgeschichte* represents the narrative control of the west over the universal past and future is undeniable. That this narrative banished from its horizon "the realm of wonder," of "myth and fantasy," and the experience of daily life (Guha 2002: 68), is less convincing. In fact, from Macpherson onwards the enlightened eighteenth century made a frenetic appeal to myth, to the remnants of the defeated, to hidden traces, to endangered traditions, to the preservation of memory, to circular time and a return to nature, to entrenched roots, to the authentic. And all this without awaiting Romanticism, which is so often depicted as the Enlightenment's conceptual overcoming, when it was in fact only one of its progressions. From the nineteenth century up until today, western museums are no longer a documentation of great men and their heroic deeds, but of the remnants of the labor and daily life of unknown men and women, the unknown soldiers—anonymous links whose destiny is lost in the infinite chain of timeless being. Similar thinking during the early twentieth century led various strands of European philosophy to express a renewed version of melancholy for lost origins, thereby giving strength to the voice of protest against the alienation of advancing modernity. The nationalist far-right-wing political and ecological neocommunitarian proposal had already been playing around with these themes for a long time before some of the left-leaning intellectuality adopted them during the twentieth century.

If community myths and community talks are so common to the west, what, then makes neocommunitarian reactions to western-led globalization plausible? To Goodhart (2003: 955–56) it is

> hardly surprising that the Lockean system of rights and liberties facilitating it [neoliberal globalization] should appear alien, selfish, atomizing, and anti-social. Nor is it surprising, given the current distribution of power in the global political economy and the coercive mechanisms employed to advance globalization, that the destruction of traditional institutions and values outside the West might manifest in a cultural conflict, as a product of clashing cultural values.

One may indeed doubt that the "supposed contrast between an 'individualist' West and communal values elsewhere" is more than an ideological representation. In a study such as the present one, in which the invention of "cultures" and other immutable group connotations is criticized, it is easy to agree on the preponderance of human similarities over differences. This should, however, be better stated without teleological references to the before and after stages of human development, as Goodhart does when suggesting that the illusion of dissimilarities stems from the contemporaneity of the non-contemporaneous. According to the author, before Polanyi's Great Transformation, Europe was no less communitarian than residual non-western areas are today. In favor of West and non-West similarities, perhaps more plausible arguments can be found in taking into consideration the ideological character of the juxtaposition of community versus society.

Premodern experience, to begin with, was only a posteriori labeled as "community" in western self-descriptions, whereas the presence of modern "society" was conceived of as a conscious arrangement among supposedly irreducibly free individuals to whom any social conditioning beyond the convenient voluntary contract would appear "unnatural." In that way, the community-society "stages" were made to fit the great western teleological narrative. What makes non-western neocommunitarian reactions against the globalization of the market economy plausible is thus primarily the parallel globalization of western methodological individualism. Otherwise, why should the negatively perceived effects of the advancement of the market economy be represented in typically western terms, that is, as the destruction of community and the emergence of an alienating individualistic and atomized society? This individualism is not merely the individualism of Locke's theorization of the social contract, or of Mandeville's plea for the social utility of egoist behavior; it also underlies the idea of the existential solitude of those who desire community in order to grasp a glimpse of their being.

Earlier individualism contained such fictitious assumptions that recently even liberal thinkers admitted "the social construction of the individual self" (Appiah 2003: 219). To counterbalance this somewhat uncomfortable evidence, a new safe haven for conceptual and methodological individualism was created under the name of "identity." The spread of terms such as "community" and "identity" is functional both for western ideological hegemony over anti-western discourses and for sociological analyses of non-western social changes through a western lens. Of course in the African experience also, for example, the image and self-image of the individual human were always "socially constructed" and strongly interrelated with group dynamics. But African conceptualization seems less problematic and contradictory on that point, as the social construction of the individual hardly requires any legitimizing explanation. What is more,

> in African morality, there is an unrelenting preoccupation with human welfare. What is morally good is that which brings about—or is supposed, expected, or known to bring about—human well-being. This means, in a society that appreciates and thrives on harmonious social relationships, that what is morally good is what promotes social welfare, solidarity, and harmony in human relationships. (Gyekye 1996: 57)

This approach is sustained by a cosmological view according to which "human life is generally perceived as a cycle. . . . The abode of the dead lacks the concept of heaven and hell. There is simply one place where all the dead go and that place is not described in terms of punishment and reward" (Sackey 2013: 159).

Does a morality that celebrates social well-being pay no attention to individual freedom? According to Brigid Sackey (2013: 161), to Africans "the truth of religion is that it must be functional, namely to be able to provide human beings with their existential needs be it food, health, shelter, or money," whereas Kwame Gyekye (1997: 118) underlines that the African traditional council permits the free and public expression of all opinions. This is not to celebrate the higher qualities of African experience or anything similar, also because I lack any competence in comparing African theories to African practices. What the above quotations show, however, is that for the profession of a principle that protects the freedom of speech and other individual rights, and morally appreciates personal and collective well-being and prosperity, a theoretical or theological system that makes an allegedly "natural" solitude of human beings the contractual basis of a society is unnecessary. Nor does the same principle need to be sustained by a historical narrative that distinguishes the bright age of "consciousness" about the true character of society from the "dark" age when consciousness was lacking regarding the superstitious character of the communitarian arrangements. In short, the scientific and religious reinterpretation of the African experience was nothing like what was really needed by the Africans themselves.

Neocommunitarian discourses and the recourse to the peculiarity of local traditions are often criticized by human-rights activists. There is little doubt indeed that neocommunitarian discourses stabilize local power relations and favor the conservation of privileges by native postcolonial elites in what used to be called the Third World. At the same time, however, the human-rights movement often shows itself to be "intolerant of competing world-views." Part of "the self-righteousness and intolerance of the rights movement is its tendency to dismiss every local cultural assertion as masking a defense of privilege and inequality at the expense of the individual rights of the disadvantaged in the same society," whereas the supporters of the movement "risk becoming blind to global privilege" (Mamdani 2000: 3). At the level of international relations, the concept of human rights refers to "the UN Charter, the Universal Declaration, and the 1966 International Covenants of Civil-Political and Socio-Economic-Cultural Rights" (Forsythe 2000: 141).

Do the rights laid down in these documents symbolize the west's success in universalizing its own moral standards? At first glance, their historical genesis seems to suggest it. As Koskenniemi (2015: 214, 230) notes, when international law "arose as a 'modern' profession" in the western dominated world of the late nineteenth century, "it was underwritten by a liberal cosmopolitism that posited free individuals as the objective of supranational law." However, according to the same author, a more complex set of motives governs the more recent evolution of international law. While "international law—like all law—contains a teleological element," the expectation behind this element is heterogeneous. Diverging political interests and normative prescriptions, as well as a variety of philosophical traditions imagine the attainment of equality differently. This is why both the UN Charter and the Declaration of Human Rights go beyond the liberal tradition, for example, insofar as the Declaration contemplates social rights.

Hence, decision-makers and interpreters of international law often move in opposite directions. As Chomsky notes, the neoliberal West contemplates the extension of personal rights to a selected group of social formations, that is, private firms and banks: "General Motors can demand 'national treatment' in Mexico, but Mexicans of flesh and blood will know better than to demand 'national treatment' north of the border." Chomsky goes on to argue that western practices were often operated in opposition not only to what they call "outdated" articles of the Declaration, but also to the west's own manifestation of ideals of democracy and personal freedom. While in the Declaration there "is no place for the 'relativist' demand that certain rights be relegated to secondary status in light of 'Asian values' or some other pretext," the most "relativist" behavior of all is that exhibited by the western superpower, as the United States indirectly, but officially, refuses substantial parts of the UN Declaration (Chomsky 2003: 52, 73). They equate human rights with personal freedom as defined by the US Bill of Rights, "and not with the broader and more complex conception found in the International Bill of Rights" (Forsythe 2000: 141).

When it comes to the factual implementation of international law in the realm of international relations, contradictions become even more striking. For the first twenty-five years of existence, "the UN agendas normally went in America's direction," with no need for the latter to veto any of its decisions (Kennedy 2006: 54). But since the 1970s not only have western powers been increasingly refuting social rights; they are also trying to impose the respect of human rights according to their own understanding, preferably onto non-western actors rather than onto themselves. On various occasions, the United States claimed exemption, seeing as "utopian, legalistic means like outside mediation, the United Nations and the World Court" that ignore "the power element of the equation," as the former US secretary of state George Shultz once stated (Chomsky 2003: 68). Accordingly, crime and punishment in the field of human rights seem to concern only weaker actors, such as local dictators who transform from allies into brutal state leaders and mass murderers overnight. Democratic leaders of the west and the great powers in general are de facto enjoying a preemptive general amnesty, no matter what they might commit in terms of kidnapping, imprisonment, murder, torture, drone strikes, cluster bombing, or waging wars of aggression. The International Criminal Tribunal for the former Yugoslavia (ICTY) swiftly dismissed all charges against

NATO members for their bombing of Serbia (Ricci 2000), while it strenuously prosecuted, in particular, Serbian military and political leaders on charges of war crimes and genocide. Ten years after the former president of Yugoslavia, Milošević, died in the Scheveningen prison, a chamber of the ICTY ruled that his government had not supported ethnic cleansing in Bosnia (ICTY 2016: 1245). As far as the International Criminal Court is concerned, some of the world's major powers never ratified the treaty, as they prefer not to see their own representatives prosecuted and tried. In 2016, "some African leaders have called the court an instrument of modern colonialism" and vowed to withdraw from the treaty (Chan and Simons 2016: A5).

What comes to the fore here is what Richard Falk (2011) has called "the persisting failures of international criminal law mechanisms of accountability to administer justice justly, that is, without the filters of impunity provided by existing hierarchies of hard power." It is under such conditions that the procedures of international jurisdiction sometimes "turn into a burden, perpetuating privilege and hierarchy" (Koskenniemi 2015: 230). If an effective international rule of law fails to be implemented thanks to "the power element of the equation," what, then, should a liberal cosmopolitan like Kwame Anthony Appiah (2003: 216) hope for in order to promote "the equal dignity of all people, their equal entitlement to respect" in the world?

Appiah (2003: 212–14) favors dialogue but refuses a "dialogue among static closed cultures, each of which is internally homogeneous and different from all the others"; he imagines instead a world in which words and art are understood "differently, because people are different and welcome to their difference," and instead imagines a world in which words and art are understood. When adding that agreement should be reached on particulars rather than universals, as universals are beliefs that should be reciprocally tolerated without fruitless discussion, Appiah's way of thinking seems to resemble Ulrich Beck's differentiation between certainty and truth. In Beck's view, every man or woman has his or her own truth about humanity, but cannot be certain that others share the same view or have other truths. We should behave consequently, be tolerant without relativistic moral concessions.

> To assert no more than one's own universalism is not necessarily to leave other universalisms just as they are; it does not entail a mutual hands-off agreement. On the contrary: only a renunciation of claims that my version of human rights is the only one enables it to contend for validity alongside other versions. (Beck 2000: 85)

At a first glance, these words may sound fair: they do not envision neither hands-off agreements nor mutuality. Beck's reasoning is however not about "if-at-all," but "how" western concepts are best adopted worldwide. Human rights and universalism, two key words for the present western worldview, are assumed as being unquestionably relevant to anyone. Making generalizing cosmological assumptions is not an exclusively western practice, but these two terms stand for a typically western way of doing it. Similarly, Brooke Ackerly (2008: 22, 26) observes that "not everywhere and at all times have people made rights claims and called them 'human rights' when doing so, but around the world, when they face oppression they have made claims through their words and actions that can contribute to our understanding of universal human rights." The same author favors "a theory of human rights whose universal justification is based on a dynamic understanding of political legitimacy where the authority of human rights as a tool for criticism is not undermined by a commitment to interrogate that authority. Nor is it undermined by its lack of legal, traditional, or charismatic authority at any given time in any given context." The feminist activist Molly Talcott delivers another variant still. She abandoned her previous poststructuralist critique of human rights as "political violence shrouded in benevolent universalism" in the course of her activity in Mexico, among "indigenous, rural and largely cash-poor women who have arguably less connection to 'Western' ways than I." These women made her "understand the real importance of 'human rights' as a tactic and a metaphor for multiple incarnations of justice" (Collins et al. 2010: 300–01). Likewise, what Ackerly calls a political theory for a nonideal world tends to reconfirm the idea that rights must be "human" and "universal" by definition. This is an assumption that must never be doubted, no matter what they are called by people who fight against oppression.

Is this a theory in a nonideal world, or rather a fact-resistant theory? Costas Douzinas argues that the idea according to which rights are gifted to people because of their humanity instead of their belonging to a collectivity is contradicted by actual "non-ideal" practices. Refugees, undocumented immigrants, imprisoned suspects of terrorism, among others, have few rights, if any. "'Bare' humanity offers no protection and whoever claims to represent it lies." The author points out that "humanity has no fixed or universally acceptable meaning and cannot act as the source of moral or legal rules." The use of the adjective "human" is not in fact as neutral as it pretends to be. While hardly offering any concrete juridical entitlement, it condenses to the eschatological promise of western religion and philosophy, and promotes the western self-righteous judgment and classification of others. In the case of spaces, races, and cultures, this manifestation was rather plain to see. Despite suggesting an egalitarian reference to every single member of the species, human rights, however, do the same. They "classify people on a spectrum between the fully human, the lesser human and the inhuman" (Douzinas 2014), a classification that ideologically validates the abovementioned "power element of the equation."

Roberto Esposito adds an interesting aspect, when stating that "never before have human rights—from the first among them, the right to life—been denied from the root as they are today." This has to do with the western concept of "person." In the tradition of Roman law, "person" (mask) refers to specific social roles and consequently to unequal rights. The Christian notion of "person" refers to the transcendent, immortal soul, while the impersonal biological matter it inhabits during its terrene existence has no intrinsic value. Until the person remains at the center of juridical entitlement, we will witness "the absolute inapplicability of a human right as such" (Esposito 2009: 8–10). A "bodily" definition of the human being, however, would contradict the transcendent meaning of "humanity" that is at the basis of moral and juridical consideration in the west.

The concept of human rights had to first be spread around the planet by western dominance before it could become a relevant matter of worldwide debate. It is to such a kind of historically and hierarchically prestructured debate that Ulrich Beck's following observation seems to refer:

> Contextual universalism does not oblige anyone, in the name of some misguided relativism, to accept human rights violations in other cultures and countries. . . . It asks: What conceptions of human rights, and what human rights groups, are there in the countries where human rights are being grossly violated? How do *they* judge what is happening in their country, from their point of view and with their knowledge of human rights? (Beck 2000: 86)

Beck states that in the globalized world it is virtually impossible for anybody not to interfere with others, and that it is ludicrous to deny the general relatedness between all elements of world society. His statement seems incontrovertible, but outlined like so it merely remains a sterile abstraction and one should ask under which conditions universal interference develops. Consider, for example, the following variant of Beck's quotation: "Contextual universalism does not oblige anyone, in the name of some misguided relativism, to accept *mana* violations in other cultures and countries. It asks: What conceptions of *mana* and what *mana* defense groups are there in the countries where *mana* is being grossly violated? How do *they* judge what is happening in their country, from their point of view and with their knowledge of *mana*?" Why is it so hard to consider seriously a version such as this one? *Mana* was conceived of as a general, unlimited (although not necessarily "universal") principle as well. The forms of violation of this principle in everyday western style of life are manifold, as discussions and juridical disputes in the Fiji Islands, New Zealand, and other places show (Baledrokadroka 2003: 30; Auckland District Health Board 2011: 4). How many *mana* promotion groups exist in the west or in other places far from the South Pacific? Western civil society associations

(Ehrenberg 1999: 238–39) defending their truths against *mana*-threatening behaviors and law codes seem not to be too numerous. Are we wrong in suspecting that under Beck's point of view it is more urgent for Melanesian and Polynesian people to make up their minds about human rights than for the Bundestag to debate and decide about the promotion of *mana* in Germany?

Undoubtedly, this is right: his statement on human rights is more relevant to the average Melanesian or Polynesian than any Melanesian or Polynesian statement would be to the average German. One explanation for this imbalance would be the intrinsic superiority of western thought: once the utopia of a "liberal cosmopolitan global society" is achieved, Greek stoics and the Enlightenment philosophers "will be looked back to with affectionate gratitude" (Rorty 2003: 233, 236). Another explanation, slightly different from this self-pleasing vision of western philosophy, is that the imbalance in the power of words straightforwardly stems from the military and economic power relations which have developed worldwide over time. Under this condition, interdependence tends to be one-sided, that is, dependence, while one-sided interference turns into dictate. What remains to be done in order to achieve a liberal utopia is the perseverance of western interference into the affairs of others, given that the interference of others in the affairs of the west is not even to be contemplated.

There is no doubt either that the hundreds of thousands of westerners who organize into associations so as to promote humanitarian aid, the proliferation of democracy, gender equality and human rights, and to oppose censorship, torture and persecution, are driven by a most sincere altruistic motivation. Their noble feelings of solidarity and compassion, which more often than not are a response to selective media representation of reality rather than autonomous enquiry, make them indignant vis-à-vis the suffering from injustice by fellow members of the "global civil society." "Claims against any one nation state by its victims are now pursued by global alliances, by expatriates but also by sympathizers abroad with no ties to that state" (Albrow and Seckinelgin 2011: 2). What had already been a feature of colonialism—auxiliary work driven by the sincere altruism of the "foreign sympathizers" for the natives—has now become a feature of western geopolitics. Not only have respectable international health and development organizations been partially transformed into a sort of embedded corpus of groups which step in immediately after humanitarian military operations of western troops take foot on the ground, several nongovernmental organizations (NGOs) and civil society promotion organizations also take up preparatory tasks. Organizations such as Freedom House, Westminster Foundation for Democracy, National Endowment for Democracy, Open Society Foundation, and others, which flourished after 1989 and were sent out in particular to former communist and Arab countries, operated as geopolitical instruments of foreign policy, influencing the internal politics of targeted countries. Hofbauer (2012) remarks that over the last few decades the civil society interventions by western organizations "are united by one goal: to direct revolutionary processes in East and South towards the western understanding of liberal democracy; to pave the way for 'constitutional liberalism'. Many democratic elections, for example in Eastern Europe, but also in the Arab world after 1989/91, did not reflect the western idea of liberal democracy" and thus required correction. Claims against democratically elected "dictators" in order to undermine their legitimacy were echoed in international media campaigns. Activists were trained and sustained in a multitude of ways so as to foster a liberal westward-looking civil society, with the aim of spreading "universal" democracy.

As the 2014 overthrow of the elected Ukrainian government by EU and NATO-backed militant groups and other examples have shown, the border between peaceful protest, civil resistance, and violent or paramilitary action is willingly malleable. When these efforts "do not fulfill the aim of 'regime change,' a military intervention can take place" (Hofbauer 2012: 1). Iran, when looked at from the point of view of western governments, is a good example of this thought, wherein on its behalf, American fantasies are populated by a wide range of options, from a rather costly military invasion to a seemingly low-cost "velvet revolution" put forward by US-friendly factions of Iranian civil society (Amuzegar 1999: 86–101; Pollack et al. 2009: 103–12). Vis-à-vis similar uses of the activists' altruistic motives, it is not surprising that a sinister connotation imbues the statement according to which "global civil society practitioners" had "to reconsider and recast their legitimacy to act in a dynamic manner" (Albrow and Seckinelgin 2011: 6).

What are the contents of their commitment and efforts? The social rights of workers, protection from unemployment, a minimum wage that allows a worker's family to live in "universal" dignity, health care, and so on, although not completely absent from the panel, are not at the center of the human-rights agenda. Over the last two or three decades, gender equality and the right for sexual self-fulfillment became a major topic of the efforts of human-rights activists. This is interesting given that historically "judgments about the sexual behavior of the people colonized by Europe played a core part in cultural othering." At the time, promiscuity was perceived to be a core feature of otherness. Today, the direction of the same prejudice seems to be inverted: "Gender equality is linked, by the spokesmen of, for example, Islamic cultures, to promiscuity in the West" (Chanock 2000: 20). However, also highlighting the other's backward view on the Christian or western self as being too relaxed in sexual habits and gender relations is a traditional form of cultural othering. Already Cervantes ([1613] 2014: 256) let one of his gypsies affirm:

> We live free and secure from the bitter plague of jealousy; and though incest is frequent amongst us there is no adultery. If a wife or a mistress

is unfaithful, we do not go ask the courts of justice to punish; but we ourselves are the judges and executioners of our wives and mistresses, and make no more ado about killing and burying them in the mountains and desert places than if they were vermin.

Effectively, even gaining legal and constitutional equality between adult men in the west has been a lengthy and turbulent process of political and social struggle. Slavery is not the only example of how liberalism did not grant equality to everyone in the nineteenth century. In many cases, it excluded male citizens, who did not hold sufficient patrimony or wealth, from political participation. Reaching at the least a formal equality between men and women in legislative and constitutional terms was an even longer process. If at the end of the seventeenth century Mary Astell had wondered "If *all Men are born free*, how is it that all Women are born slaves?" (Ward Scaltsas 1990: 141), going beyond a generic attribution of dignity would not occur for centuries later. Even arguments in favor of a limited equality that had been proposed within the moderate liberal perimeter struggled to garner support. Once again, we need to remember that in accordance with such a way of thinking, holding "natural right" to be equal to freedom did not at all mean legal or social equality; neither did it mean an absence of power or of a hierarchy of command.

Thanks to philosophical sophistication, the basic assumption safely lived side by side with an essentialism distantly derived from Christianity that insisted on a "natural disparity" between men and women (Ward Scaltsas 1990: 140). These were the premises accepted by most of the eighteenth century's elite and literary feminism, who intended on giving good society women an education that would make the most of the "typical female nature" for the common good. Militant thinkers like Mary Wollenstonecraft and Harriet Taylor Mill later surpassed a similar vision. The latter indiscriminately extended her liberal principles to women, claiming for every individual an equal right to test their capabilities in earning a responsive role in society.

Whereas some of the pioneers of liberal thinking, with Locke, imagined there to be a natural and divine commitment to the disparity between men and women, others, such as Hobbes, ignored such association. Along theoretical lines, Hobbes did not preclude women from any role of command; it was entirely a matter of individual ability. However, seeing as even based on this premise an equal natural right did not imply an equal ability to exercise it, relationships of command and subordination between men and women also seemed to be characterized by a reciprocal rational convenience for Hobbes: "The most common situations are, according to Hobbes's reasoning, those where the woman is either the wife or a servant of a male family sovereign" (Pietarinen 1990: 134). The pronounced power relationships between genders that ruled eighteenth- and nineteenth-century European societies did not necessarily contradict the theories of liberalism, just as, on the other side, the calls for equality of rights advanced by Taylor Mill in the mid nineteenth century did not either.

However, gender equality cannot be considered a mere matter of formal laws and rights; it is also one of customs and behavior. In the early eighteenth century, Catherine Trotter Cockburn denounced the insult against the dignity and honor of women that was disguised behind the gallant attention of men. She claimed that compared with similar humiliation inflicted by men upon women there was "nothing more unjust, more base, and barbarous" (Cockburn 1751: 141). Using this last adjective, the author tried to strengthen her claim through appealing to the philosophy of history. Although with more ambiguous and nostalgic tones, at the end of the eighteenth century the writer Justine Wynne confirmed that "the barbarous man who is absolutely savage does not choose a companion nor does he care for the sweetest bond that nature teaches us to covenant; to him it is not worthy of consideration or formality" (Rosenberg Wynne 1798: 52). In addition to their numerous other flaws, the enlightened writers also charged the barbarians with humiliation, or little consideration, of women. And likewise, they were in fact comforted by the opinions of their male colleagues. Among the errors that distinguished the first, savage, epoch of history, Condorcet (1796: 28) recalled "the prejudice that consigns the female part of society to a sort of slavery." And even where civilization had left behind the stage of savagery, such as was the case in the Orient, the barbarian heritage of disregarding and oppressing women was still vivid. According to Voltaire (1761: 148), the "greatest difference between us and the Orientals is the manner of treating our women." The most remarkable sign of distinction of European men, in the French philosopher's eyes, was treating their women better and on a more equal basis.

Western gender talks on backward and oriental societies were a product of not only the most common savage–barbarous–civilized stages theory, but also of another classification effort according to which both nature and the book of Genesis provide basic evidence for a clear gender differentiation. Men and women were most often referred to by the collective singulars man and woman, similarly to the treatment reserved to national ("the Turk"), religious ("the Jew"), racial ("the Negro"), and social ("the Worker") groups. Yet more than two hundred years after Voltaire, another prominent French philosopher, Michael Foucault, wondered:

Do we truly need a true sex? With a persistence that borders on stubbornness, modern Western societies have answered in the affirmative. They have obstinately brought into play this question of a 'true sex' in an order of things where one might have imagined that all that counted was the reality of the body and the intensity of its pleasures. (Foucault 1980: vii)

Drawing on the will of God and the findings of biological and medical sciences, common sense was educated to accept the allegedly unequivocal division of humans and animals into exactly two sexes.

Binary gendering became a major bureaucratic, juridical, scientific, and moral practice of social discipline, which not only favored the exclusion of women from the public and political spheres with the only exception of charity activities (Heywood 2000: 55–57), but also marginalized those who for one reason or another felt that they did not really belong to just one, or rather none, of the two sexes. The rule was that humans "should be assigned to one of the two categories, or removed from society" (Judson 2003: 178). We are not exactly talking about infinitesimal phenomena. Without even speaking about the various sexual preferences that have become the preferred targets of criticism regarding the "promiscuity" of others, researchers have estimated that the group of people for which medical science registers any deviation from the primary or secondary canonic characteristics of gender can occur in one in fifty births. This up to 2 percent of humanity would currently correspond to around 194 million people. However, according to the same estimate, in the general perception 184 million of these are not perceived in their irregularity toward the M/F distinction, perhaps because the irregularity does not particularly stand out, or because they adapt to avoid negative consequences (DGTI 2001). Vis-à-vis the repressive effects of socially created gender stereotypes, criticism targeted the M/F configuration as a whole (Butler 1993:7–8), and consequently not just male chauvinism, but also feminism. Queer theorists highlight "feminist essentialism's minimization of women's autonomy, capacity for self-definition, and self-knowledge" (Ettinger 2013: 107) and refute that "a unitary, 'essential' women's experience can be isolated and described independently of race, class, sexual orientation, and other realities of experience" (Harris 1990: 585).

Apart from the evolution of scholarly debate, the persistent contribution of the book of Genesis in shaping westerners' worldview should not be underestimated. In the self-declared "world's largest community for sharing questions and answers" on the internet, to the question "Why we are called human and not huwoman?" we read the answer: "We are called human because in the story of Adam and eve [sic], Adam was created as the first living thing on earth. If it had been eve [sic] maybe we would be huwomans" (wikiAnswers® n.d.). Explicit male chauvinism continues to be powerfully pervasive in nearly all societies and not only western ones; in the west, however, it has been banned from public consensus and marked as politically unacceptable. Feminist discourse, however, at least in its popularized media version, has become a widely accepted serial producer of sexist commonplaces. As a powerful stronghold of collective singulars which resisted postmodern deconstructionist attacks far better than others did, it transformed "the woman" into a *topos* for positive features and virtues, and hence into the primary agent for the eschatological fulfillment of history. Since the woman-singular is expected to incorporate the more valuable capabilities and behaviors of human beings and makes these better human features "feminine" by definition, it is "the woman" and other people of "typically feminine" attitudes who can best pave the way for everlasting peace and universal sisterhood.

As a result, feminism has achieved a central position in the western universalist taxonomy. The preceding cursory remarks on western gender discourses may help explain why after 9/11 feminist stances have been integrated into racist, militarist, and neocolonialist political projects (Haritaworn 2012: 73–78). To quote a particularly blatant example, one may recall the propaganda effort made by the Bush administration "to further galvanize US public support, which was already at an all-time high after 9/11," which consisted of "a media campaign with Laura Bush as its newly minted feminist spokesperson. The media campaign rationalized the military invasion as a moral 'war of necessity,' given the human rights abuses committed against Afghani women and girls by the Taliban" (Collins et al. 2010: 305). These were partially the same political and religious forces that had been helped since 1979 by the United States in their military and terrorist efforts of fighting not only the pro-Soviet government, but also its gender-equality agenda and efforts for girls' schooling.

Numerous other examples could be cited concerning hypocritical media campaigns against adversaries who disregard or ignore women's claims for equality. In the meantime, the method has been extended. For example, "Israeli pinkwashing is a potent method through which the terms of Israeli occupation of Palestine are reiterated—Israel is civilised, Palestinians are barbaric, homophobic, uncivilised, suicide-bombing fanatics. It produces Israel as the only gay-friendly country in an otherwise hostile region" (Puar 2010). As Lentin and Titley (2010: 89, 213–14) put it, "co-optation of discourses of gender and LGBT equality, both by the state and in the name of a global military interventionist politics, pits them against racialized minorities who find themselves increasingly alone in the struggle for equality." They quote an open letter "to white, non-Muslim feminists" by Fatemeh Fakhraie who writes: "Let me be clear: you do not know more about us than we know about ourselves, our religion, our cultures, our families, or the forces that shape our lives. You do not know what's best for us more than we do." The authors laconically add: "But liberalism *does* know better."

4

A craving for goodness

For the general delineation of imperialist sentiment, the altruistic conception is one of the most prominent, recurrent, and vivid ones. . . . This altruistic principle is completed by the second formula: the wellbeing of humanity is the only purpose of imperial action.

GIOVANNI AMADORI VIRGILJ,
IL SENTIMENTO IMPERIALISTA (1906)

The West is not merely an idea, it is a factual reality. For centuries it was a colonial conqueror and dominated worldwide trade, industries, and markets. Under its rule, and as a consequence of such, economic disparities among the world's populations grew substantially. Whereas at the beginning of the nineteenth century the richest 5 percent of the human population was on average seven times richer than the poorest 20 percent, by the end of the twentieth century it was sixteen times richer (Jolly 2006: 1). In 2000 "the richest 2 percent of adult individuals own[ed] more than half of all global wealth, with the richest 1 percent alone accounting for 40 percent of global assets" (Davies et al. 2008: 7). In the same year, North America and Europe possessed 66.9 percent of total world household wealth; until 2015 this share had slightly decreased, to 65.5 percent (Davies, Lluberas, and Shorrocks 2016: 34, 94). It has to be seen whether this almost unperceivable reduction is a short-lived cyclical setback, or a signal that the centuries-old tendency of wealth to increase disproportionally in the west might be inverted in the future.

A previous moment of doubt regarding the solidity of western predominance occurred in the middle of the twentieth century, when Europe's colonial empires were definitely dismantled under the pressure of anticolonial movements.

During the same period the American geopolitical hegemony emerged in a more apparent role. Western military interventions against decolonization in Algeria and Vietnam, and the support for bloody insurgencies and toppling of "third world" governments, like in Iran, Indonesia, and Chile, continued. However, up until the 1980s the fight for independence of the colonies and the military capabilities of the world's largest country in terms of territory, the Soviet Union, generated some obstacles to the western desire for worldwide control. During and after Soviet decline, the global strategic equilibrium became biased again, even if it never fell back to the level of nineteenth-century western command, when the British-dominated system expressed "as much a 'world empire' as it was a 'world-economy'" (Arrighi 1994: 59). But the United States grew to be the most forceful superpower in human history ever. In 2008–09 it counted 716 overseas military bases and facilities in 38 countries (Department of Defense 2009), 190,000 troops placed in 46 nations and territories, and some type of military presence in 151 of the 192 United Nations Member States (Johnson 2010: 120–28). In 2011 the United States spent 44 percent of the world's military expenditure on its own, and 65 percent together with its North Atlantic allies (Nazemroaya 2012: 356). While the world became further militarized and more deeply entrapped in endless war, the main instrument of power of the US-led Western Alliance, the NATO, openly disengaged from its former supposedly defensive character and took on an "undivided global responsibility" (Kryshkin 2010). It has a self-assigned "responsibility" to interfere if necessary beyond the norms of international law, because, if "governments will not be willing or able to safeguard their citizens" against the threat of atrocities, "the world must respond" (Albright and Williamson 2013: 26).

After recovering from the setback caused by decolonization and bloc confrontation, the US-led system of western powers increasingly has turned to claim for themselves the right to wage war anywhere in the world, by any means. The latter include the use of "terror and repression to foster freedom" (Valentine [1990] 2000: 332), as was the case with programs such as the Phoenix Program and Operation Condor. They also involve "funding and supply of arms and explosives" for local terrorists (Imposimato 2012: 341) to destabilize the political situation in insubordinate countries. And they include an openly conducted, if not declared, war that leaves behind "the horror of destroyed villages, murdered individuals and mutilated bodies," and which is conducted by the use of missiles and bombing campaigns and "the latest terrible weapons: drones, which are synonymous with terrorism and absolute impunity" (Chomsky and Vltchek 2013: 172). The United States even threatens non-nuclear countries with a "tactical" nuclear first-strike (Joint Chiefs of Staff 2005: I3–I5). Already before the proliferation of interventions since the dawn of the twenty first century, no less than 120 American military operations had been conducted abroad between 1890 and 2000, despite only one significant instance of military aggression against an overseas territory under American sovereignty occurring in the same period (Grossman 2014).

Economic wealth and military force belong to the strong arguments that "western values" still have in their favor. What interests us in the present context is to understand the high degree of ideologization that distinguishes western foreign policy. According to the most influential theories, in a post-Westphalia setting international relations are by definition amoral, since sovereign states may be obliged by persuasion or by coercion to respect some international treaties, but ultimately behave like Hobbesian savages who have no superior law above them. Against this "realist" vision, morally driven "liberals" object that "practical problems, such as the environment, humanitarian intervention and asylum issues [require] a rethinking of many taken-for-granted assumptions about the morality of the sovereign state" (Lawson 2012: 160). That is, the sovereignty of non-western states that do not accept western definitions of "universal values," may be put into question for ethical reasons. Actually, the Hamletian dilemma between "cynical" power politics and "ethically" driven interventions, are self-comforting representations. In western foreign policy ethically motivated interventions were never free from crude power calculations, neither were rough-and-ready power politics ever free from ethical convictions.

Throughout the twentieth century, the most influential spin-doctors of Anglo-American foreign policy and strategy, from Nicholas John Spykman (1942) to Zbigniew Kazimierz Brzezinski (1997), continued to refer to some of Halford John Mackinder's basic geopolitical conjectures. The British geographer suggested that for their "great replanning of human society," the "Westerners and the Islanders" must struggle against the emergence of any unified power in the Euro-Asiatic heartland, where "it is only with the aid of a conscious ideal, shaping political life in the direction of nationalities, that we shall be able to entrench true freedom" (Mackinder 1919: 6, 254–55). In the early 1990s the US secretary of state James Baker informally promised Gorbachev that there would be "no extension of NATO's jurisdiction for forces of NATO one inch to the East" (Goldgeier 1999:15). This was a trustworthy statement in the sense that the extensions went far beyond just one inch alone. It actually went so far as to leave no neutral inch between NATO and substantial parts of the Russian Federation's western and southern borders. What is more noteworthy than the dubious trustworthiness of western informal promises, is the degree to which the post-1989 western, especially Anglo-American, geopolitical strategies of encirclement of Russia and China appear to be in line with Mackinder's ideas. As Brzezinski (2004: 124) put it, in order to maintain its "global leadership," America must be prevented from losing "its strategic preeminence in Eurasia." The fueling of nationalism, separatism, religious sectarianism and hatred, the conduction of hybrid warfare, the adoption of crowd control psychology in social network operations during "color revolutions," the support of violent regime changes or illegal government overthrow, the favoring of dismantling state structures—from Yugoslavia and Somalia to Iraq, Syria and Libya—in addition to the sowing of seeds for a "civil society" in what some generations earlier was called the "Tartary plains" so as to entrench "true freedom," all appear to be actions in line with Mackinder's ideas. As Chomsky points out, money, drones, and nuclear bombs do not, however, act alone. Their owners "must also be assured a compliant intellectual class to interpret what they do as right and just, possibly a 'mistake' if 'benign intentions' go awry" (Chomsky 2003: 71). When ideology is taken into the equation, what appeared to be a blood toll to pay for cynical power calculations in fact turns out, first and foremost, to be the price for the supposed moral superiority of the west.

The heavy-handed military, political, economic, and cultural actions of the west have been widely summarized within the term "imperialism," which has also been discussed in its possible diversity from "hegemony" (Maier 2006: 59–77). In this chapter it is perhaps not worth dwelling too much on the ins and outs of the term. If we "suggest that 'real empire' requires effective final authority" (Lawson 2012: 36), the term applies to many situations, while to many others it does not. According to Gray, the United States "has few attributes of an imperial regime," as it conditions many world regions but "does not govern any of these regions and its forces have minimal contacts with their peoples" (Gray 2008: 232–33). However, world history has seen so many different forms of what then was called empire, that it seems wise to avoid any approach that "falsely creates an ideal type of empire based on formal acquisition of territories, an established imperial ruling class, hostility to decolonization, and the treatment of colonial peoples as dependents" (Tyrrell 2010: 2). Maybe it is better to look to the Latin root *imperare*, that is, the act of commanding by one social group over another, and the faculty to direct other people's fate. In that case western universalism—in the different forms we have come across up until now—does not lack justification for being deserving of the term.

It would be naïf to deny that powerful economic interests of small but mighty financial, industrial, military, and technocratic oligarchies, that is, a global elite of less than 1 percent of world population, have the decisive say in international political decisions, and that the western share in the decision power is still predominant. However, it would be just as erroneous to overlook the profound ideological commitment behind the "political violence of the modern West," which "can only be understood as an eschatological phenomenon" (Gray 2008: 48). And it would be even more erroneous to minimize the capacity of western universalism for penetrating the feelings and faiths of the society's majority, which should not be seen as a mere victim of powerful manipulations. Universalism is not only able to mold mass behaviors under manipulation "from above," but is also perfectly capable of being regenerated "from below," when the feelings which surround and nurture the west's global commitment seem to transform it into an irrepressible political impulse. The most important of these feelings is not selfishness. It is altruism.

4.1 A fair amount of killing

The argument of ideas and moods conditioning international political and military decisions is also the axiom of Dominique Moïsi's study *The Geopolitics of Emotion*, where he attempts to "map globalization in an emotional way." Identifying the prevailing macro-areas of hope, fear and the sense of humiliation, he also analyzes what he believes to be the west's "identity crisis." Under the Shakespearian motto *And make us lose the good we oft might win / By fearing to attempt*, he laments the culture of fearing the prey to which the west is succumbing in his view. It cannot be a wrong observation, we could say, if the fear is that of no longer being able to judge, educate, teach, help, lead, free and approve, that is, carry out all those actions driven by the mission of a West that has been charged by history to preempt and accompany the progress of all humanity. Moïsi observes:

> The identity crisis that confronts the Western world may be summarized by the concept of fear. But a single word may describe very different realities. The fear that today dominates America is quite different from that which permeates Europe. Yet it is not an oversimplification to say that it is fear that unites the two branches of the West, the American and European. And it is precisely the fear factor that may separate us tomorrow if America, under the leadership of a young president, sheds its culture of fear to recover its traditional culture of hope, while Europe . . . stumbles further into an ever-deepening loss of confidence. (Moïsi 2009: 7, 90–91)

What Moïsi apparently admires is the American capacity of reacting optimistically to the risks faced by the west seen as a whole. This, at least, was the prevailing outlook at the beginning of Obama's first term in the presidential office. Obama would hardly operate any substantial breach with the (bipartisan) neoconservative foreign policies of his predecessors, for reasons that are both ideological and structural, as Gray notes: "The United States is the last militant Enlightenment regime and the only advanced country that is still unshakably Christian. The two facts are not unrelated and help explain the peculiar qualities of neo-conservatism and its rise to power" (Gray 2008: 170).

In the spring of 2011, in a speech to the British House of Commons, immediately defined by the press as historic, a Barack Obama fresh from having eliminated, through what is hard to call a fair trial, the King of Terror, states that "after a difficult decade that began with war and ended in recession" the global economy is now "stable and recovering," and then goes on to claim that "in a world where the prosperity of all nations is now inextricably linked, a new era of cooperation is required to ensure the growth and stability of the global economy." The then still "young president of hope" vigorously faces the culture of fear produced by the achievements of new economic and political powers:

> It has become fashionable in some quarters to question whether the rise of these nations will accompany the decline of American and European influence around the world. Perhaps, the argument goes, these nations represent the future, and the time for our leadership has passed. That argument is wrong. The time for our leadership is now. It was the United States, the United Kingdom, and our democratic allies that shaped a world in which new nations could emerge and individuals could thrive. And even as more nations take on the responsibilities of global leadership, our Alliance will remain indispensable to the goal of a century that is more peaceful, more prosperous and more just. (Obama 2011)

In order to reflect on these words we can call upon the work of Italian sociologist Giovanni Amadori Virgilj, who, under the influence of the French sociology of his time, published an original analysis dedicated to the "imperialist sentiment" in 1906, at the dawn of a prosperous century, which would in fact see little peace, and at the height of what is today considered to be the first wave of globalization (Hertner 2002: 37–38). Many of his observations can in fact be read as a commentary of current events:

> In popular psyche there is a dogma according to which the empire speaks on behalf of civilization, of a universal good: a dogma that can be fought or accepted but not be discussed. Certain of their dogma, and enclosed in their unilateral ways, the imperialist peoples do not understand opposition of contrary actions. As an immediate result they move from the rigid conviction of *having to overturn* those actions even with extreme brutality in the name and in the interests of civilization. In addition to fundamentally depending on the collective character of such *sentiment*, the violence which is often come across in the actions of such peoples also depends on these logical-dogmatic relationships that individuals sketch out within their mental constitution. The American people tolerated and approved the carnage in the Philippines, and the English the massacres in Transvaal, because they

considered these events, if not necessary ways, certainly the quickest ways to gain a decisive victory for civilization. (Amadori Virgilj 1906: 110)

At that time, the "consent without consent" doctrine was invented

> by an American sociologist justifying the slaughter of hundreds of thousands of Filipinos by their liberators. "We have the consent of our own consciences," President McKinley explained, and in "obeying a higher obligation" the 'liberator' should not 'submit important questions . . . to the liberated while they are engaged in shooting down their rescuers," failing to comprehend God's will. (Chomsky 2003: 60)

The later Nazi jurist Carl Schmitt ([1932] 1991: 55) learned from similar examples that it is easier to tolerate a war when it is humanitarian, as it means that the enemy is not human, and that war can therefore be driven "to the most extreme inhumanity."

Disregarding established rules and laws such as state sovereignty or *habeas corpus* was a common feature of colonial warfare long before the Second World War (Gilroy 2004: 24). The same pattern also dominates recent warfare against terrorists and "rogue states." Commenting on the war imposed on Iraq in 2003 by the so-called Coalition of the Willing, Noam Chomsky observes that "it is uncontroversial that Bush and associates did commit the 'supreme international crime'" according to the terms defined by Robert Jackson, chief of Counsel for the United States at the Nuremberg Trials. "An 'aggressor,' Jackson proposed to the Tribunal in his opening statement, is a state that is the first to commit such actions as '[i]nvasion of its armed forces, with or without a declaration of war, of the territory of another State.'" Chomsky chooses

> to recall Jackson's eloquent words at Nuremberg on the principle of universality: "If certain acts in violation of treaties are crimes, they are crimes whether the United States does them or whether Germany does them, and we are not prepared to lay down a rule of criminal conduct against others which we would not be willing to have invoked against us." (Chomsky 2011)

Jackson did not imagine, it appears, the measures that future presidents of the United States would be able to take for the sake of peace, justice, and human rights in the world. The argument that "the notion of state sovereignty can change in international relations" (Forsythe 2000: 20) was not accepted in the Nuremberg trials, whereas in recent pro-western literature on human rights, it is.

On January 23, 2009, the BBC reported that

> two missile attacks from suspected US drones have killed 14 people in north-western Pakistan. . . . These are the first drone attacks since Barack Obama was inaugurated as US president on Tuesday. . . . The second attack was aimed at the house of a Taleban commander about six miles from the town of Wanna, local reports said. But officials told the BBC that the drone actually hit the house of a pro-government tribal leader, killing him and four members of his family, including a five-year-old child. (BBC 2009)

This, however, was only one of a long series. Until late 2012 they had already provoked some hundreds, others estimate thousands, of casualties: "The Bureau of Investigative Journalism issued a report detailing how the CIA is deliberately targeting those who show up after the sight of an attack, rescuers, and mourners at funerals as a part of a 'double-tap' strategy" (Taylor 2012). The tradition of drone strikes continued after the end of the Obama administration. On January 29, 2017, a "Navy's SEAL Team 6, using armed Reaper drones for cover, carried out a commando raid" in which thirty people were reported killed, "including 10 women and children. Among the dead: the 8-year-old granddaughter of Nasser al-Awlaki, Nawar, who was also the daughter of [American citizen] Anwar Awlaki," earlier killed by a drone strike. US military officials "had been planning and debating the raid for months under the Obama administration, but Obama officials decided to leave the choice to Trump" (Greenwald 2017).

It is Chomsky (2011) again who reminds us that not only the killings of civilian bystanders, but also of suspected terrorists are equal to "planned assassination" and the violation of "elementary norms of international law." Is it admissible to equate acts whereby, although materially similar in their extrajudicial action and identical in their lethal outcome, one is a "terrorist attack" and the other a "targeted removal" carried out by the special forces of democratic nations? One is a "barbaric assassination" and the other a "surgical operation"? One is a "heinous crime against humanity" and the other "deplorable collateral damage" carried out for the greater good? Amadori quotes Theodore Roosevelt, a US Republican president of his time, who in 1904 stated to the Senate that the purpose of his country and all other "enlightened nations" was to approach the day in which peace and justice would prevail in all the world; and who in *The Strenuous Life* of 1899 had written that peace can often only be achieved at the cost of war. To support the expansionism of a great civil power which represented law, order, and righteousness meant therefore to favor peace in the world (Amadori Virgilj 1906: 108). One hundred and twelve years later, when talking to British members of parliament, US Democrat President Obama affirmed that

Our two nations know what it is to confront evil in the world. . . . Precisely because we are willing to bear its burden, we know well the cost of war. That is why we built an Alliance that was strong enough to defend this continent while deterring our enemies. At its core, NATO is rooted in the simple concept of Article Five: that no NATO nation will have to fend on its own; that allies will stand by one another, always. And for six decades, NATO has been the most successful alliance in human history. Today, we confront a different enemy. . . . In that effort, we will not relent, as Osama bin Laden and his followers have learned. (Obama 2011)

Even in his time Amadori had warned that "the scale of thought is the world, this is the field of action and the result of fighting," a field in which an "idea of universal good" was disseminated. He had not yet known of institutions such as the International Criminal Court and the International Criminal Tribunal for the former Yugoslavia at The Hague, established in order to place ousted dictators, military personnel, and other executors of heinous war crimes against humanity on trial—as long as, so it seems, they are not representatives of what Amadori called "imperalist peoples." He already warned, however, that "the idea of sovereignty and freedom of States is weakening and is about to be abolished" (Amadori Virgilj 1096: 70–71, 106). Following the end of conflict between the two superpowers, regulated by intangible international law norms for better or for worse, such as state sovereignty, the western block has on various occasions, with the American military force and the reformed organization of NATO at its center, bypassed the regulatory norms of the United Nations and the Security Council; as it happened in 1999, when it started its "first 'humanitarian war'" attacking Serbia "unilaterally without any UN approval," removing the province of Kosovo with force, and appointing it a de facto "NATO protectorate" (Nazemroaya 2012: 96–97).

The American section, in particular, globally widened its potential field of political, military, paramilitary, and terrorist interventions, allowing itself "prerogatives" that, in addition to the war of aggression against sovereign states, also included kidnapping and torture. If the abolition of torture had been "the result of an Enlightenment campaign that began in the eighteenth century," it was "used at the start of the twenty-first as a weapon in an Enlightenment crusade for universal democracy" (Gray 2008: 271). The war of the just includes also "extrajudicial" murder of people who appear on a premeditated kill list: "Those individuals who are being nominated for killing have been discussed at a weekly counter-terrorism meeting at the White House situation room that has become known as Terror Tuesday. Barack Obama, in the chair and wishing to be seen as a restraining influence, agrees the final schedule of names" (Cobain 2013). In 2013 a poll stated that 75 percent of American voters approved, and 13 percent disapproved, of the extrajudicial murders (Roberts 2013). For disciples of the eschatological political religion, apparently "torture and terror are acceptable if they assist in the global war against evil" (Gray 2008: 203).

What had happened in the meantime was that the "murder of thousands of civilians on 11 September 2001 brought apocalyptic thinking to the centre of American politics." A massive attack on Afghanistan was promoted immediately after 9/11 under the name of "war on terror." Both name and action were "a symptom of a mentality that anticipates an unprecedented change in human affairs—the end of history, the passing of the sovereign state, universal acceptance of democracy and the defeat of evil" (Gray 2008:150, 259). Based on a systematic deception of public opinion (which in the name of good is also perfectly legitimate), an earlier planned attack with long-lasting social and political effects was moved on Iraq by President George W. Bush. The move was reported by general Wesley Clark (2003: 130) to be part of a five-year campaign plan according to which, "there were a total of seven countries, beginning with Iraq, then Syria, Lebanon, Libya, Iran, Somalia, and Sudan." The full execution of the plan delayed, but as the proxy war against Syria suggests (Anderson 2016), it was not completely abandoned.

The neoconservative current, which successfully conditions both Republican and Democrat administrations, goes back to the Cold War Era becoming very influential in the years of Soviet decline. In 1997 its apocalyptic "faith in America's redemptive role in history" (Gray 2008:157) took the organizational shape of a nonprofit organization called "Project for the New American Century." At that time many of its ideas had already penetrated the formerly "realistic" strongholds of military doctrine. In a contribution originally published in 1997 on the US Army War College quarterly *Parameters*, Lieutenant Colonel Ralph Peters (2001: 141) predicted that

> there will be no peace. At any given moment for the rest of our lifetimes, there will be multiple conflicts in mutating forms around the globe. Violent conflict will dominate the headlines, but cultural and economic struggles will be steadier and ultimately more decisive. The de facto role of the U.S. armed forces will be to keep the world safe for our economy and open to our cultural assault. To those ends, we will do a fair amount of killing.

4.2 An over-accumulation of benevolence

The astonishing aspect is how, even in view of the unprecedented asymmetry in the worldwide distribution of military potential and economic wealth, the leaders and populations of western countries manage to victimize themselves as inhabitants of a geographical area "under threat." This representation, which seems to turn upside down the factual balance of powers, is probably a fruit of the enduring efforts of educators, media, and intellectuals, as discussed in the previous chapters. In recent years also the fear of terrorism proliferated thanks to spectacular media representation of terror crimes. The imposition of bureaucratic directives "to prevent terrorism" that occur on a daily basis and increasingly resemble Orwell's dystopian control over society, tend to be accepted as a fair price for "security." Still unsatisfied, the political elite, and often interventionist journalists also, take pride in painting the west to be far too indulgent with its adversaries. All of this could, at first glance, appear to be a grotesque performance of fantasies, purely instrumental for a vicious policy of strength. It is a policy that has to face various criticisms both from left-leaning and conservative political forces. The latter include, for instance, a libertarian minority standpoint in American patriotic tradition, which draws parallels between the US and Roman decline and fall. They refer to Roman history as a record of how the armed freeman–citizen had used his "liberty to establish empire over others but had been corrupted by that empire to the point where he had lost liberty first and empire afterwards" (Pocock 2003: 555). Chalmers Johnson, who was one of those conservatives who believed that it is necessary to dismantle the empire before it is too late for reestablishing the original virtues of the American republic, commented on the foreign policy of the power establishment of his country with the following words: "They start believing that they are the bearers of civilization, the bringers of light to 'primitives' and 'savages' (largely so identified because of their resistance to being 'liberated' by us), the carriers of science and modernity to backward peoples, beacons and guides for citizens of the 'underdeveloped world.'" (Johnson 2010: 89). However, while this comment is clearly embraceable, it comes under the title of *An Imperialist Comedy*, whereas what has been said so far in these pages does not seem to warrant a similar ironic interpretation; it seems to instead testify in favor of the hypothesis that it is all carried out with the most earnest conviction of acting for the "universal good." It is this ever-relevant, sincere conviction of representing the good which gives shape to the imperialist sentiment of today.

This conviction continues to be not just an American but a western one. Alarmed by utterances made by Donald Trump during the US electoral campaign of 2016, former secretary general of NATO, Anders Fogh Rasmussen, wrote a passionate pamphlet on "America's indispensable role in the global fight for freedom," warning the American voter against isolationist tendencies and imploring him not to make a "fatal mistake" and "turn away from the world and pretend that its problems are not America's problems. Whenever the United States steps back, the actors of evil are emboldened to step forward" (Rasmussen 2016: 5–6). After Trump's election in November 2016, former prime minister of Belgium and member of the European Parliament, Guy Verhofstadt, declared in an interview: "Let's create a European defence union, let's take on our responsibilities . . . . Let's become an empire, an empire of the good and not of the bad" (Silvera 2016). Whether Europe would have the necessary economic and political means to supplant the United States in the role of the empire of the good has to be seen. What we can take for granted is that a substantial share of Europe's population and of its ruling elites is not destitute of the necessary ideological conviction.

Recalling the "logical-dogmatic relationships that individuals sketch out within their mental constitution," Amadori already raised a key aspect of the matter he called "imperialism," comparing it partly with the experience of colonialism. Even early Portuguese and Spanish colonialism, which from the outset saw the Catholic Church playing a primary role as missionary of the Word of God, yet seeker of its own economic interests at the same time (Magalhaes Godinho 2001: 56), was more often than not seen as a cynical betrayal of a fundamentally good religious message due to a greed for profit. This is a narrative device which allows to criticize not colonialism as such, but its hypocrisy and brutality. Also Condorcet had given shape to this discursive modus operandi, commenting on the beginning of transoceanic colonialism. According to the Marquis, although the great explorers

> gave promise of advantages highly important to the progress of the human species, if a noble curiosity had animated the heroes of navigation, a mean and cruel avarice, a stupid and brutal fanaticism governed the kings and robbers who were to reap the profits of their labour. The unfortunate beings who inhabited these new countries were not treated as men because they were not christians. This prejudice, more degrading to the tyrants than the victims, stifled all sense of remorse, and abandoned, without controul, to their inextinguishable thirst for gold and for blood, those greedy and unfeeling men that Europe disgorged from her bosom. The bones of five millions of human beings have covered the wretched countries to which the Spaniards and Portogueze transported their avarice, their superstition, and their fury. (Condorcet 1796: 152)

Thus, already during the colonial era, European colonizers were conceptually subdivided into exploiting hypocrites and sincere humanists who meant their colonial conquest as an act of liberating the backward populations from their blameless ignorance and irrationality. The same division between interests of economic exploitation and a sense of the civilizing and progressive mission can be found in the critiques of imperialism advanced during our centuries. From the late nineteenth to the early twentieth century, moral reform groups and missionaries "often thought of their work as analogous to empire—but a kind of Christian moral empire that rose above 'nation,' and one nobler in aspiration than the grubby motives of gold and glory" (Tyrrell 2010: 4).

The most qualified theories of imperialism from between the end of the nineteenth and the beginning of the twentieth century do not ignore the importance of moral sentiment, but they gave it little credit in terms of explaining the phenomenon itself. In his piece from 1902, John Atkinson Hobson remarked on the fervor of the well-meaning philanthropists. Ethically motivated reformers and missionaries "who were not simply pawns in their governments' imperial gambits, nor did they typically seek to enrich themselves" (Gott 2002: 24), avidly and devotedly followed the work of even the most ferocious imperialists such as King Leopold of Belgium, who in any case, when talking about the Congo, did not hesitate to declare that "our only plan is the moral and material regeneration of the country." These people, Hobson argued, are "ill-trained for the most part in psychology and history." They believe

> that religion and other arts of civilisation are portable commodities which it is our duty to convey to the backward nations, and that a certain amount of compulsion is justified in pressing their benefits upon people too ignorant at once to recognise them. Is it surprising that the selfish forces which direct Imperialism should utilise the protective colours of these disinterested movements? Imperialistic politicians, soldiers, or company directors . . . simply and instinctively attach to themselves any strong, genuine elevated feeling which is of service, fan it and feed it until it assumes fervour, and utilise it for their ends. (Hobson 1902: 208–09)

Some decades later, Carl Schmitt ([1932] 1991: 55) stated that "'humanity' is a particularly useful ideological tool of imperialist expansion, and in its ethical-humanitarian form it is a specific vehicle of economic imperialism." Similarly, when the United States, with approval from most of its allies, invaded Iraq over a hundred years after Hobson's work in order to unearth Saddam Hussein's weapons of mass destruction, bring freedom to its people, and hang the "new Hitler" of the moment, they were reproached for their goal of "bringing democracy to the Middle East" (Gibney 2006: 85), representing nothing but an intentional lie. According to critics, the matter was in actual fact one of a war that was assembled through the American petrol aristocracy so as to place their hands on the oilfields between the Euphrates and the Tigris, or to at least prevent the Iranians, Russians and Chinese, or Saddam Hussein himself, from placing their hands on those in Kuwait. Even should American interests have not gained direct control over Iraqi oilfields, the underlying geo-strategic goals were nonetheless all about oil: "Whoever controls the Middle East controls the global oil spigot and whoever controls the global oil spigot can control the global economy, at least for the near future." (Harvey 2003: 19). In all cases, the tale of exporting democracy would only have been invented in order to gratify the west's goodwill.

For Amadori, however, the true naivety lies with the critics of imperialism who believe in the exploitative and manipulative use of goodwill by other individuals and groups who only look to gain an economic advantage and political and military power. He admits it to be true that these groups exist, and that "the sentiment-driven declaration of disinterest completes their circle of justifications," but that does not mean that their craving for goodness is only a fake reason behind imperialism. "Along the general lineation of imperialist sentiment this altruistic concept" is one of the main "factors of moral confidence and faith in the destiny of empire." For this reason the Italian sociologist criticizes "the absolute inadequacy of all definitions that explain the phenomenon as a result of political and economic tendencies." (Amadori Virgilj 1906: 63, 104–05).The message's pretence of goodness is therefore completely inseparable from the sinister action which it calls forth, and it is in fact the good intention in itself that is the core problem of imperialism.

According to the author, it is also perfectly futile to accuse power-hungry groups and leaders of cynicism, because the leader is only such in as much as he is able to give a voice to collective feelings. For Amadori Virgilj (1906: 63, 70) imperialism "is a feeling, a general feeling of the people," and the collective concept of domination "is that of moral hegemony; that is, the people do not identify their sovereignty in any political-military or economic matter, but rather in a moral empire that must also extend to the intellectual, political and economic field." Incidentally it might be noted that Hobson and other critics of his time "shared the view that present circumstances were unifying the nations of the world into a moral whole." (Lang 2011: 754). The moral empire is a cause that Obama also knew how to play out, when in 2011 in front of British representatives and TV viewers worldwide he declared:

> In this century, our joint leadership will require building new partnerships, adapting to new circumstances, and remaking ourselves to meet the demands of a new era. That begins with our economic leadership. Adam Smith's central insight remains true today: there is no greater generator of wealth and innovation than a system of free enterprise that unleashes the full potential of individual men and women. . . . In other words, we live in a global economy that is largely of our own making. And today, the competition for the best jobs and industries favors countries that are free-thinking and forward-looking; countries with the most creative, innovative, entrepreneurial citizens. That gives nations like the United States and the United Kingdom an inherent advantage. (Obama 2011)

Quoting Adam Smith was an able rhetorical move by the speaker or his ghostwriter because it firstly meant paying homage to the host country's intellectual heritage. However, it also meant welding the west's moral superiority with the free-market principle, inasmuch as the Scottish philosopher claimed that even before *The Wealth of Nations*, his masterpiece was actually the less-quoted *Theory of Moral Sentiments*, in which he had explained how the motivation behind human actions consisted of a desire for recognition. This brings us to consider another of Amadori's observations, where "there is therefore a profound and precise concept of an apostolate to be carried out in imperialist sentiment" (Amadori Virgilj 1906: 111). It is this apostolate, which just days after September 11, 2001, brings the American President George W. Bush to exclaim in front of the American people's representatives that "This is not, however, just America's fight. . . . This is the world's fight. . . . This is the fight of all who believe in progress and pluralism, tolerance and freedom" (Gibney 2006: 84).

Thus the apostolate remains that of a universal progress of humanity, which lived one of its topical moments on August 26, 1789. On this day, acting on a proposal made by hero of American independence, General Gilbert du Motier de La Fayette, the National Assembly of Paris enacted the Declaration of the Rights of Man and Citizen with the intention of not simply establishing a preamble to the future constitution of France. On the contrary, it was to be "the catechism of 'all men, of all times, of all countries.' The Revolution began French only to become universal" (Diagnopsy 2001: 6). Illustrating this moment, a telling allegoric drawing appeared on a leaflet in circulation during the days after May 15, 1791, when a—soon-after-revised—decree ruled that free-born *gens de couleur* should be admitted to primary assemblies in the colonies (Cormack 2011: 161). The drawing—which is reproduced on the front cover of this book—shows a scene bathed in the light of the blazing star Sirius, a (not only) Masonic symbol of divinity, universe, knowledge, and power. One divinity, Nature, banishes the demons of aristocracy, avarice, injustice, and encourages the other divinity, Reason, to hand over the Declaration of Rights and the decree of May 15 to a man in a French army uniform, who passes it on to another man of dark complexion partially covered by a loincloth. Hanging down from Reason's level, a cornucopia gifts the savage with wealth. It could be said that the apostolate of the west is entirely encapsulated within this allegory.

4.3 A rescue from the limbo of history

Another variant of the western sense of history, promoted to being a foundation of the international law we know today, is the principle of "self-determination of the peoples," launched as a "reaction to the conquests of Belgium, Serbia, and other small European states" (Kennedy 2006: 178) by the American president Woodrow Wilson. It became a guiding force of the 1919 Versailles Peace Treaties and the League of Nations. The same principle was somewhat invoked by the signatories of the Munich Agreement in 1938, when they recognized how the creation of Czechoslovakia in terms of the Peace Treaties had discarded the right to self-determination of the German, Hungarian, and Polish minorities. Apparently drawn up with the purpose of safeguarding peace, the Munich Agreement notoriously became a step toward the beginning of the Second World War, following which the principle of self-determination of the peoples prominently merged into the 1946 United Nations Charter. From then on, at least at first (before legitimizing separatist movements in the various States, from Yugoslavia and onwards), it would go on to serve as a judicial backing for the claims of the independence movements, and for States emerging from the process of decolonization, often conflicting with the interests of the western colonial or mandatory countries.

Yet despite the reticence of the latter, because of "premature times," on principle that right was never denied to the man in loincloth. On the contrary, it was conceived of as a universal goal by the philosophy of human progress, even before that distant leaflet of 1791. However, in order to exercise that right, the human associations were to first abandon the stage of tribal infancy and of barbaric customs, and develop a minimum amount of civilization and cultivation that would allow them to become a "nation" and finally a "sovereign people." How long that journey would take was to essentially depend on two things for every population from all corners of the globe: on the historical distance covered, with respect to the original state of nature, that is, on the stage of civilization reached, and on the capability of the "advanced," modern, European and Western nations—basically, the soldier on the leaflet—to exercise their responsibility to help them in accelerating the process of developing their civil capabilities, and their ability to self-government.

A clear example of such Western benevolence is provided by Article 22 of the Covenant of the League of Nations. This article attempts to deal with the difficult matter of how to manage power over the territories that had been taken from the defeated powers after the First World War, in particular, the Ottoman Empire. It states that territories:

> which are inhabited by peoples not yet able to stand by themselves under the strenuous conditions of the modern world, there should be applied the principle that the well-being and development of such peoples form a sacred trust of civilisation and that securities for the performance of this trust should be embodied in this Covenant. The best method of giving practical effect to this principle is that the tutelage of such peoples should be entrusted

to advanced nations who by reason of their resources, their experience or their geographical position can best undertake this responsibility, and who are willing to accept it, and that this tutelage should be exercised by them as Mandatories on behalf of the League. The character of the mandate must differ according to the stage of the development of the people, the geographical situation of the territory, its economic conditions and other similar circumstances. Certain communities formerly belonging to the Turkish Empire have reached a stage of development where their existence as independent nations can be provisionally recognized subject to the rendering of administrative advice and assistance by a Mandatory until such time as they are able to stand alone. The wishes of these communities must be a principal consideration in the selection of the Mandatory. Other peoples, especially those of Central Africa, are at such a stage that the Mandatory must be responsible for the administration of the territory under conditions which will guarantee freedom of conscience and religion, subject only to the maintenance of public order and morals, the prohibition of abuses such as the slave trade, the arms traffic and the liquor traffic, and the prevention of the establishment of fortifications or military and naval bases and of military training of the natives for other than police purposes and the defence of territory, and will also secure equal opportunities for the trade and commerce of other Members of the League. There are territories, such as South-West Africa and certain of the South Pacific Islands, which, owing to the sparseness of their population, or their small size, or their remoteness from the centres of civilisation, or their geographical contiguity to the territory of the Mandatory, and other circumstances, can be best administered under the laws of the Mandatory as integral portions of its territory, subject to the safeguards above mentioned in the interests of the indigenous population. (League of Nations [1924] 2008)

Returning from that early example of "global governance," which comprised the great powers' obligation "to inspect—or at least to report on—their 'mandated' territories" (Kennedy 2006:11), to current times, following what now is depicted as an exceptional period of unchallenged strength of the nation-state's sovereignty, with the little-debated decision of NATO not to dissolve after the crumbling of the Soviet Union, but to instead transform itself into a global military and political institution, western philosophy concerning international law generally appears to have been "reset" to the principles of 1919, inflicting the geopolitical agenda of the west increasingly upon the sovereignty of the militarily weaker states. While the rules of the United Nations that had emerged from the anti-Axis alliance during the Second World War were based on the paradigm of a reciprocally inviolable principle of state sovereignty as defined by international law, these principles then eroded in favor of other values and juridical goods such as the prevention of genocide or the preservation of human rights even against possible sovereign state prerogatives. Thus, the exclusive role of state sovereignty was put into question, at least in the case of states that were neither western, nor democratic, nor economically or demographically strong, nor holding an atomic or other military deterrent that could be convincing in terms of costs of a military intervention. The matter of "security" was configured around the confirmation that in many realities, through the pressure of globalization, of the regional, ethnic, religious and tribal divisions, and of the emergence of organized crime, militia, and uncontrollable terrorist groups, the strength of the peripheral state was no longer able to provide any guarantee of credible security to its citizens, or to the "international community"; the latter being interpreted, as per usual, by the west, which once again holds the "heavy burden" of taking action.

In order to abide by their "responsibilities," the west's political elite discovered the usefulness of an anthropological and historical concept of the nation as a cultural construct. Nation building is no longer only being talked about in books inspired by Eric Hobsbawm or Benedict Anderson, which were critical about both nationalism and the very idea of nation. For some time now, it has been frequently talked about in an apologetic way in the military academies and among the institutions for political and strategic consultancy, as another typically western "inescapable responsibility" (Dobbins 2003: 1). Of course, the purpose is not to dismantle and reconstruct the American, French, or German nations, and so on, as these are considered strong democratic states and mature civilized countries. According to the west's spatial–cultural hierarchies, it is the "artificial" postcolonial nations or the remains of the Soviet Empire that should be dismantled so as to remodel the more "natural" and more easily controllable pieces. It is suggested that nations such as ex-Yugoslavia, Iraq, or Libya cannot be grouped together for ethnic, religious, or historical reasons. The same applies to populations torn apart by civil and tribal wars, such as Somalia, that is, lands inhabited by populations who are "not yet able to stand by themselves."

The hope that the independent nation-state might function as "a driver of development and security" in many cases had to be abandoned, as "many postcolonial leaders gradually became more interested in redistributing wealth to themselves and their cronies than in creating growth and wealth for the nation at large" (Stepputat, Andersen and Møller 2007: 9). It should however be added that also western economic and financial policies were not so irrelevant to the failure of the post-colonial projects. The West is now attempting to react to the their disappointing performance, understanding that still more time and "aid" is needed until the former colonies are "able to stand by themselves." Almost a hundred years after the 1919 Covenant of the League of Nations, "fragile statehood" and "fragile security" have once again become the focal points of the debate for the military elite and for western policies, when they exert their "peacekeeping" and "humanitarian" interventions. As a consequence, in what was to be baptized the "Third World" after decolonization, in several cases we can see the return to a sort of informal "mandate" system, "benefiting" countries that do not have sufficient demographic, political, or military strength to protect themselves against interference.

In this context it is taken for granted that Iranian NGOs, or North-Korean troops, or Zimbabwean legal advisers cannot be sent to substitute the state authorities that are either missing or have been destabilized under the impact of civil war and intelligent bombings, nor to reconstruct a "civil society." As states such as Iran, North Korea, or Zimbabwe do not represent humanity's universal values, there is not a perfect symmetry or equality between the states when it comes to interventions by the "international community." This task mainly falls on western troops and organizations, or their regional allies. In all of this a mere political and military commitment is not sufficient. It requires comprehensive coordination of interventions, donations, and investments, all combined in a packet of coordinated measures that involves military and private security organizations just as much as it involves other commercial and financial businesses, as well as NGOs that work in the social, medical, educational, and legal fields.

These latter associations are often nonprofit, and their activists are—now as ever—motivated by authentic charitable sentiments and altruistic impulses of solidarity. And now as ever—if not more now than ever—they are framed within an overall political strategy of global hegemony, at times being forced to dirty their hands directly, other times observing impotently, for example, when they see that "unfortunately for Afghans, despite considerable improvements in certain areas, human rights abuse continued unabated in the aftermath of the Taliban's removal." And even if it is not easy to attribute this deplorable state of affairs solely to the immature and uncivil customs of the indigenous peoples, inasmuch as the American treatment "of their prisoners has been probably worse than their Afghan allies" (Lafraie 2006: 125), we are invited to have a certain understanding for the complexity of the enigmatic situations that occur in "different cultures," and to act with the necessary flexibility in that context: "The key challenge for external actors who wish to strengthen human rights and improve access to security and justice may thus be to contextualize—without necessarily relativizing—human rights" (Scheye and Andersen 2007: 241).

4.4 Imperialism: A popular sentiment

The globalization of NATO may transcend its original anti-Soviet purpose, but it does not betray the declarations of the Brussels Treaty of March 17, 1948, drawn one year before the North Atlantic Pact's foundation. The signature states of the Treaty reaffirmed "their faith in fundamental human rights, in the dignity and worth of the human person" and united their efforts "to fortify and preserve the principles of democracy, personal freedom and political liberty, the constitutional traditions and the rule of law, which are their common heritage" (Löwenstein and Zühlsdorff 1975: 355). After September 11, 2001, the language was updated, but the underlying sense remained identical. The "international community" remains deeply convinced of acting in the name of universal humanity. It acts in preparing "armies for peace" and international organizations with the aim of educating the populations which are not yet capable of being nations or of governing their countries on their own, at least not in the way they should or how the "modern world" requires: democratically, without relapsing into tribal wars, without placing themselves in the hands of cruel tyrants, without carrying out genocide on minorities, without discriminating women or gay people, and without providing shelter for international terrorism.

As Amadori Virgilj (1906: 106) already pointed out, progressive nations which do not intend to detract from their responsibilities to history, work for

> a worldwide educational reconstruction based on similar concepts, which will produce goodness, and advantages for imperial domination. Strength made from energy, but at the same time also from justice, vigor of morally good conscience, clear and decisive will in carrying out responsibilities and in seeking their own wealth: these will be the foundations of the education of the world's peoples; whereas an immense development of all material energies will accompany this moral elevation.

With similar words, aimed at revealing what lies beneath the name of imperialism, the author actually sketched one of the innermost aspects of western ideology from at least the second half of the eighteenth century.

With imperialism being essentially a popular sentiment, according to Amadori Virgilj (1906: 63), "in its social generality, in its almost passionate nature, lie its only peculiarities, which individualize the phenomenon through history, and which make it incomparable to the conquests that formed the monumental empires of past ages." The author seems to suggest that a link exists between the craving for universal goodness and supremacy on the one hand, and a people's sovereignty founded on consent and shared feelings on the other. It is difficult to deny that with the emergence of modern concepts of nation, the mythological legitimizations of power in the eighteenth and nineteenth centuries underwent change, with respect to those that held up the dynastic and imperial powers previously. Placing sovereign power on *un plébiscite de tous les jours* (Renan), the participation, the conscience, and the sense of duty of every single person are called upon directly. With a similar political necessity, the role of "political religion," of patriotism, of the sense of sacredness of the nation and its universal mission were destined to expand. Political action more than ever required the investiture to be on the side of goodness.

We have, after all, mentioned in various ways how in contemporary times the idea of nation and the sense of a universal mission are intertwined: there is no western nation which intends for its existence to be justified purely in being itself, neither does it feel satisfied in itself as it is; each of them believes itself to be charged with a universal mission that transcends its own reality and finds its original position within the philosophies of history paved out by Christianity and Enlightenment. Regarding the United States, the country which was "ranked at the top of national pride rankings" during the 1980s and 1990s, it has been observed that "two centuries after Alexis de Tocqueville set foot in the United States, his observation that 'there is no country in the world where the Christian religion retains a greater influence over the souls of men' still holds" (Gibney 2006: 87). The secular sense of the mission of an elected people seems to thus be made up of eschatological delays which are not only earthly, and seems to be combined with a sacred sense of mission in which secular pathos and religious pathos merge so far as to no longer be distinguishable. "Mission" means that America, and the west in general, do not just want to gain dominance, but to win the people over. The education of the world's populations, according to what was said by an experienced Pentagon official during the heyday of the Cold War, "isn't merely a question of stronger battalions or a higher standard of living, or, indeed, of material values at all. As General Donnelly put it, 'You can't win the souls of men without a faith—faith in a power that transcends this world.'" (Löwenstein and Zühlsdorff 1975: 331).

5

Ecology and apocalypse

Shall I then praise the heavens the trees, the earth
Because their beauty and their strength last longer
Shall I wish there, or never to had birth,
Because they're bigger, & their bodyes stronger?
Nay, they shall darken, perish, fade and dye,
And when unmade, so ever shall they lye.
But man was made for endless immortality.

ANNE BRADSTREET, CONTEMPLATIONS (1678)

During the twentieth century certain narratives emerged which tended to translate western teleology into a sort of nostalgic account of loss. At the same time, the temperament of historical optimism that also so characteristically belongs to western teleology, after the Second World War ended up being ever more strongly projected onto the economy. It was as if the greatest happiness could originate from the consumption of goods. This at least is what is suggested by the fact that the last comprehensive paradigm of universal history was offered up in 1960 by an economist. In addition to declaring that history is a succession of predictable stages, right from the title, *The Stages of Economic Growth* by Walt Whitman Rostow also contains a reference to the tradition of the philosophy of history in the subtitle, in stating its intention of being *A Non-Communist Manifesto*. The author's idea was that the "age of high mass consumption, where, in time, the leading sectors shift towards durable consumers' goods and services," was supposed to stop the supporters of Marxism in their tracks. History promised that the working class would no longer need to achieve happiness in that communist other world, but could have it at arm's reach, just on the other side of the revolving doors of the department store. Not that this was necessarily the end of history, yet "beyond, it is impossible to predict" (Rostow [1960] 1991: 10–11).

The dream of unrelentingly high economic growth rates was interrupted in the 1970s in those same western societies. However, the comparatively fewer opportunities for consumption in socialist countries and their economic stagnation during the 1980s contributed to the implosion of communist-led political systems which were unable to enter into the age of high mass consumption, as predicted by Rostow two decades earlier: "Its citizens hunger for it; but Communist leaders face difficult political and social problems of adjustment if this stage is launched" (Rostow [1960] 1991: 11). Nonetheless, the Rostowian confutation of the *Communist Manifesto* in a certain sense was by now ideologically and conceptually idle. Many Marxist intellectuals had for some time been extending the concept of alienation from the sphere of production—where it indicates a precise mechanism of appropriating the work of others, as such independent from the salary level and the possibilities of consumption that that level offers—to a broader, more generic and, dare I say, spiritual field. This field was in fact already well populated by numerous others, differing masters of thought among them, who also shared this negative evaluation of the empty hedonism of the *homo œconomicus*. If a Jesuit priest such as Teilhard de Chardin ([1959] 2004: 304) could write that the "believers in progress think in terms of a Golden Age, a period of euphoria and abundance; and this, they give us to understand, is all that Evolution has in store for us," the Marxist intellectuals mentioned above were no less skeptical about the consumerist rituals driven by commodity fetishism. Calling again upon the tradition of the philosophies of history, they turned their critique against the expulsion of Man from his authentic condition as worker, and thus interpreted the future liberation from exploitation in terms of a return.

This shift in focus within Marxist theorizing had been on its way since the nineteenth century. It consisted in a transposition of the concept of alienation that demonstrated what may have been a fairly biased analogy with respect to the path taken by Rousseau concerning the same concept, but in relation to property and not work. In Marx's core analysis, to alienate the worker from his own work was the mark of "capital," a term that wholly embraces what is more commonly called the capitalist mode of production; more in general, in his historical stages theory the emergence of a class society is tightly interrelated with the analysis of technical change and the division of labor. Although "the eschatological promise" was an element of this theory from the outset, it was formulated "in more 'secular' terms" in the *Communist Manifesto* (Balibar 2015: 236–37). When in the later nineteenth century Marxists moved the focus as outlined above, the precise mechanism of exploitation acquired a more pronouncedly transcendent meaning. Man is no longer a beast because he is a worker, and therefore to alienate him from the result of his creative activity means to distance him from his authentically human condition. So, in harmony with parallel shifts in the cultural and political atmosphere of the late nineteenth century, over the initially prevailing analytical aspects of a specific mode of production's functioning, the transcendent one was imposing itself with increasingly greater strength. After reflecting on the work of American anthropologist Lewis Henry Morgan, Friedrich Engels, in an annotation to the English 1888 edition of the *Manifesto*, came to the conclusion that the parable of human history originated from a "primitive communistic society" (Marx and Engels [1848] 1970: 42]), which had never been mentioned in the *Manifesto*. On that basis, a wide range of possible intersections of "official" Marxism opened up during the transition toward the twentieth century, with elaborations of various philosophical molds, from the post-Romantic perspectives to existentialism, and to Christian theology. In this way, Man, who was downgraded to the appendix of the machine, from bearer of a practical critique of the mode of production was transformed into a witness against his own progressive alienation from authentic Being. This was a theoretical landing point, which after 1945 was shared by several circles of intellectuals, to the west just as to the east of the "iron curtain."

It is important to emphasize how this nostalgic readjustment of western philosophical discourse on the history of the human species, despite reflecting alternate seasons of prevalent optimism or prevalent pessimism (which in turn reflect vicissitudes and *res gestae* of the west), does not represent a radical ideological change, nor a real inversion of the temporal perspective. It in fact seems virtually impossible within the horizon of western ideology to hypothesize any utopia without nostalgia, and vice versa. Ultimately, the mythopoesis of the past and the mythopoesis of the future are not only reciprocal preconditions, they are also interchangeable, and have in fact exchanged roles more than once. What unites them is the myth of an origin that already contains every possible future meaning: "The new logos is always an ancient logos" (Ricœur 1986: 308). Phrases such as "we must know the past in order to know ourselves and where we are going" are the popular translation of this idea, and are, as Dubuisson (2003: 21) maintains, the fruit of the prevailing Platonism in western thinking. Modern ecology and the postmodern critique, which imbue a large part of public discourse and of current common sense, take their lead from here. That is, from an idea of origin, of nature, of essence, of authenticity, and of the dramatic erosion of these in the process of civilization, which inexorably leads to alienation. It brings, nonetheless, hope for a return, and for a repossession of one's own self and place in the world.

5.1 Nature

In contrast to Europe, where the ecologist movements can be traced back to the nineteenth century not only as an idea and cultural association, but also as political action, the beginnings of the American movement are only made to coincide with "the successful fight against damming the Grand Canyon in 1966." Despite being at odds with America's proverbial economic optimism, and its insatiable hunger for raw materials, in less than half a century the US ecologist movement has grown to become a powerful political and cultural factor, as well as a laboratory of cultural expressions that are significant to the entire West; we find, for example, "deep ecology," which intends to redefine the man–nature relationship on a cosmic–psychological level, "social ecology," which advances neocommunitarian social models deemed to be more suitable for nature, and "ecofeminism," which places the relationship between women and nature at the center of attention and of normative regulations (Merchant 2007: 199, 206).

In his *History of Environmental Ethics*, also centered on the American situation, Roderick Frazier Nash provides the diagram of two inverted cones, one referred to the development of ethics and the other to the development of rights. The vertex of the first originates in the Self, in the layer of the pre-ethical past—and therefore, it would seem, in the immoral, selfish, and isolated wilderness of the Hobbesian imagination—and it expands through the ethical past (family, tribe, region) and the present (nation, race, humans, animals) toward the future, when Man will take on moral responsibility for the plants, rocks, ecosystems in general, the planet, and ultimately, the universe. Similarly, the cone of the rights originates from "natural rights" and develops through the rights of the *Magna Carta* "freemen," American colonists, slaves, women, native Americans, workers, blacks, among others, so as to arrive at the inalienable rights of Nature with the Endangered Species Act of 1973. As the author points out, "the relatively recent emergence of the belief that ethics should expand from a preoccupation with humans (or their gods) to a concern for animals, plants, rocks, and even nature, or the environment, in general," marks "the farthest limits of American liberalism" (Nash 1989: 4). A glimpse of the change in the "ethic climate," which is underway as a consequence of similar discourses may be caught by observing the present campaign to prevent global warming. Distinguished climate scientists who argue that the public debate and political decision making should not simply ignore the inevitably high degree of uncertainty regarding both causality and forecast reliability (Curry and Webster 2011), "are routinely recast as climate-change *deniers*, an insidious echo of the phrase 'Holocaust deniers'" (Cooke 2016). That they have also been labeled "heretics" by members of their own academic community indicates that quasi-religious fervor increasingly supplants scientific argumentation.

Leaning on the work of nineteenth-century predecessors such as Henry David Thoreau and John Muir, in the second half of the twentieth century the US ecologist movement also contested the utilitarianism and anthropocentrism of the official policies of protection and conservation of nature, which considered nature only as a resource for human society. It was necessary to project the concepts of ethics and rights onto other living beings and the whole of nature, almost as if it was about minority rights. The environmentalists

> recognize that wolves and maples and mountains do not petition for their rights. Human beings are the moral agents who have the responsibility to articulate and defend the rights of the other occupants of the planet. Such a conception of rights means that humans have duties toward nature. . . . When environmentalists began in the 1960s to talk about the rights of nature and the need to liberate this new oppressed minority from human tyranny, they used the language and ideals of liberalism. (Nash 1989: 10).

But are the concepts of the "new environmentalists" truly less anthropocentric than those of previous approaches? Some doubts may be justified. On the one hand, they express the presumption of belonging to an animal species which is "superior" based on its capacity for forming ethical judgment, despite Frederick Turner warning not to "define Nature as the unreflexive, the unpremeditated, and thus distinguish it from human cultural activity," or to find human "uniqueness in the possession of motives and values" (Turner 1991: 55). On the other, a strong sense of mission can be felt, one that once again descends from the ethics of the civilized man who places nature within the role of the naive savage whom he must protect.

Can this mission refer to the Darwinian revolution, a revolution which raised the question as to whether the human species was "truly the favored creation of a supernatural creator, itself endowed with a supernatural spirit, and set upon earth to rule creation?" (Oelschlaeger 1991: 107). Following the words of Darwin himself, his conceptual revolution attributes a subordinate and internal role to humans with respect to nature and to its merciless principle of selection. The latter "is a power incessantly ready for action, and is as immeasurably superior to man's feeble efforts, as the works of Nature are to those of Art" (Darwin [1859] 2010: 40). Indeed, this was not merely a statement that would be hard to define as being anthropocentric. It was also difficult to attribute to an ethical foundation whereby man is held responsible for the preservation of nature. Darwin's nature rather looks like Φύσις in the sense of Heraclitus, "as a title for the world as a whole" (Mikulić 1987: 234), that is, as that totality which *has been*, *is*, and *will be*, and which is, therefore, indestructible.

Neither can we easily presume there to be condemnation of technology in this vision, or exclusion of the idea that it might be understood as a physical means employed by one of the animal species in its "natural fight" for reproduction and survival. However, if the intrinsic selfishness of the species, shaped through the process of selection, turns out to be ethically insufficient, and if man is truly the exploiting tyrant of nature, how could the matter be approached under a non-anthropocentric point of view? Should it not simply push such an ethic until man takes his leave, leaving nature alone and in peace with itself? On the contrary, "the problem now, as most ecologists agree, is to find ways of keeping the human community from destroying the natural community, and with it the human community" (Rueckert 1996:107). And when it is discovered through the most up-to-date scientific paradigms that ecosystems can not only be dismantled by human intervention, but also by other natural events, the ecological ethical imperative is retrieved, projecting it onto the harmony of action: "Both humans and nonhumans disrupt nature, and both can work in partnership to restore it" (Merchant 2007: 190). Basically, man is once again at the center as the self-nominated protector in the struggle for the salvation of the world. "Apocalypse is, after all, an anthropocentric myth" (Gray 2008: 296).

Various approaches to holistic environmentalism are sensitive to this anthropocentric concern. For example, those that are moving in the tradition of Baruch Spinoza, who "put forward the pantheistic notion that every being or object—wolves, maple trees, humans, rocks, stars—was a temporary manifestation of a common God-created substance. . . . A tree or a rock had as much value and right to exist as a person" (Nash 1989: 20). Even more sensitive to it are the ecologists who instead deny "that culture is a purposive expression of nature so that whatever it does is *natural*" and therefore underscore the difference: "The word nature by itself at least implies a culture that can conceive of and name it." So it "does not work to counter the destructive separation of humans and nature with the notion that humans can be one with nature" (Boschman 2009: 11, 14). From this point of view, whatever happens, humanity carries on down its path. It is a metaphysical path, that is, a path that conceptually conducts beyond Φύσις, toward a spiritual infinite. Therefore, we can conclude that not just the landscape, as Simon Schama (1995: 61) maintains, but nature itself turns out to be "a construct of the imagination projected onto wood and water and rock."

Löwith also referred to the word "nature" as a sign of human uniqueness, in quite an interesting way: "We can put into question only what we have taken a distance from. But whoever is able to distance himself from every natural condition, including his own, is not univocally nature, but instead *possesses* a nature, in a polyvalent meaning, and within the limits defined by nature itself" (Löwith [1957] 1981: 285). As Ludwig Marcuse (1960: 8) observed, for Löwith such an estrangement "is not an original sin, neither is it inhuman, but on the contrary is the most considerable trait of the human species. Or, we can say, of that living being which is capable of 'distancing himself' from his environment and from himself." But then adds an apodictic sentence: "Animals do not know of estrangement from themselves" (Marcuse 1960: 8). With this, human exceptionalness seems to once again have been rescued, even if this operation appears to be dubious in its effectiveness: following George Herbert Mead, reflexive distancing from one's Self is not only possible, but inevitable for all organisms equipped with a sufficiently differentiated nervous system that allows a time–spatial anticipation or postponement of experience due to memorization of the past fact, and anticipation of the future act (Mead [1932] 2002: 54). This implies a transcending of the present, incorporated into the general relationality between organism and environment, which does not need to be explained in terms of any human exceptionalness, let alone in terms of a transcendent concept of "humanity."

Ever since its earliest days, however, the ecology movement has taken the opposite road. In the German speaking area of the late nineteenth century, the concepts of *Heimatschutz* and *Umweltschutz*, that is, the protection of the homeland and the protection of the environment, were conceptualized together, and were often understood as being one and the same thing, particularly in extreme right-wing political movements and cultural circles. Race, nation, nature, culture, and personality ideally mingled into one single wholeness, through *Heimat*, the place where man could come closer back to his natural condition from which civilization had expelled him. The ecological disposition was what the philosopher Eduard Spranger (1923: 14) meant by the self's interiorization of his surrounding world. Through appropriation of the place of dwelling, the child or adolescent becomes a conscious part of it, and therefore moves closer to his or her true nature. Following Spranger's suggestions, a holistically envisaged *heimatology* was inserted into the programs of elementary school teaching. Not only the conservative Spranger, but also other intellectual leaders of the *Heimatschutz* and *Umweltschutz* movement, such as Walther Schönichen (1929, 1934, 1950) personified the conceptual continuity among German ecology movements throughout the Weimar Republic, the Third Reich, and the early Federal Republic.

The ethical imperative of ecology cannot easily be presented as an altruistic principle from the point of view of the species. "Even Heidegger's phenomenological concept of 'world' remains too anthropocentric for Löwith," Wolin (2001: 77–78) states, to continue that the "sublimity of the 'world' in Löwith's sense lies in the fact that, like the aforementioned mountain and river, it is without a goal and without a purpose." Considering the intrinsic purposelessness of Φύσις, what, then, is the "preservation of nature" all about? Simply a more refined version of Darwin's innate natural survival interest and selfishness of all species? It rather seems another generalization of the eschatological load of western ideology.

Even if we abandon the German context of the nineteenth and early twentieth century, and its political specificities, the philosophical assumptions about nature and the ethical imperative of its preservation remain similar elsewhere in western societies. According to William Howarth (1996: 69), "the *oikos* is nature, a place Edward Hoagland calls 'our widest home,'" while the British scholar of Shakespeare, Sir Jonathan Bate (2000: 75), underlines that the "eco" in ecology "is derived from the Greek *oikos*, 'the home or place of dwelling.'" It is also a place where "the farthest limits of liberalism" seemingly overlap with views shared by German *völkisch* thinking. As a reviewer noted, the Heideggerian syllogism "if mortals dwell in that they save the earth and if poetry is the original admission of dwelling, then poetry is the place where we save the earth" lies "at the heart of what Bate calls 'ecopoetics'" (Gilbert 2002: 293). Jimmie Killingsworth (2004: 5) observes that Martin Heidegger's essays have been "widely cited in environmental rhetoric, philosophy, and politics if not in ecocriticism before Bate. Heidegger's 'Question Concerning Technology' illustrates how German Green thinking links back to Muir's experience." Max Oelschlaeger (1991: 178) confirms that the Scottish–American naturalist John Muir had understood wilderness as home "in the most fundamental sense of the word." Civilization, "rather than defining the locus of human beingness, was something to be tolerated, not celebrated. He wrote that 'going to the woods is going home.'"

The creator of the expression "ecology" seems to be Ernst von Haeckel, the German biologist. It has been claimed that his "racist construction of human evolution had contributed to the work of the Nazis"—unjustly, according to Robert Richards (2008: 148; 2013), who in his meticulous studies breaks the line traced by others between Darwin and Haeckel and Nazism. The German biologist's studies highlight in particular the close ontogenetic kinship in the embryos of animal species such as reptiles, birds, and mammals, that is, the kinship between lizards, hens, mice, and men. It is likewise difficult to hold Darwin responsible for later political transpositions of statements such as "there must in every case be a struggle for existence, either one individual with another of the same species, or with the individuals of distinct species, or with the physical conditions of life" (Darwin [1859] 2010: 41). In the same way in which Herbert Spencer "was the most influential exponent of Social Darwinism, a system of ideas that owes little to Charles Darwin" (Gray 2008: 124), it must also be excluded that Haeckel had a similar interpretation to that of Heidegger in mind when coining the term "ecology"; Heidegger was in fact *philosophically* aligned with the Nazi Party, in addition to formally joining this party on May 27, 1933.

Haeckel (1866b: 286–87) defined ecology as the "science of the external relationships of the organism" and of its position "within the economy of the nature as a whole." Similarly, Darwin ([1859] 2010: 40) had spoken of the "whole economy of nature, with every fact on distribution, rarity, abundance, extinction, and variation" of species. For the two biologists, a metaphorical conceptualization of *oikos* was thus mediated by a common sense of "economy," understood as the distribution and exchange of resources, and the effort to acquire them. With economy and ecology they intended on indicating a dynamic context of action and interaction, probably without purposes other than survival (as also Ghiselin 1994 maintains, contrary to Lennox 1993). This setting, if anything, was more defined by action than by a "dwelling" on an existential ground. Bate's (2000: 56) statement—"Here we see how the line from Rousseau to Romanticism runs on into the twentieth century"— is therefore perhaps even better adapted to the author's own interpretative approach, rather than to Haeckel to whom Bate here in fact refers, and who indeed shared the Romantic belief whereby "God and nature were one" (Richards 2008: 9).

Not only for Romantic literature is homecoming an intimate and existential experience. According to Spranger, nature as a homeland is a place where the external world is partially "dragged into my inner life (*Innenleben*)" (Spranger 1923: 14). This statement, closely aligned with the pedagogy and developmental psychology of the late nineteenth century, privileges spatial dimensions through which the individual is invited to compose an atemporal image of himself. Historical time and the changes it brings about are seen as a potential menace to the integrity of the oneness of the individual being. The temporal dimension provokes emotive tension, an existential nostalgia for the passing of time, and for the distance that separates the fictitious "I" from the observing self through this passing of time. The only remedy, according to this approach, is for the spectator to look at the impenetrable entity of his own "I" through the mirror of the environment, and to be able to find his "own" inner self thanks to this reflective gaze. This idea probably drew on the studies of another biologist, the ethologist Jacob von Uexküll's research on the behavior of animal communities. According to von Uexküll, a constant in the behavior of individuals and communities is the creation of an *Eigenwelt* through signs perceived in the surrounding space. The *Eigenwelt* appears, therefore, to coincide with that part of *Umwelt* that surrounds the body, and which every individual physically comes in touch with. *Eigenwelt* is the recipient of the objects through which the individual—the animal for the ethologist, the child for the psychologist—acquires a concept of himself that is otherwise unattainable. Without the mapping and bordering of the environment as one's own territory, it is not possible to have an experience of oneself: this was the most politically useful conclusion to be drawn from his findings.

The *Umwelt/Eigenwelt* dichotomy introduced by von Uexküll (1934) in some ways overlaps with the distinction that Haeckel (1866a: 238) had employed between "the physiology of the relationships of animal organisms and the external world (ecology and geography of animals)" and the "physiology of the relationships of the various parts of the animal organism and its other parts (physiology of muscles, nerves, etc.)." It does not therefore sound too astonishing that Uexküll's "environment" remained a subject matter in ecology studies as defined by Haeckel. What appears transformed is the other side of the dichotomy: here we can detect a shift from Haeckel's closed physiological system called "organism" to an open psychophysiological one, which Uexküll calls *Eigenwelt*.

Similar findings by biologists of the nineteenth and early twentieth century, according to whom the creation of any specific individual dimension is the result of interaction rather than introspection, were picked up in quite different ways. On the one hand, George Herbert Mead and other scholars developed a theory that conceived of the mind as an open field of social interaction rather than a personal interior dimension, and of the "I" as a fantasy product of memory and anticipation rather than something present beyond imagination (Mead 1912: 401–06; [1932] 2002: 93–94). On the other hand, an increasing number of scholars of psychology, pedagogy, and philosophy, interpreted the same findings in terms of a "complex set of relationships between humankind and environment, between mind and world, between thinking, being and dwelling" (Bate 2000: 73). As long as humankind and mind remain conceptually separate from a "world" that is seen as their outside "environment," nature will stand for a desire of homecoming, repossession, and identity.

5.2 Identity

Before investigating some aspects of "identity" in further detail, a brief excursus regarding the popularity and the context of the word may be useful. What is the impact of the key terms discussed in the present chapter on public discourse? Using the cumulated internet frequency of the expressions reported in Graph 1 as a rough proxy, one discovers that the use of "nostalgia," "apocalypse," "utopia," and "alienation" is relatively restricted, if clearly not to specialist contexts only, however to a more limited group of interlocutors.

At the same time, the data seem to confirm the great impact of "nature" among web users, followed by the words "god" and "spirit," which also enjoy great popularity on the internet. It should be noted that for one word not represented in Graph 1, yet significantly important not just for this chapter, but for the book as a whole—"history"—a frequency of 3.61 billion was detected, which equals "nature" and "god" summed together, that is, around two-thirds of the total frequency of all the above quoted items. Perhaps it is too arduous to conclude on the basis of such a limited set of data that "history" functions as nodal point of semantic intersection between nature, god, spirit, nostalgia,

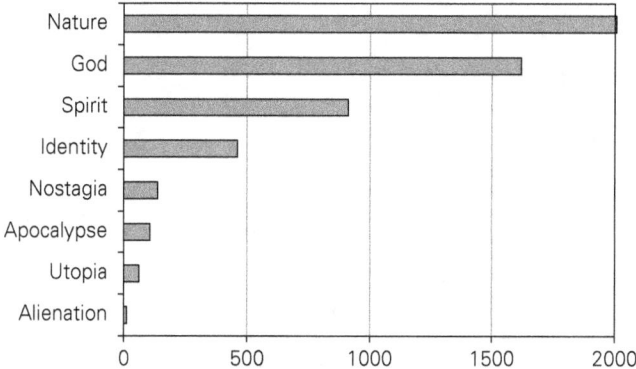

GRAPH 1 *Internet frequency (in millions) of key terms in western public discourse. Source: Google search engine, January 15, 2017*

utopia, alienation, and apocalypse. What seems undeniable, however, is the semantic centrality of "history" for public reasoning on the web, presumably often within the same contexts in which words such as nature, god, spirit, identity, nostalgia, alienation, and apocalypse are also used.

Within the sample, "identity" is a particularly interesting concept, especially when we consider that its present meaning is comparatively new. Today it is hardly possible to open any newspaper or listen to any politician's speech or even a conversation in the street, without encountering the word. Most of the time, it is not used by its speakers or writers as a mathematical expression for a particular form of equation, but is charged with psychological, philosophical, or political connotations and with nostalgic sentiment.

Graph 2 considers the occurrence of "nature" and "identity" in entry titles of the Online Computer Library Center, a worldwide network of over 70,000 libraries. The curve progression over the period 1900–2010 is not a valuable proxy for the terms' frequency in public discourse, as it probably reflects the absolute growth in book and article production over more than a century, as well as possible lacunae in the bibliographical data collection of earlier decades. The comparison with "nature," still the popularity champion today among the terms considered above, allows, however, some interesting inferences regarding the history of "identity's" vogue. The most significant is that the term seems to be an almost absolute newcomer to the broader public of the late twentieth century. As the popularity gap with "nature" still varies between the internet and the book market, it looks as if "identity" was introduced to the broader public by an insistent media spillover of scholarly debate. Whereas during the first three decades its use in book and article titles hovered around only 4 percent of the total use of "nature," it slowly started to increase after 1930, and began rising significantly only after 1960, seemingly spreading beyond specialist milieus.

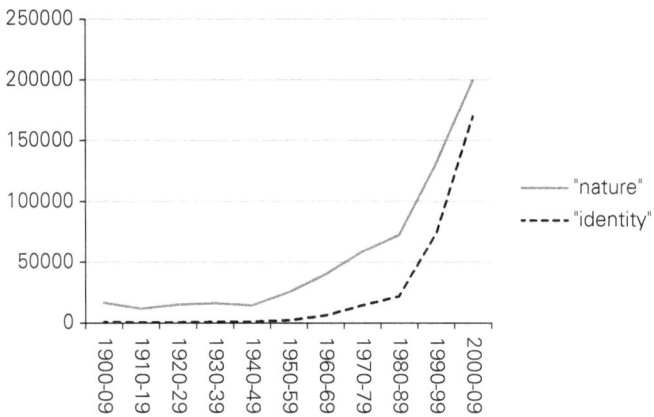

GRAPH 2 *Frequency of "nature" and "identity" as title word entries in OCLC catalogues. Source: WorldCat search engine, January 4, 2015*

From 1980 a sharp increase can be detected, from 30 percent during the 1980s to 56 percent throughout the 1990s, and 85 percent during the first decade of the new millennium. What did this veritable identity mania stem from?

If the use of "identity" began to soar in the 1960s, first among scholars of psychology, sociology, and other disciplines, then spilling out to the broader public during the 1980s, it was likely due to Erik Erikson's book *Young Man Luther*, at least in part. The text introduced the concept of "identity crisis" into a broader debate on personality, community, society, and history. The author reconstructed Luther's life according to a Freudian scheme of "steps in psychological maturation which every man must take" to achieve the "safe establishment of an identity as a worker and a man." Erikson underlined the construed character of "identity," as any young human "must detect some meaningful resemblance between what he has come to see in himself and what his sharpened awareness tells him others judge and expect him to be" (Erikson [1958] 1993: 14, 213). In the words of Horowitz (2014: 102), it is the awareness "of the self as a continuous and, usually, coherent entity that perceives, thinks, feels, decides, and acts. Conscious identity rests upon the belief structures of unconscious self-organization," and Erikson had the ambition to unveil these structures in the case of young Luther.

Nonetheless, young Luther's personality was not "deconstructed" by Erikson in terms of what Pierre Bourdieu (1986) would characterize as a "biographical illusion," consisting in the attempt of a person to give his life a transcendent sense through a coherent history of himself, full of events and gestures all aimed at a superior purpose which goes beyond his own end. According to the French sociologist, the illusion consists of a coherence that is fictitious rather than real, but which is, however, awarded by a society inclined to assign a safely established identity license to anyone capable of giving a coherent narrative account of his own life. Whereas for Erikson this coherence was not at all illusionary, but essential, just as the underlying finalist narrative was. Apparently, the hard labor of fortification and reconstruction was a matter of adolescence, and not destined to last beyond entry into adulthood, as is instead claimed by Dan McAdams (1999: 486), according to whom "the life storymaking process will continue apace through the healthy adult years and well into old age." Man as defined by Erikson (similarly to Freud) just needs to "mature," seeing as it is in becoming an adult that he can safely define his own identity, unless he carries it out by falling backward and succumbing to pathological regression. It looks as if he is forced to retrace what are seen to be the collective stages of human development, which go from the primitive state to the civilized state of humanity, all in the compressed period of one single life. The path to maturity, riddled with crises and not immune to failure, for Erikson therefore represents "a developmental root for the basic human values of faith, will, conscience, and reason—all necessary in rudimentary form for the identity which crowns childhood" (Erikson [1958] 1993: 254). Man is then made, and if all goes as planned by western philosophies of history, he even comes out pretty well, as he is supposed to.

However, if something goes wrong, a strong discomfort surfaces, as Charles Taylor points out: "Without a cohesive identity, one is on the edge of crisis: not only are we unhappy, but in fact incapable of behaving normally." According to this philosopher of community, in the premodern era there was no identity problem because the meaning of the life cycle was seen as premeditated. "The modern identity, on the other hand, although its basic elements may indeed be predetermined, must be accepted by the individual. My identity belongs to me only in as much as being accepted by me, something which leaves room for negotiations with my environment, my history, my destiny" (Taylor 1995: 11, 13).

Taylor's reflections on that point replicate the thought of early-twentieth-century German *Heimat* philosophers, such as Eduard Spranger, Kurt Stavenhagen, Martin Heidegger, and Ernst Jünger. Their concern was the individual and the "acceptance of his identity" on the basis of a "free" choice between keeping faith to, or betraying, one's self. As in their eyes technical civilization produced man's estrangement from being, the question arose as to how every single individual could tackle the existential loneliness of a senseless life. In their view *Heimat*, that is, the reunion of nature and community, was the element that enabled a certain encounter between existence and being. As Jünger ([1959] 1991: 52–53) stated, every individual grasps intuitively that he possesses a "unique destiny and, consequently, a peculiar position in the universe." This intuitive understanding, however, evokes a feeling of absence. According to Heidegger (1960: 27), "*Heimat* does not exist on this earth. *Heimat* is at each case a specific one, and as such destiny." It is the *je meinige Heimat*, the innermost place of the self, his part of the whole and its center of *Dasein*. As such, it represents the potentiality for our being in the world, "even if in the mode of inauthenticity" (Heidegger [1927] 1962: 224). As Stavenhagen (1939: 107–08) added, "through *Heimat* man achieves the closest attainable vicinity to being." Therefore, *Heimat* is another word for the place "that we have been assigned to in the cosmos." It is important to underline that the abovementioned thinkers did not envisage a return to an "authentic" togetherness, which was fantasized to have been present in pretechnical times; rather, they envisaged a compelling choice of keeping faith to oneself, that is, to one's own non-otherness. What could be conceived in this way actually was a community of nothing, "inhabited by an absence of subjectivity, of identity, of property" and completely devoid of meaning, as Esposito (2010: 138) explains. What made this community discourse so vigorously political was the idea of "existential loners" who shared with millions of their fellow-loners the same feeling of *absence*, that is, of something that *is not* but *should be*.

Why did these themes so powerfully re-emerge between the 1970s and the 1990s under the booming label "identity"? A standard explanation would be that if something goes wrong in the development of so many men and women, the pathology must also be attributed to society. Or even that the pathology in fact *is* society, according to a variant of such an explanation, which is in fact close to becoming mainstream. Crucially, "society" here is understood in terms of a Tönniesian set of relationships among individuals, which is driven away from shared forms of living by "modernity." If community means "sharing of a common history, culture, and a heritage of values and symbols absorbed from birth, profound enough to determine the shaping of the individuals' identity" (Pazé 2004: 12), then an identity crisis, however individual, is at the same time a mass phenomenon and as such collective. And if a "lack of identity" is not a good way to live, and this deficit depends on a social pathology—like technology, consumerism, loss of cultural memory—rather than just a personal one, then the remedy appears to consist of a "return" to communitarian forms of living. As Zygmunt Bauman explains, this communitarian revival is in response to "a most genuine and poignant issue of the pendulum shifting radically—perhaps too far away—from the security pole in the dyad of *sine qua non* human values. For this reason, the communitarian gospel can count on a large audience-in-waiting." Up until the second half of the 1970s, a territorial bond connected workforce and capital in the west, making it possible to lead a life which was relatively protected by decent salaries and public-welfare benefits. The loosening and eventually the dissolution of that bond during the neoliberal period of globalization, and the "seminal changes subsumed under the rubric of liquid modernity," caused those solid and long-lasting social ties to be dragged into an abyss, along with any self-certainty (Bauman 2000:170–71, 184).

Similarly to what happened to ecology, in this new season the community, despite bearing the historically indelible mark of a right-wing discourse, also expanded to the left wing of the political spectrum. Here it was acknowledged that "a positive answer to the question of whether an attachment to the place of origin (in German, *Heimat* means place of origin)—or in any case the place where one feels at home—belongs to the fundamental values." These were values that "throughout the complex societies of today" must be defended against the "irreversible standardization," or the "eradication" through forced mobility, the "triumph of calculated rationality," the "eradication of the welfare-state," the "loss of the features of communitarian living and the spread of a sense of self-insecurity." Opposing these developments means preserving an "environment with which the subject has acquired deep familiarity," and rebuilding it as a territory "of trust and hope" and as a field of "subjective and social action," as personal identity is seen as being "intimately connected to the participation of the individual in the symbolic system that we call culture" (Pasinato 2000: 3–6).

Since the earlier days of the identity discourse, around the end of the nineteenth century and the early twentieth, the concept was sporadically used in the later sense of a "We" related to space, history, and community (Holmén 2015: 15–17). But similar uses were not yet universally accepted. As Ludwig Wittgenstein wrote it was obvious that identity could not define a relation between objects.

> One could of course say that in fact *only a* has this relation to *a*, but in order to express this we should need the sign of identity itself. . . . Roughly speaking: to say of *two* things that they are identical is nonsense, and to say of *one* thing that it is identical with itself is to say nothing. (Wittgenstein 1922: 69–70)

Such statements, which should have been interpreted in the wider context of Type Theory, stimulated a long sequence of critiques such as: "But who said it had to do with two *objects*? Identity is characterized precisely by the fact it is a relationship with the Self, and not with a stranger" (Beckmann 1996: 374). Also according to Heidegger, Wittgenstein missed the point:

> The more fitting formulation of the principle of identity "A = A" would accordingly mean not only that every A is itself the same; but rather that every A is itself the same with itself. Sameness implies the relation of "with" that is, a mediation, a connection, a synthesis: the unification into

a unity. This is why throughout the history of western thought identity appears as unity. But that unity is by no means the stale emptiness of that which, in itself without relation, persists in monotony. . . . Since the era of speculative Idealism, it is no longer possible for thinking to represent the unity of identity as mere sameness, and to disregard the mediation that prevails in unity. Wherever this is done, identity is represented only in an abstract manner. (Heidegger 1969: 24–25)

Heidegger raised an eminent question: the inadequacy of conceiving of identity as mere sameness. The dialectics of identity can, however, be "resolved" in two opposite directions. One consists of detecting the impossibility of building personal and collective "identities" without "swallowing" the Other, and absorbing it into the "I." As the anthropologist Francesco Remotti shows, building "identity does not entail simply reducing, removing variety, marginalizing alterity; it also means appealing to, utilizing, introducing and incorporating alterity (whether it is desired, or not, whether it is stated or not) in the formative and metabolic processes of identity." Identity therefore "needs to be continuously negotiated with time first of all, as well as with the others" (Remotti 1996: 63), seeing as we do that alterity inevitably resurfaces through those same operations that construct and reconstruct identity. As if invoking identity as a condition which is dramatically missing were the best way to create an unsolvable and perpetual problem. Clearly uncomfortable with this trend of the postmodern age, Remotti gave a programmatic title to his essay: *Against Identity*.

Heidegger went in the other direction. What he suggested against Wittgenstein's logic was not that the term "identity" merges objects, which are different, ambiguously into one, as Remotti suggests. On the contrary, he maintained that "identity" signals the belonging together of what is artificially divided and forced to drift apart. In other words, he denounced the absence of identity, which he places at the core of the present disease. Joan Stambaugh commented that the

> manner in which man and Being concern each other in the world of technology Heidegger calls the framework. The framework is far more real than all atomic energy and all machines. But it is nothing necessarily ultimate. It could be a prelude to what Heidegger calls the event of appropriation. The event of appropriation is the realm in which man and Being reach each other in their very core. They lose the determinations placed upon them by metaphysics. Metaphysics thinks identity as a fundamental trait of Being. For Heidegger, Being and thought belong to an identity whose acting nature stems from the letting *belong* together which is called the event of appropriation. (Stambaugh 1969: 13–14)

5.3 Alienation

Away from home, away from nature: "Western man's alienation from nature" (Bate 2000: ix) is the great "tragedy." Western hope relies on homecoming, identity, authenticity, whether or not that may be achieved through "linear" or "cyclical" temporality, through a "historical" or a "natural" path to redemption, which eventually allows access of the realm of authentic being. Regarding the possibilities of redemption, once taken for granted, skeptical, if not pessimistic, expectations tend to prevail since the late nineteenth century. Outside the realm of sciences, "linear temporality" is mostly associated with teleology, transcendent meaning, and eschatology. "Cyclic temporality" is instead associated with "nature," that is, determinism, reversibility, steadiness, equilibrium, perfection. But without the divine design instilled into human soul and reason, "nature" also means unreflective purposelessness. A purposelessness that scares is what remains after the "death of God"; Nietzsche states this as: "Let us think this thought in its most terrible form: existence as it is, without meaning or aim, yet recurring inevitably without any finale of nothingness: '*the eternal recurrence*'" (Nietzsche [1887] 1967: 35).

Nietzsche's "nihilism" turns out to be an extremely frightened anti-nihilism, a mere horror of nothingness. What will happen to Man if history no longer has a transcendent meaning? Will any form of redemption or return ever be possible? As Kermode ([1966] 2000: 5) explains, "apocalyptic thought belongs to rectilinear rather than cyclical views of the world, though this is not a sharp distinction." Also Nietzsche seems to remember that every redemption in fact resembles the ending of a cycle. Perhaps then, the eternal return can become a return to eternity. "Nietzsche intended on bringing Man back . . . and housing him within nature and the cosmos. If Man were to readapt to the cosmic laws rather than lose himself in the impractical labyrinths of religious views on history and morality, he would regain the properties of the natural world, including the innocence of Becoming" (Danzer 2011: 135). In the context of western eschatology, Nietzsche's proposal is not so exceptional as it was often depicted, as according to all its variants, reunification and the "event of appropriation" coincide in a moment that must signal the end of history and extend beyond that end.

Before taking a closer look at this event, we should consider what opposes appropriation or repossession throughout historical times: alienation. According to Heidegger, man is thrown out of Being into existence, and this provokes his desire for identity as he suffers the difficulty of attaining the entirety to which he belongs, from which he was estranged, and from which he feels attracted. This generates a feeling of estrangement and displacement, as psychiatrist Eugenio Borgna (2004: 59) observes: "The alien soul on earth seems to me to be the unfathomable figure that stands at the root of all nostalgia." Svetlana Boym (2003: 9) also added that modern nostalgia hinges on a sense of double estrangement: as a "pathological" sadness that is expressed through "a feeling of grief for the impossibility of a mythical return," or as a desire for redemption which, through an apocalyptical catharsis, gives hope of a return to the "edenic unity of time and space before entering into history."

As has already been pointed out, the theme of the soul seen as a stranger on earth had originally been used by right-wing cultural circles. An important contribution in the popularization of the same topic in left-wing intellectual milieus came from György Lukács, who agreed with Novalis that the "I" is still incomplete and cannot fully grasp the transcendent meaning of its existence. He shares the *not-yet* contended "longing [*Sehnsucht*] for the great synthesis between unity and universality" (Lukács 1911: 106), even though he then criticizes the romantic poetical strategy of offering an illusory resolution. Similarly, the bourgeois novel is "the epic of an era in which the broad totality of life is no longer apparent, and so the vital immanence of meaning is jeopardized, although the mental disposition of this era is pending towards totality nonetheless" (Lukács [1916] 1982: 47). The alienating loss of meaning catapults the life of Man into a state which Lukács describes as being a transcendental homelessness. Anatoly Vasil'evich Lunacharsky, the first Soviet People's Commissar of Education under Lenin, maintained that socialism should "take over and ennoble, not destroy" what religion had expressed, namely "man's need for community, his yearning to transcend himself, and his unity with nature and all mankind" (quoted from Thrower 1983: 112). His work of 1908–11, *Religiia i sotsializm*, is considered by Roland Boer (2014) significant for a tradition of Marxist engagement with religion that anticipated later works by Ernst Bloch. After the Great War, similar concepts penetrated an ever-increasing left-wing culture which was learning to share this yearning for the utopian place where Man is to find himself after overwhelming the alienating conditions that surround him. During the period between 1938 and 1947 Ernst Bloch (1959: 1608) summarized his *Prinzip Hoffnung* with the utopian logos of *Heimat*. It is in fact this word which he uses to indicate the *not-yet* of his utopia, and which closes his dense philosophical dissertation after more than 1600 pages. Like Nietzsche and Heidegger, also Lukács, Lunacharsky and Bloch mourned the "death of God," that is, the disappearance of a transcendent purpose of life and history.

These are only some of the rivulets through which a romantic concept of alienation and a nostalgic sense of utopia flow toward political and cultural areas that were once characterized by an apparently unconditioned trust in the future. Now these same political and intellectual circles welcomed the intuitions of what stood out in the nineteenth century first as conservative and romantic notions, and later as nationalist and populist slogans. In the second half of the twentieth century these concepts become so widespread that they came to be translated within actions against the cultural leveling effects of globalization and the destruction of ecological equilibriums. Today they are manifested in a sort of neocommunitarian reformism, striving to develop "the conditions required for realizing *Heimat* . . . which must be carried out by defending cultural singularities from whatsoever homologation," and which ends up disheartened because "the potential of *Heimat* has been exploited by nationalism" (Pasinato 2000: 7, 9).

The meanings of homelessness, of nothingness, and of purposelessness within the (anti-)"nihilist" position are so similar that they overlap under some points of view. For existentialists like Sartre and Camus "nothingness is the source of not only absolute freedom but also existential horror and emotional anguish" (Pratt n.d.). The lament of alienation, which in fact grew in the wake of Nietzsche's writings, seems to reach its peak in the discourse on the postmodern and global era, where difference is said to be substituted by indifference, and history, memory and time supplanted by speed. However, this "dizzying whirl of the acceleration of reality" (Virilio 2005: 3) runs idle so as to produce a permanent present, de facto a standstill which inhibits any move toward a foreseeable future, and annihilates any expectation of the better. It is a never-ending, stressful today that has been stripped of any past or future, of any expectation, certainty, or hope of goodness. This speed represents the mere overexcitement of a techno-culture suspended in an empty and fragmented present. It is the age of networks in a state of continuous decay and rehashing, of indifferent liquefaction of differences, of a breaking down of barriers, of the large and powerful global disorder, and of the transitory nomad and virtual communities of the cyberspace, which are by now populated by a humanity pulverized into an accumulation of bytes. The philosophers of postmodernity accuse their era of expressing only inhumane rights whereby the evaluation of moral good and evil is handed over to extra-human mechanisms. A present that is only present with no future expectations, denies what "we call human in humans" (Lyotard 1991: 3). This is the dramatic diagnosis of the *philosophes* of postmodernity, which states that we are living in an apocalyptic era which is also, already, and at the same time, a post-apocalyptic era, in as much as any possibility of Goodness has already been eradicated.

The absent-minded cacophonous chaos of a fragmentary and invalidating coexistence between past, present, and future may well be a postmodern era, but it is not yet one of post-alienation. According to these readings, the suspension of history, of memory, and of time that we are currently experiencing has not been able to delete the modern disease. Although it has now been pushed outside of time toward the space where an accelerated present is not going anywhere, Benjamin's Angelus Novus still has "its face facing the past" and intends on continuing to "hold back, awaken the dead and reconnect the shattered pieces." Why? The reason is that the "storm that snagged his wings, and which is so strong that the angel can no longer close them" continues to inevitably take breath "from paradise" (Benjamin [1940] 2003: 12). This is also the hope of Scott Lash (1998: 159–60), according to whom the angel of history, pushed by the winds of progress toward the de-futurized future of the postmodern world, continues to look back with melancholy "to past objects, to disused things, to the ruins of the city." He looks back "on not just the *Erlebnis* of individual memory, but onto and through the retrieval of collective memory, into the *Erfahrung* of the collective symbolic and imaginary. . . . Through his work of mourning, through his chronic inability to forget, the melancholic may be our best hope of retrieval of any sort of politics of value." It appears that under the smoking ruins of post-modernity a past which brings with it a promise of redemption still smolders.

Through much of postmodern condemnation, an incipient hope for an anti-relativist, neocommunitarian, or even authoritarian future seems to shine, which in fact insistently invades, and ever-increasingly adds to the determination of cultural and political discourse of the "liquid modernity" of our era: "The community of the communitarian gospel is a home writ large (the *family* home, not a *found* home or a *made* home, but a home *into which one is born*, so that one could not trace one's origin, one's 'reason to exist', in any other place)" (Bauman 2000: 171). While after facing the loss of confidence in the future during the late-modern age nothing seemed to be left to the westerners but to agree on the *Prinzip Hoffnung* along with Bloch or to establish that "only a God can save us" along with Heidegger ([1966] 1976: 193), Max Oelschlaeger (1991: 344) is confident that "a postmodern hierophany is at least possible and that Postmodernism will entail some old-new image of the human project."

> Today we are thousands of years away from the Paleolithic mind, the modern ego swollen with pride in our cultural achievements. We cannot see the heavens wheeling overhead in their cosmic course—our city lights and smog have rendered them indistinct. And from inside our human-made habitats we cannot feel the winds and rain, smell the flowers and animal herds, or hear the running water and singing birds. Yet we remain, in spite of the myths of modernity that blind us to primordial insights into the mystery of existence, the human animal, bound with the cosmic flux. . . . Through space and time speaks the voice of that nineteenth-century genius Henry David Thoreau: *In wildness lies the preservation of the world*. Only when we are lost—and isn't the testimony of the twentieth century evidence that humankind is lost amid the very splendor and potential of the civilization it has created?—can we begin to find ourselves. (Oelschlaeger 1991: 333–34)

Oelschlaeger (1991: 353) ultimately wonders: "Is salvation possible? . . . Is there hope for the plant and animal people? Is there hope for us all? These are questions that must be answered by the postmodern mind, for only through that exercise of consciousness can our modern dilemma be transcended." As can also be grasped from these quotes, along with the persistence of preserving a hope of a return to Nature, to the Garden of Eden, to God, to the One, to Being, to Communion and Community, to Authenticity and Full Humanity, the difficulties are carefully elaborated under the sign of doubt, and of premonition of apocalypse.

Since the latter implies the revelation of a truth that was latent "from the beginning," a historical tale which takes inspiration from eschatological hope, yet one that does not cultivate nostalgic visions at the same time, is hardly conceivable. According to La Capra (2004: 47), "at the limit the utopian may be empty, vacuous, or totally open-ended and even defended as such insofar one desires a complete rupture with the existing conditions and a radically different form of life or civilization." Perhaps in similar borderline conditions, all of history that had come before would be abhorred without regret, without, however, being forgotten, but equally and necessarily narrated in the name of, and in conflict with, the hope of overcoming it. It is not easy, however, to imagine what could ever foster in the western mind such a hope outside of a ratifying memory that is tied to the desire of a return.

We could furthermore wonder whether at least Derrida's messianic wait without messiah is untainted by the disease of nostalgia. Derrida (2002: 70–81) believes that messianism represents a universal structure of human experience. All of humanity should share that encapsulation of anticipation and anxiety that is in itself neither religious nor utopian. This slightly emphatic statement of Derrida's reminds us of a present that is "shifting" between Kosellek's space of experience and horizon of expectation, and to which Ricœur (2004: 381–82) refers when he explains that: "People of the past once were, like us, subjects of initiative, of retrospection, and of prospection. The epistemological consequences of this consideration are substantial. Knowing that people of the past formulated expectations, predictions, desires, fears, and projects is to fracture historical determinism by retrospectively reintroducing contingency into history."

If contingency and indeterminism were to be understood in terms of autopoiesis (Maturana and Varela 1972), or of the self-organization of complex systems (Prigogine 1980), it would be convincing to claim that here nostalgia is irrelevant. The author goes on nonetheless: "If, in fact, the facts are ineffaceable, if one can no longer undo what has been done, nor make it so that what has happened did not occur, on the other hand, the sense of what has happened is not fixed once and for all" (Ricœur 2004: 381). The construction of the past is therefore not supposed to begin with a new event "which in its relation to other events gives structure to time" (Mead [1932] 2002: 51), but with the nostalgic narrative recovery of a memory of possible, desired, but unattained, yet perhaps still desirable, past futures. Historical indeterminism, in this case, seems entirely relegated to the realm of sense-making. In western discourse, the exclusiveness assigned to the "meaning" as that which builds time through narration seems to trace back to the dichotomy between history and nature, spirit and matter, soul and body, man and beast, already widely discussed in this book. It is a concept, which conflicts with a vision such as Mead's, whereby human knowledge and its practical results are inherent to a broader evolution of *Φύσις*, in which a retrospective determination of the past is an intrinsic principle that can be conceived of as existing also independently from human cognition and language (Joas 1985: 178). On the contrary, history remains at the center of western reflections, yet it is not understood as an intrinsic reflexive principle of change in all complex environments, but as a way of assigning to that change a meaning that transcends the presence and the contingency of the act, and engulfs its experience with a sense of incompleteness and loss.

Right from the beginning, therefore, melancholy has constantly accompanied even the most optimistic visions of the future. Thus, not even Rostow was able to avoid a melancholic hypothesis concerning what could happen after the fulfillment of the hedonistic and consumerist cravings felt by men and women who had emerged from millennia of poverty and scarcity: "Beyond lies the question of whether or not secular spiritual stagnation will arise, and, if it does, how man might fend it off" (Rostow [1960] 1991: 12). The fear of such a stagnation seems to be a more general western distress that can hardly be healed by an "active engagement" of the organism "with its environment" within the unspiritual horizon of "an unplanned evolution" (Joas 1985: 169). Neither can it be reconciled with the equally simple idea of inevitable extinction, both on an individual level and as a species, as it would be in the most plausible hypothesis of observable things. However, no, that singular animal elected by nature in order to overcome itself must never die. Mankind, which represents both the self-reflective part, and spiritual counterpart, of nature, "cannot acquiesce in its total disappearance without biologically contradicting itself" (Teilhard de Chardin [1959] 2004: 298).

5.4 Apocalypse

Apocalyptic thinking tends to put all beginnings under the spell of an "end" that has to be understood in its dual significance of cessation and purpose. We may say that this dual significance informs the innermost conception of western eschatology and philosophy of history. The expected revelation of the last hidden truths of human destiny induces both hope and fear, however real or metaphoric, predetermined or moving, the revelatory "event" may be imagined. On the one hand, the hope for redemption projects human life optimistically beyond the very horizon of history; on the other, it contains a pessimistic dread of cessation and nothingness. This is because in western tradition, however open or predetermined a future might be imagined, the "final outcome" of history is thought to be dialectically dependent on the erratic behavior of the animal that was gifted with reason and free will, and of whom we cannot trust that he will actually succeed in fulfilling his transcendent purpose. "Consequently, the 'apocalyptic imagination' . . . has a tendency to conceive the world in starkly dualistic terms" (Walliss 2004: 16) and divide it into the forces of good who know their duty and the forces of evil who deny it. It easily induces a readiness for destruction and violence in the name of good. In the era of nuclear armament the endeavor to achieve redemption from evil may in its ultimate paradoxical consequence drastically anticipate the "natural" extinction of our species.

Before elaborating further on this somewhat worrisome perspective, it may be worth reflecting on the range of variants in which apocalyptic thinking pervades our life. It is important to underline that in eschatological terms, both the denial of human extinction by nature and its translation into a merely spiritual survival have a similar function. According to the "heterodox" Teilhard de Chardin, nature is different from the most truly human dimension, given that nature can transcend itself by reasoning about itself precisely through humanity. Nature is therefore something else when compared with culture and artifacts, with woolen textiles, synthetic materials, computers, machines, polluted refuse, and cities of men. In order to nurse the fullness of their being human, men must in any case form a pact with nature and defeat the all-consuming monster in them which incessantly presses the accelerator of entropy, removing the foundations of life from future generations. This reference to future generations represents the hope for humanity to achieve eternal life: "In order that the end of Mankind may be deferred *sine die* we are asked to believe in a species that will drag on and spread itself indefinitely" (Teilhard de Chardin [1959] 2004: 302).

Spirit and matter, god and nature, soul and body, remain separate from one another also in Enlightenment and rationalist thought, as long as "humanity" exists, that is, as long as it preserves its difference and autonomy from both and as a mixture of both. Through the emancipation of the secular man and the transnatural temporality of mankind that Koselleck talks of, the end becomes *immanent* and so "has perhaps lost its naïve *imminence,*" as Kermode ([1966] 2000: 6–7) observed, underlining, however, that there can hardly be any escape from under its shadow. This holds certainly for individuals, who "need fictive concords with origins and end" to make "sense of their span." When this sense consists of a contribution to the immortality of mankind, that is, the infinite procrastination of its end through increasing humanization, also the modern transformation of imminence into immanence reveals its eschatological character. For Nicholas Georgescu-Roegen (1976: 5) conceiving of mankind as an immortal species is more than anything a loss of realism. The father of bio-economics observed that it seems "below man's dignity to accept the verdict . . . that the most certain fate of mankind is the same as that of any other species, namely extinction." The ideologically instilled need for sense-making, however, renders such a disenchanted realism idle. The same need assigns to both the secularized illusion of endlessness and the millenarian sense of ending a quite similar function within the overall rational of apocalyptic thinking.

Another example comes from the present debate on global warming. Dipesh Chakrabarty advances "the proposition that anthropogenic explanations of climate change spell the collapse of the age-old humanist distinction between natural history and human history." What is said to risk a collapse here is the artifice of western thinking that splits Φύσις into spirit and matter, body and soul, nature and culture, beast and human, and so forth. Were it to really occur, it would probably be perceived as a conceptual confusion rather than a conceptual rectification. It would seem dramatic, because conceiving of humankind as of a biological species would cede ground, as Chakrabarty believes, "to a more deterministic view of the world" where little room remains for free will. And it would seem apocalyptic, because according to scholars of deep history, given the human destructive potential capable to menace all live on the planet, "humans constitute a particular kind of species." So it is, once again, thanks to their peculiarity that they can, "in the process of dominating other species, acquire the status of a geologic force. Humans, in other words, have become a natural condition, at least today" (Chakrabarty 2009: 201, 214). This return to nature looks like a repossession of the apocalyptic kind indeed.

Of course, there are many variants in which the "event of appropriation" can be located, on the humanity asymptote which is tangent to the end at infinity, or in the infinity which extends beyond the end of history. There seems to be no great theoretical concern regarding the natural end of the species for Father Teilhard, whose concept of nature appears to be similar to that of Schelling ([1799] 1858: 279), who wrote: "If all is reciprocally sustained and supported in every organic totality, then this organization must preexist with respect to its parts; the whole could not be born from its parts, but its parts must have been born from the whole." Teilhard de Chardin ([1959] 2004: 256, 303) also starts from the idea of the design being preceded by the design's creator, and therefore, human history with all its artifacts is only the historical progression and culminating phase of the natural search for a return to the original unity between creation and creator. It is on account of this that he can write "that Evolution is rebounding on itself through the fact of human totalization," and can consequently highlight "the profound identity existing between the forces of civilization and those of evolution." For Teilhard de Chardin, *homo sapiens*, with his culture, artifacts, synthetic materials, cities, and so on, becomes a technological inventor "of a collective global mind" (Black 2010: 83) who heralds a movement toward the recomposition of all the parts in the One, and therefore toward going beyond these parts. Here the autonomy of humanity and of its time is not preserved as it is in the secularized and Enlightenment tradition, but this same humanity vanishes, overcome, and remunerated by a return to God. As Schelling ([1799] 1858: 309) had remarked, when there is no longer any self-distinction of the absolute in opposites, "identity, absolute tranquility" dominate. With humanity having returned and being absorbed from this primordial identity, for Teilhard de Chardin ([1959] 2004: 310), the "astonishing adventure of the world will have ended" in a "now tranquil ocean."

Up until here, therefore, we have that which has been recognized by authoritative sources as an updated interpretation of Christian worship (Ratzinger 2000: 29). As such, it might also be seen as a remodeling of that vision which provided the blueprint of western philosophies of history, both secular and atheist philosophies included. And it might suggest that the cycle of dominant "secular versions of apocalyptic myth has come to an end" because "old-time religion has re-emerged at the heart of global conflict" (Gray 2008: 260). Whether John Gray's forecast will be confirmed in the near future or not, is, however, not so central to the conceptual history of western ideology. As already Löwith had suggested, the most profound characterization of western tradition does not consist of a description of *which* transcendent meaning it assigns to history, but of the acknowledgment of the fact that it is assigning a meaning to history *at all*. A similar point was also made by Teilhard when he wrote,

> Is the Universe utterly pointless, or are we to accept that it has a meaning, a future, a purpose? On this fundamental question Mankind is already virtually divided into the two camps of those who deny that there is any significance or value in the state of Being, and therefore no Progress; and those, on the other hand, who believe in the possibility and the rewards of a higher state of consciousness. (Teilhard de Chardin [1959] 2004: 33–34)

The clearly spiritual configuration of this statement must not distract us from the more general significance of finalistic thought for western ideology, which, as in Kant, harmonizes natural order with the needs to have a moral life. An intrinsic finality to be successfully deployed over time also dwells in the elements of the Enlightenment philosophy of nature, and from it originates a sense of responsibility that men are obliged to accept. A "historical conscience" therefore holds men responsible without promising them any immediate return. We thus see a dialectic materialist philosopher such as Alexander Spirkin (1983: chapter 5/7) writing that "an important form of responsibility is responsibility for the future, both near and distant, which is built on the sense of responsibility for the present and the past."

According to Hans Jonas, there is a human duty arising from procreation "that is involved in a responsibility for future mankind. It charges us, in the first place, with ensuring that there *be* a future mankind." However, it cannot just descend from procreation in the way in which a similar duty is taken over by procreating animals. One of Jonas's "imperatives" declares: "Act so that the effects of your action are compatible with the permanence of genuine human life" (Jonas 1984: 11, 40). It is worth humankind surviving because of its genuine character, which is more than just the biologically intrinsic imperative of survival; the genuine character of this species consists in its very capacity for taking responsibility on the basis of free will. Man therefore has a mission to fulfill, which transcends mere survival and which, as Reyes Mate (2006: 34) explains, links back to the double dimension in the ethics of responsibility: Kant's dimension based on the freedom of choice in obeying or violating moral law, and Hegel's, which considers the future consequences. Jonas's imperative, he argues, "would be the final episode in this Hegelian view." Seeger (2010: 125) adds "that the relation between the responsible and those for whom he is responsible is not reciprocal but one-sided" as future generations will not have the possibility to punish the past ones for their misdeeds. The judgment of their deeds applies to moral law, which derives, if not from God, then from the final order and final purpose of Nature.

Since taking responsibility is considered to be an option only made available to humans, according to Herder, the supreme finality of history can in fact be summarized within the very concept "humanity." The *History, Humanity, Responsibility* curriculum title developed by the Holocaust Museum Houston (n.d.) effectively highlights this nexus. Intuitively, it is difficult not to share the idea that the memory of an event as traumatic as that recorded by the Holocaust Museum should serve as a way of making future generations feel responsible so that such an event should never repeat itself. On account of this, however, is it necessary to appeal to concepts such as history and humanity? One of the problems in fact lies within the polyvalent and problematic practical implications that these concepts manifest on the political level.

The appeal for responsibility in the face of progress, history, and humanity has always been part of the mobilizing rhetorical arsenal throughout the twentieth century. In 1914, for example, German Social Democrats justified their support of the imminent war by asserting that "the terror of an enemy invasion looms over us" and that "our people and our future of freedom risk greatly, if not altogether, should a Russian despotism that is already stained with the blood of its own people reach victory. We must stop this danger and bring our culture and the independence of our country to safety" (Reichstag 1916: 8–9). Here an often-repeated standard discursive structure becomes apparent: first, the charge against the enemy of despotism and *inhuman* brutality, obviously placing the Us on higher cultural and civil ground; second, the conjecture that this enemy has aggressive intentions and is ready to go to war from one moment to the next; third and last, an appeal to whoever needs to finance, or go to their death, to take *responsibility* in the face of *history* for the wealth and freedom of *future generations*.

When wars were waged between European or western powers, this type of argumentation was more or less symmetrically encountered on both sides. Following 1989, however, the Good was often declared to stand united on one side, the Evil on the other. With the strength of this conviction behind them, western powers militarily intervened more than once with the argument of needing to take responsibility in order to protect defenseless populations against despots whose actions were compared to the crimes of the Second World War. Various "new Hitlers" appeared on western television screens, passing the relay torch among them during the race of propaganda campaigns. This media curtain fire over the representative of Evil of the moment is by now a habitual practice in preparation of military interventions. The wake of death and destruction that such interventions leave behind do not seem to nullify the contentment of the western public, who remain convinced of doing, or supporting, "the right thing." At the most, they grieve for the fallen victims as unavoidable necessities in the fight for the Good. It, however, goes without saying that the protagonists of these slaughters, which are, when discovered, attributed to errors made in good faith, do normally not need to take responsibility in front of any *super partes* judge.

Similarly, and as was already mentioned in the previous chapter, the forced movement of the juridical axis from international law to human rights is backed by the "responsibility to protect" campaign. The two most important aims of such a campaign, as their spearheads declare, are "changing the paradigm of civilian protection from a right to a responsibility, and legitimizing the use of force as a last resort" (Human Rights Center 2007: 2). Western military interventions "in the periphery" and in conditions of "asymmetrical war" have been defined by Herfried Münkler (2004: 184) as wars of pacification. "At the base of these interventions are geo-strategic, economic, and humanitarian motives, and it is often difficult to decide which of these factors was the decisive one in deciding to intervene." All things considered, it indeed seems to be futile to distinguish between these factors given that under a western point of view, everything that strengthens the west automatically increases the rate of "genuine humanity" on the planet.

However, perhaps the idea of the twenty-first century being the century of asymmetrical wars will not end up as having been so well predicted. The dream of progressing humanity in steps, by cutting evil into slices like meat, so we could say, seems more an idea belonging to the likes of independent intellectuals than one of strategic think tanks, of those who really count. The latter in fact do not at all exclude a confrontation between the major state powers, but on the contrary, more than likely think of this as an ultimate battle, and plan accordingly. It is still the case here that strategic, economic, and humanitarian motives blend together so as to become indistinguishable. However, with all the asymmetry among the military powers, which in fact continues to work in favor of "genuine humanity," the game radically changes for practical reasons. Should war break out between nuclear powers, even the weakest adversary possesses the capacity for reacting sufficiently so as to go down the path toward Armageddon, perhaps within hours or even minutes. Here the words of a man of peace such as Teilhard de Chardin ([1959] 2004: 256) once again come to mind, in which he predicted the inevitability of a final conflict:

> Again, if it be true that Evolution is rebounding on itself through the fact of human totalization, it must, becoming conscious, fasten passionately upon itself: which is to say that Man to progress further, will need to be sustained by a powerful collective faith. According to whether we believe in it or reject it, the totalizing process, from which there is no escape, will either infuse new life into us or destroy us.

Upon which theoretical fields and in which areas of action can the seeds of similar eschatological discourses on human totalization take root? Only those concerning the recycling of refuse, the rights of rocks, and the conservation of energy for future generations? Or that of prayer, and of humble and faithful anticipation of the end of all time? Or in others also? It remains an unsettling question mark. We are living in an era of massive destructive potential of nuclear weapons, exceedingly enough for a multiple destruction of human and other forms of life on earth. The Mutual Assured Destruction (MAD) is the deterrence rational of great nuclear powers. Unfortunately it works as a peacekeeping deterrent only until all sides agree that a cathartic destruction is neither a desirable nor an obligatory passage for the victory of the Right and the Good they think they represent. Once political and military decision makers stick to an ideology that makes them believe the contrary, things might drastically change.

> We have explosive power at our disposal in all magnitudes of which nuclear weapons are capable, from small charges for the local battlefield to the

behemoth city incinerators of Armageddon. . . . One day the drill *could* turn out to be the real thing and the hardware, personnel, doctrine, and élan ("yes, sir, it is necessary, lawful, and just to fire this missile") *could* come together as planned. The worst-case *scenario* of planners' nightmares could simply be the worst case global devastation. We have ensured that all of this is entirely possible. (Lindberg 2004: 324–25)

Evidently, important decision makers were already fanatic enough to make this all happen. Or should we say "optimistic" enough? Or "illusionary" enough? More than ten years after the thoughtful words mentioned above were written, a rather far-going "Eurasia defense strategy" assessment came to the conclusion that contrary "to the global apocalypse envisioned in the wake of a superpower nuclear exchange during the Cold War, there will very likely be a functioning world after a war between minor nuclear powers." Since according to the Mackinderian doctrine the "defense" of the Eurasian world island is the core issue of world politics, there "is a need to rethink the problem of limited nuclear war in which the United States is a direct participant" (Krepinevich 2017: 91).

In addition to the worrisome mental landscape that opens behind similar utterances, imagine the enduring pervasiveness of "the apocalyptic nationalism of the seventeenth century" (Madsen 1998: 9) under the auspices of which the first New England colonies were founded; imagine the influence of "evangelical American Christians who especially like to emphasize the end of history" (Boschman 2009: 19); imagine the heritage of America's so-called second awakening that occurred in the early nineteenth century, disseminating the ideas "of the Rapture, when believers will ascend into the heavens to meet Christ," and "that the final battle between Christ and the hosts of the Antichrist will occur on the plains of Armageddon in modern Israel" (Gray 2008: 166); finally, imagine decision makers who are influenced by these traditions and whose spiritual nightmare is the vacuity of meaning. It does not take much fantasy to believe that in certain circumstances they might opt in favor of annihilation rather than let "nihilism" prevail, especially when they trust in the promise that following the end of history, and the death of the world, the just will be rewarded, and the good (who they imagine to be) "may be absorbed with it in God" (Teilhard de Chardin [1959] 2004: 310). Paradoxically, their move would anticipate "natural" extinction through the fulfillment of another of Georgescu-Roegen's (1976: 35) pungent hypotheses: "Perhaps, the destiny of man is to have a short, but fiery, exciting and extravagant life rather than a long, uneventful and vegetative existence. Let other species—the amoebas, for example—which have no spiritual ambitions inherit an earth still bathed in plenty of sunshine."

Afterword

As the reader might have noticed, I engaged with my enterprise of writing a critical account of western ideology by looking almost exclusively at the object of my criticism through the lenses of western thought. For reasons of biography, education, and linguistic capabilities, that is, due to my own limits and faults, the only sources available to me were western ones. While this is clearly a limit, it may nevertheless be acceptable. That the core of western ideology remained unvaried over some four centuries does not mean that western thought is in general invariant or homogeneous, nor that all westerners converge toward one single view. In exposing the fragility of the western sense of superiority I have been preceded by many in the west. It was also possible to refer to several critics of teleology, and I even could affirmatively refer to a few authors who earlier and more brilliantly than myself have located the eschatological and apocalyptic vision of history at the core of western ideology.

That I could rely on western sources, however, did not only depend on the possibility of agreement. It did perhaps even more depend on the possibilities offered by the critical method. Many authors whose ideas I rely on would probably not agree with my overall conclusions, but this is no good reason for not being inspired by them. In my view, criticism departs from an attempt to understand someone else's thought, and proceeds toward a different conclusion by a reflective re-elaboration of that thought. Were I to write another book that contains only ideas which I agree with, many of the authors whom I repeatedly subjected to my criticisms in the present pages would nevertheless be inserted in that other reference list too. Western intellectual history is rich in ideas that do not pertain to an eschatological view of history, and others which explicitly or implicitly reject it, even if on political subjects they remain marginalized by hegemonic ideology.

Over the past decades, I drew inspiration from developments in twentieth-century science, especially from texts that de facto revise the humanist view of "nature." Particularly important to me as a historian have been theories which tackle irreversible change in complex environments, and the high degree of self-organization that these environments entail. I also use to refer affirmatively—although less densely in this work—to scholars of humanities and social sciences who in one way or another come close to the same "thermodynamic" understanding of change. In short, I think that many concepts, theories, and methods that belong to the western tradition, do not stand and fall with the eschatological view of history.

Something analogous may even be said regarding the realm of political thought, which we normally consider contiguous to that of ideology. I maintain that it is well possible to prefer consent over coercion, for example, or freedom of speech over censorship and surveillance, without any need for a transcendent foundation of individual rights. The principle of checks and balances between powers and the rule of law can also be seen as a basic legal arrangement that does not require a mythical legitimization of sovereign rule. It would be presumptuous to think that before reading "thou shalt not kill" in the Decalogue, people comprehended killing as an amusing leisure activity. In the same way it would be presumptuous to maintain that people need to rely on a transcendent concept of the inherent dignity of the human person to favor free speech, habeas corpus, or fair trial; nor must they necessarily subscribe to the axioms of natural justice to appreciate in their own ways the advantages of a division of powers capable of containing their potential of arbitrary violence. What "justice" concretely means has been always decided by struggles and negotiations subjected to change in time and place; so it will be, I guess, as long as there is a need and a desire for it.

The presumptuous premise of western ideology is, however, exactly this: that without a transcendent purpose of history, without a "higher meaning" behind our "being in the world," and without the recognition of the "responsibility" that this meaning bestows upon us, no moral standard can be justified and no rightful law established. Should there ever be a time when all the infamous bugaboos of the west are eliminated, there will still remain the western boogeyman of the last resort, which they call "nihilism." Even if there is no agreement regarding its meaning and hardly any affirmative "nihilist" theory, the general feeling is overwhelming that whatever it means, it is totally unacceptable. Because, there *must* be something! I am afraid I will conclude this book without offering another alternative version of that "thing." This book was written to draw attention to the nefarious consequences of the very expectation that some "thing" of the kind has been or will be revealed, and of western ideology's self-instilled horror of its absence.

Apparently we are living in one of those periods of transition from a more stable set of world affairs to something else. We are witnessing growing turbulence, which is typical for periods of transition. Were perhaps decolonization and the implosion of communism the early ground motions of a "world-historical" tectonic shift, somehow away from western hegemony? Nobody knows, as the shape of the future is in the making and cannot be foreseen yet. Nobody knows by which rules and means human affairs will be regulated, which standards will prevail, which agreements or disagreements will emerge, and what the major lines of concord and conflict will be. But I dare to make one prediction: if we persevere in our self-righteousness over the meaning of history, and in the presumption that we know better and line up "against evil" better than others do, then we will make everything worse. For the sake of ourselves and of millions of fellow-humans whose desire is to live just their life with its joys and grievances, and tackle injustice and uncertainty in their own ways, it would be far better to dismiss our deceptive philosophy of history.

References

Abbas, A. (2010), *Liberalism and Human Suffering: Materialist Reflections on Politics, Ethics, and Aesthetics*, New York: Palgrave Macmillan.
Abbott, C. (2006), *Frontiers Past and Future: Science Fiction and the American West*, Lawrence: University Press of Kansas.
Achleitner, W. (1997), *Gott im Krieg: Die Theologie der österreichischen Bischöfe in den Hirtenbriefen zum Ersten Weltkrieg*, Wien: Böhlau.
Ackerly, B. A. (2008), *Universal Human Rights in a World of Difference*, Cambridge: Cambridge University Press.
Agazzi, E., and V. Fortunati (2007), "Introduzione," in E. Agazzi and V. Fortunati (eds.), *Memoria e saperi. Percorsi transdisciplinari*, 9–24, Roma: Meltemi.
Ahmad, A. (2000), "Between Orientalism and Historicism," in A. L. Macfie (ed.), *Orientalism: A Reader*, 277–85, New York: New York University Press.
Albright, M. K., and R. S. Williamson (2013), *The United States and R2P: From Words to Action*, Washington: United States Institute of Peace.
Albrow, M., and H. Seckinelgin (2011), "Introduction: Globality and the absence of justice," in M. Albrow and H. Seckinelgin (eds.), *Global Civil Society 2011*, 1–7, Basingstoke: Palgrave Macmillan.
Althusius, J. ([1603] 1995), *Politica: An Abridged Translation of Politics Methodically Set Forth and Illustrated with Sacred and Profane Examples*, Indianapolis: Liberty Fund.
Amadori Virgilj, G. (1906), *Il sentimento imperialista. Studio psico–sociologico*, Milano: Sandron.
Amuzegar, J. (1999), "Iran's Future: Civil Society or Civil Unrest," *Middle East Policy*, 7 (1): 86–101.
Anderson, B. (1991), *Imagined Communities. Reflections on the Origin and Spread of Nationalism*, London: Verso.
Anderson, T. (2016), *The Dirty War on Syria: Washington, Regime Change and Resistance*, Montréal: Global Research.
Appiah, K. A. (2003), "Citizens of the World," in M. J. Gibney (ed.), *Globalizing Rights. The Oxford Amnesty Lectures 1999*, 199–232, Oxford: Oxford University Press.
Aristotle ([~ 350 BC; 1885] 2000), *Politics*, translated by B. Jowett [1885], Mineola: Dover Publications.
Arndt, E. M. (1814), *Blick aus der Zeit auf die Zeit: Germanien*, Frankfurt am Main: Eichenberg.
Aron, S. (2006), *American Confluence: The Missouri Frontier from Borderland to Border State*, Bloomington: Indiana University Press.
Aron, S. (2011), "Frontiers, Borderlands, Wests," in E. Foner and L. McGirr (eds.), *American History Now*, 261–84, Philadelphia: Temple University Press.

Arrighi, G. (1994), *The Long Twentieth Century: Money, Power, and the Origins of Our Times*, London and New York: Verso.
Auckland District Health Board (2011), "Show respect when using the mortuary lift," *Nova: The Official Newsletter*, September, available online http://www.adhb.govt.nz/documents/Nova_Sept_2011.pdf (accessed November 14, 2016).
Baldwin, R. E., and P. Martin (1999), *Two Waves of Globalisation: Superficial Similarities, Fundamental Differences*, Working Paper 6904, Cambridge (MA): National Bureau of Economic Research.
Baledrokadroka, J. (2003), *The Fijian Understanding of the Deed of Cession Treaty of 1874*, Dunedin n.n., available online http://www.fijileaks.com/uploads/1/3/7/5/13759434/joeli_baledrokadroka_deed_of_cession_thesis.pdf (accessed November 14, 2016).
Balibar, E. (1991), "Racism and Nationalism," in E. Balibar and I. Wallerstein (eds.), *Race, Nation, Class: Ambiguous Identities*, 37–67, London: Verso.
Balibar, E. (1994), *Masses, Classes, Ideas: Studies on Politics and Philosophy before and after Marx*, New York: Routledge.
Balibar, E. (2015), "Marxism and the Idea of Revolution," in H. Trüper, D. Chakrabarty and S. Subrahmanyam (eds.), *Historical Teleologies in the Modern World*, 235–50, London: Bloomsbury.
Baraka, A. (2003), "Beginnings: Malcolm," in A. Baraka, *Somebody blew up America & other poems*, 3–5, Philipsburg: House of Nehesi.
Barcellona, P. (2001), *Le passioni negate. Globalismo e diritti umani*, Troina: Città aperta.
Barker, E. (1937), *Oliver Cromwell and the English People*, Cambridge: Cambridge University Press.
Bassin, M. (2008), "Eurasianism 'Classical' and 'Neo': Lines of Continuity," in T. Mochizuki (ed.), *Beyond the Empire: Images of Russia in the Eurasian Cultural Context*, 279–94, Sapporo: Slavic Research Center.
Bate, J. (2000), *The Song of the Earth*, London: Picador.
Bauman, Z. (2000), *Liquid Modernity*, Cambridge: Polity Press.
BBC One–Minute World News (2011), *Deadly Missiles Strike Pakistan*, http://news.bbc.co.uk/2/hi/south_asia/7847423.stm (accessed December 30, 2011).
Beck, U. (2000), *What is Globalization?*, Cambridge: Polity Press.
Beckmann, J. P. (1996), "Entdecken oder setzen? Die Besonderheit der Relationstheorie des Duns Scotus und ihre Bedeutung für die Metaphysik," in L. Honnefelder, R. Wood and M. Dreyer (eds.), *John Duns Scotus. Metaphysics & Ethics*, 367–84, Leiden: Brill.
Benhabib, S. (2000), *The Reluctant Modernism of Hannah Arendt*, Oxford: Rowman & Littlefield.
Benjamin, W. ([1940] 2003), *Über den Begriff der Geschichte*, Kassel: Offene Uni.
Bernier, F. [Anonymous] ([1684] 2000), "A New Division of the Earth," in R. Bernasconi and T. L. Lott (eds.), *The Idea of Race*, 1–4, Indianapolis: Hackett.
Black, W. (2010), *Beyond the End of the World*, Raleigh: lulu.com.
Bloch, E. (1959), *Das Prinzip Hoffnung*, vol. 2, Frankfurt am Main: Suhrkamp.
Blount, H. (1636), *A Voyage into the Levant with particular observations concerning the moderne condition of the Turks, and other people under that Empire*, London: Andrew Crooke.
Blumenbach, J. F. ([1795] 2000), "On the Natural Variety of Mankind," in R. Bernasconi and T. L. Lott (eds.), *The Idea of Race*, 27–37, Indianapolis: Hackett.

Blumenbach, J. F. (1828), *The Elements of Physiology*, London: Longman.
Blumenberg, H. (1983), *The Legitimacy of the Modern Age*, Cambridge (MA): MIT Press.
Boer, R. (2014), "Religion and Socialism: A. V. Lunacharsky and the God-Builders," *Political Theology* 15 (2): 188–209.
Borgna, E. (2004), *L'arcipelago delle emozioni*, Milano: Feltrinelli.
Borgolte, M. (2001), "Perspektiven europäischer Mittelalterhistorie an der Schwelle zum 21. Jahrhundert," in M. Borgolte (ed.), *Das europäische Mittelalter im Spannungsbogen des Vergleichs*, 13–27, Berlin: De Gruyter.
Boschman, R. (2009), *In the Way of Nature*, Jefferson: McFarland & Company.
Boucheron, P. (2005), "'Tournez les yeux pour admirer, vous qui exercez le pouvoir, celle qui est peinte ici:' La fresque du Bon Gouvernement d'Ambrogio Lorenzetti," *Annales HSS*, 60 (6): 1137–99.
Bourdieu, P. (1986), "L'illusion biographique," *Actes de la Recherche en Sciences sociales*, 62/63 (Juin): 69–72.
Boyer, P. S. (2012), *American History: A Very Short Introduction*, Oxford: Oxford University Press.
Boym, S. (2003), "Ipocondria del cuore: nostalgia, storia e memoria," in F. Modrzejewski and M. Sznaiderman (eds.), *Nostalgia. Saggi sul rimpianto del comunismo*, 1–88, Milano: Bruno Mondadori.
Boym, S. (2010), *Another Freedom. The Alternative History of an Idea*, Chicago: University of Chicago Press.
Bradstreet, A. (1678), "Contemplations," in A. Bradstreet, *Several poems*, Second edition, 221–29, Boston: John Foster.
Brice, C. (2012), "La storia culturale del politico," *Memoria e Ricerca*, 40: 55–74.
Bron, G. (2016), "Learning lessons from the Iberian Peninsula: Italian exiles and the making of a Risorgimento without people, 1820–48," in M. Isabella and K. Zanou (eds.), *Mediterranean Diasporas. Politics and Ideas in the Long 19th Century*, 59–76, London: Bloomsbury.
Brunner, O., W. Conze, and R. Koselleck (1984), *Geschichtliche Grundbegriffe. Historisches Lexikon zur politisch–sozialen Sprache in Deutschland*, 9 vol., Stuttgart: Klett-Cotta.
Brzezinski, Z. K. (1997), *The Grand Chessbord: American Primacy and its Geostrategic Imperatives*, New York: Basic Books.
Brzezinski, Z. K. (2004), *The Choice: Global Domination Or Global Leadership*, New York: Basic Books.
Butler, J. (1993), *Bodies that Matter: on the Discoursive Limits of Sex*, New York: Routledge.
Cana, F. R. (1911), "Cape Colony," *The Encyclopædia Britannica*, vol. 5, online: http://en.wikisource.org/wiki/1911_Encyclop%C3%A6dia_Britannica/Cape_Colony#cite_ref-3 (accessed July 30, 2014), 225–48, New York: The Encyclopedia Britannica Company.
Canetti, E. ([1960] 1985), *Masse und Macht*, Frankfurt am Main: Fischer.
Cardini, F. (1997), Le *radici cristiane dell'Europa. Miti, storia, prospettive*, Rimini: Il cerchio.
Cervantes, M. ([1613] 2014), *The Exemplary Novels of Cervantes*, Auckland: The Floating Press.
Chakrabarty, D. (2009), "The Climate of History: Four Theses," *Critical Inquiry*, 35 (Winter): 197–222.

Chan, S., and M. Simons (2016), "South Africa to Leave International Court," *The New York Times*, October 22: A5.

Chanock, M. (2000), "'Culture' and human rights: orientalising, occidentalising and authenticity," in M. Mamdani (ed.), *Beyond Rights Talk and Culture Talk: Comparative Essays on the Politics of Rights and Culture*, 15–36, New York: St. Martin's Press.

Chomsky, N. (2003), "'Recovering Rights': A Crooked Path," in M. J. Gibney (ed.), *Globalizing Rights. The Oxford Amnesty Lectures 1999*, 44–80, Oxford: Oxford University Press.

Chomsky, N. (2011), "The Imperial Mentality and 9/11," *tomDispatch.com*, September 6, http://www.tomdispatch.com/blog/175436/ (accessed December 30, 2011).

Chomsky, N., and A. Vltchek (2013), *On Western Terrorism: From Hiroshima to Drone Warfare*, London: Pluto Press.

Clark, W. (2003), *Winning Modern Wars*, New York: Public Affairs.

Cobain, I. (2013), "Obama's secret kill list: The disposition matrix," *The Guardian*, July, 14, http://www.theguardian.com/world/2013/jul/14/obama-secret-kill-list-disposition-matrix (accessed January 25, 2014).

Cockburn, C. (1751), "Extracts from Mrs. Cockburn's works," *The Monthly Review or New Literary Journal*, (August): 184–94, London: Griffith.

Collins, D., S. Falcón, S. Lodhia, and M. Talcott (2010), "New Directions in Feminism and Human Rights," *International Feminist Journal of Politics*, 12 (3–4): 298–318.

Comte, C., and C. Dunoyer ([1817] 2012), "Foreword" [to *Le Censeur Européen*], in R. Leroux and D. M. Hart (eds.), *French Liberalism in the Nineteenth Century*, 49–60, Abingdon: Routledge.

Condorcet, J. A. N. (1796), *Outlines of an Historical View of the Progress of the Human Mind*, Philadelphia: Lang & Ustick.

Confino, A. (2006), "Lo local, una esencia de toda nación," *Ayer. Revista de Historia Contemporánea* (64): 19–31.

Constant, B. ([1819] 2012), "The Liberty of the Ancients and the Moderns," in R. Leroux and D. M. Hart (eds.), *French Liberalism in the Nineteenth Century*, 68–82, Abingdon: Routledge.

Cooke, C. W. (2014), "The Climate Inquisitor," *National Review*, May 5th, http://www.nationalreview.com/article/376574/climate-inquisitor-charles-c-w-cooke (accessed June 13, 2016).

Cormack W. S. (2011), "Revolution and Free–Colored Equality in the Îles du Vent (Lesser Antilles), 1789–1794," *Proceedings of the Western Society for French History*, 39: 155–65.

Cortelazzo, M. (1988), "Il nome Europa," in G. Bazoli (ed.), *Europa. Storie di viaggiatori italiani*, 48–59, Milano: Electa.

Cotton, J. (1630), *Gods Promise to his Plantation*, London: Bellamy.

Crafts, N., and A. Venables (2003), "Globalization in History. A Geographical Perspective," in M. D. Bordo, A. M. Taylor and J. G. Williamson (eds.), *Globalization in Historical Perspective*, 323–69, Chicago: University of Chicago Press.

Croce, B. (1932), *Storia d'Europa nel secolo decimo nono*, Bari: Laterza.

Crouch, C. (2004), *Post–Democracy*, Cambridge: Polity.

Curry, J. A., and P. J. Webster (2011), "Climate Science and the Uncertainty Monster," *American Meteorological Society*, December: 1667–82.

Danzer, G. (2011), *Wer sind wir? Auf der Suche nach der Formel des Menschen*, Heidelberg: Springer.

D'Arcy McGee, T. (1869), *A Popular History of Ireland: From the Earliest Period to the Emancipation of the Catholics*, Glasgow: Cameron & Ferguson.

Darwin, C. ([1859] 2010), *The Origin of Species*, Red Wing: Cricket House Books.

Davies, J., R. Lluberas, and A. Shorrocks (2016), *Global Wealth Databook*, Zürich: Credit Suisse Research Institute.

Davies, J. B., S. Sandström, A. Shorrocks, and E. N. Wolff (2008), *The World Distribution of Household Wealth*, Discussion Paper 03, Helsinki: World Institute for Development Economics.

de las Casas, B. ([1552] 1821), *Breve relación de la destrucción de las Indias Occidentale*, Filadelfia: Juan Hurtel.

de Staël, G. ([1818] 2012), "Of the love of Liberty," in R. Leroux and D. M. Hart (eds.), *French Liberalism in the Nineteenth Century*, 61–7, Abingdon: Routledge.

Debord, G. ([1967] 1994), *The Society of the Spectacle*, New York: Zone Books.

Declaration of Independence (1776), in *National Archives. America's Founding Documents*, https://www.archives.gov/founding-docs/declaration-transcript (accessed November 7, 2016).

Defoe, D. ([1719] 2010), *Robinson Crusoe*, London: Haper Collins.

Degler, C. N. ([1959] 1984), *Out of our Past. The Forces that Shaped Modern America*, New York: Harper & Row.

Delanty, G. (1999), "Die Transformation nationaler Identität und die kulturelle Ambivalenz europäischer Identität," in R. Viehoff and R. T. Segers (eds.), *Kultur–Identität–Europa. Über die Schwierigkeiten und Möglichkeiten einer Konstruktion*, 267–88, Frankfurt am Main: Suhrkamp.

Department of Defense (2009), *Base Structure Report: Fiscal Year 2009 Baseline*, https://www.defense.gov/Portals/1/Documents/pubs/BSR2009Baseline.pdf (accessed March 18, 2017).

Derrida, J. (2002), *Marx & Sons*, Paris: PUF Galilée.

Destutt de Tracy, A. L. C. ([1811] 2012), "A commentary and Review of Montesquieu's 'Spirit of Laws'," in R. Leroux and D. M. Hart (eds.), *French Liberalism in the Nineteenth Century*, 34–43, Abingdon: Routledge.

Devji, F. (2015), "Catching up with oneself: Islam and the representation of humanity," in H. Trüper, D. Chakrabarty and S. Subrahmanyam (eds.), *Historical Teleologies in the Modern World*, 301–20, London: Bloomsbury.

DGTI (2001), "Intersexualität," in *DGTI Deutsche Gesellschaft für Transidentität und Intersexualität*, http://www.dgti.org/erstehilfe/intersexualitaet.html#1 (accessed August 6, 2014).

Diagnopsy (2001), *La révolution française*, 6: Les droits de l'homme, http://www.diagnopsy.com/Revolution/Rev_011.htm (accessed January 4, 2012).

Dobbins, J. (2003), "Nation–Building: The Inescapable Responsibility of the World's Only Superpower," *Rand Corporation*, Santa Monica, http://www.rand.org/publications/randreview/issues/summer2003/nation1.html (accessed October 27, 2016).

Dostoyevsky [Dostojewski], F. ([1877] 1917), "Zur Orientfrage," in F. Dostojewski, *Politische Schriften*, 445–71, München: Piper

Douglas, R. (2005), *Liberals. The History of the Liberal and Liberal Democratic Parties*, London: Hambledon.

Douzinas, C. (2014), "Human rights and the paradoxes of liberalism," *Open Democracy. Free Thinking for the World*, August 8, https://www.open democracy.net/costas-douzinas/human-rights-and-paradoxes-of-liberalism (accessed on August 21, 2014).

Duara, P. (1995), *Rescuing History from the Nation. Questioning Narratives of Modern China*, Chicago: University of Chicago Press.

Dubuisson, D. (2003), *The Western Construction of Religion. Myths, Knowledge and Ideology*, Baltimore: Johns Hopkins University Press.

Dunn, J. (1979), *Western political theory in the face of the future*, Cambridge: Cambridge University Press.

Duso, G. (2010), "Il potere e la nascita dei concetti politici moderni," in S. Chignola and G. Duso (eds.), *Sui concetti giuridici e politici della costituzione dell'Europa*, 159–93, Milano: Franco Angeli.

Ehrenberg, J. (1999), *Civil Society. The Critical History of an Idea*, New York and London: New York University Press.

Erikson, E. H. ([1958] 1993), *Young Man Luther: A Study in Psychoanalysis and History*, New York: Norton & Co.

Esposito, R. (2009), *Concepire l'impersonale. Verso l'originaria unità dell'essere vivente*, Modena: Paginette Festival Filosofia.

Esposito, R. (2010), *Communitas: The Origin and Destiny of Community*, Stanford: Stanford University Press.

Eton, W. (1799), *A Survey of the Turkish Empire*, London: Cadell & Davies.

Ettinger, M. (2013), "Color Me Queer: An Aesthetic Challenge to Feminist Essentialism," *Berkeley Journal of Gender, Law & Justice*, 8 (1): 106–21.

Falk, R. (2011), "Kuala Lumpur tribunal: Bush and Blair guilty. A war crimes tribunal in Malaysia offers a devastating critique of international criminal law institutions today," *Al-Jazeera*, November 28. Available online http://www.aljazeera.com/indepth/opinion/2011/11/20111128105712109215.html (accessed August 26, 2014).

Fanon, F. ([1952] 1986), *Black Skin, White Masks*, London: Pluto Press.

Febvre L., ([1945] 1999), *L'Europa. Storia di una civiltà*, Roma: Donzelli.

Ferguson, A. ([1767] 1793), *An Essay on the History of Civil Society*, London-Edinburgh: Cadell et al.

Forrest, A. (1989), "The Revolution and Europe," in F. Furet and M. Ozouf (eds.), *A Critical Dictionary of the French Revolution*, vol. 1, 115–23, Cambridge (MA): Harvard University Press.

Forsythe, D. P. (2000), *Human Rights in International Rights*, Cambridge: Cambridge University Press.

Foster, R. F. (1989), *Modern Ireland, 1600–1972*, London: Penguin Books.

Foucault, M. ([1978] 2007), "What is Critique?," in M. Foucault, *The Politics of Truth*, 41–81, Los Angeles: Semiotext.

Foucault, M. (1980), "Introduction," in H. Barbin, *Being the Recently Discovered Memoirs of a Nineteenth-Century French Hermaphrodite*, vii–xvii, New York: Pantheon Books.

Franchetti, L. (1891), *L'Italia e la sua colonia Africana*, Città di Castello: Lapi.

Frank, R. (2002), "The Meaning of Europe in French National Discourse," in M. af Malmborg and B. Stråth (eds.), *The Meaning of Europe*, Oxford and New York: Berg.

Franklin, B. ([1771] 1903), *The Autobiography of Benjamin Franklin*, Chicago: Donnelley.

Freeden, M. (1996), *Ideologies and Political Theory: A Conceptual Approach*, Oxford: Clarendon Press.
Freeden, M. (2015), *Liberalism: A Very Short Introduction*, Oxford: Oxford University Press.
Fried, A. H. (1908), *Internationalismus und Patriotismus*, Leipzig: Dietrich.
Fröbel, F. ([1821] 1862), "Grundsätze, Zweck und inneres Leben der allgemeinen deutschen Erziehungsanstalt," in *Friedrich Fröbel's gesammelte pädagogische Schriften*, vol. 1, 242–62, Berlin: Enslin.
Galimberti, U. (1999), *Psiche e techne*, Milano: Feltrinelli.
Gallant, T. W. (2016), *Modern Greece: From the War of Independence to the Present*, London: Bloomsbury.
Gamble, A. (2006), "The Idea of the West: Changing Perspectives on Europe and America," *UC Berkeley Institute of European Studies*, http://escholarship.org/uc/item/6f02368k (accessed November 5, 2015).
Gamble, A. (2009), "The Western Ideology," *Government and Opposition* 44 (1): 1–19.
Geertz, C. (1973), *The Interpretation of Cultures*, New York: Basic Books.
Gelernter, D. (2007), *Americanism: The Fourth Great Western Religion*, New York: Doubleday.
Gemelli, A. (1917), *Il nostro soldato: Saggi di psicologia militare*, Milano: Treves.
Georgescu-Roegen, N. (1976), *Energy and Economic Myths. Institutional and Analytical Essays*, New York: Pergamon Press.
Ghiselin, M. T. (1994), "Darwin's language may seem teleological, but his thinking is another matter," *Biology and Philosophy*, 9 (4): 489–92.
Gibbon, E. ([1776–89] 1907), *The History of the Decline and Fall of the Roman Empire*, vol. 6, New York: Fred De Fau & Company.
Gibney, J. (2006), "Globalization, American exceptionalism and security," in R. G. Patman (ed.), *Globalization and conflict. National Security in a "New" Strategic Era*, 79–94, London and New York: Routledge.
Gilbert, R. (2002), "The Song of the Earth by Jonathan Bate," *Modern Philology* 100 (2): 293–97.
Gilroy, P. (1992), "The end of antiracism," in J. Donald and A. Rattansi (eds.), *"Race," Culture and Difference*, 49–61, London: SAGE.
Gilroy, P. (2004), *After Empire: Melancholia or Convivial Culture?*, Abingdon: Routledge.
Gobineau, J. A. ([1855] 2000), "The Inequality of Human Races," in R. Bernasconi and T. L. Lott (eds.), *The Idea of Race*, 45–53, Indianapolis: Hackett.
Goldgeier, J. M. (1999), *Not Whether But When. The US Decision to Enlarge NATO*, Washington: The Brookings Institution.
Goodhart, M. (2003), "Origins and Universality in the Human Rights Debate: Cultural Essentialism and the Challenge of Globalization," *Human Rights Quarterly*, 25 (4): 935–64.
Gott, G. (2002), "Imperial Humanitarism: History of an Arrested Dialectic," in B. E. Hernandez-Truyol (ed.), *Moral Imperialism: A Critical Anthology*, 19–38, New York and London: New York University Press.
Graumann, C. F. (1999), "Soziale Identitäten," in R. Viehoff and R. T. Segers (eds.), *Kultur Identität Europa. Über die Schwierigkeiten und Möglichkeiten einer Konstruktion*, 59–74, Frankfurt am Main: Suhrkamp.

Gray, J. (2008), *Black Mass. Apocalyptic Religion and the Death of Utopia*, London: Penguin.
Greenwald, G. (2017), "Obama Killed a 16–Year–Old American in Yemen. Trump Just Killed His 8–Year–Old Sister," *The Intercept*, January 30, https://theintercept.com/2017/01/30/obama-killed-a-16-year-old-american-in-yemen-trump-just-killed-his-8-year-old-sister/ (accessed February 5, 2017).
Grimm, D. (2012), *Die Zukunft der Verfassung II: Auswirkungen von Europäisierung und Globalisierung*, Frankfurt am Main: Suhrkamp.
Grossman, Z. (2014), *A Century of US Military Interventions*, http://academic.evergreen.edu/g/grossmaz/interventions.html (accessed February 4, 2017).
Grundtvig, N. F. S. (1808), *Nordens Mytologi eller Udsigt over Eddalæren for dannede Mænd der ei selv ere Mytologer*, København: Schubothes Forlag.
Grundtvig, N. F. S. (1844), *Vom wahren Christenthum*, Leipzig: Gebauer.
Guha, R. (2002), *History at the Limit of World–History*, New York: Columbia University Press.
Gut, P. (2014), "The Legacy of Spinoza. The Enlightenment according to Johnathan Israel," *Diametros*, 40: 45–72.
Gyekye, K. (1996), *African Cultural Values: An Introduction*, Accra: Sankofa.
Gyekye, K. (1997), *Tradition and Modernity: Philosophical Reflections on the African Experience*, New York: Oxford University Press.
Habermas, J. (1984), *The Theory of Communicative Action*, vol. 1, Boston: Beacon Press.
Habermas, J. (2009), *Zwischen Naturalismus und Religion. Philosophische Aufsätze*, Frankfurt am Main: Suhrkamp.
Habermas, J. (2012), *Nachmetaphysisches Denken II. Aufsätze und Repliken*, Berlin: Suhrkamp.
Haeckel, E. (1866a), *Generelle Morphologie der Organismen*, vol. 1, Berlin: Reimer.
Haeckel, E. (1866b), *Generelle Morphologie der Organismen*, vol. 2, Berlin: Reimer.
Haken, J. (2011), *Transnational Crime In The Developing World*, Washington: Center for International Policy.
Hall, S. (1992), "New Ethnicities," in J. Donald and A. Rattansi (eds.), *"Race," Culture and Difference*, 252–9, London: SAGE.
Haritaworn, J. K. (2012), "Women's rights, gay rights and anti-Muslim racism in Europe: Introduction," *European Journal of Women's Studies*, 19 (February): 73–8.
Harrington, J. ([1656] 1992), *The Commonwealth of Oceana*, edited by J. G. A. Pocock, Cambridge: Cambridge University Press.
Harris, A. P. (1990), "Race and Essentialism in Feminist Legal Theory," *Stanford Law Review*, 42: 581–615.
Harris, M. L. and T. S. Kidd (2012), "The Founding Fathers and Religion," in M. L. Harris and T. S. Kidd (eds.), *The Founding Fathers and the Debate over Religion in Revolutionary America: A History in Documents*, 3–23, Oxford: Oxford University Press.
Harvey, D. (2003), *The New Imperialism*, New York: Oxford University Press.
Haumann, H. (2002), *A History of East European Jews*, Budapest: Central European University Press.
Heidegger, M. ([1927] 1962), *Being and Time*, Oxford: Blackwell.
Heidegger, M. (1960), "Sprache und Heimat," *Hebbel–Jahrbuch*, 27–50, Heide: Boyens.

Heidegger, M. ([1966] 1976), "Nur noch ein Gott kann uns retten," *Der Spiegel*, 23 (May 31): 193–219.
Heidegger, M. (1969), *Identity and Difference*, New York: Harper & Row.
Heisig, J. W. (2001), *Philosophers of Nothingness: An Essay on the Kyoto School*, Honolulu: University of Hawai'i Press.
Herder, J. G. ([1784–91] 1914), *Ideen zur Philosophie der Geschichte der Menschheit*, Berlin Deutsche Bibliothek.
Herodotus (~ 450 BC [1942]), *The Persian Wars*, translated by G. Rawlinson, New York: Random House.
Hertner, P. (2002), "Unterschiedliche wirtschaftliche Integrationsphasen," in A. Schüller and H. J. Thieme (eds.), *Ordnungsprobleme der Weltwirtschaft*, 27–43, Stuttgart: Lucius & Lucius.
Hesmivy D'Auribeau, P. (1795), *Memoires pour servir a l'histoire de la persecution françoise*, vol. 1.2, Rome: Louis Perego Salviani.
Hessel, S. (2010), *Indignez-vous!*, Montpellier: Indigène,
Heywood, C. (2000), "Society," in T. C. W. Blanning (ed.), *The Nineteenth Century*, 47–77 Oxford: Oxford University Press.
Higuchi, Y. (1998), "The concept of the nation–state viewed from the outside its birthplace," in *The transformation of the nation-state in Europe at the dawn of the 21st century*, 145–50, Strasbourg: Council of Europe Publishing.
Hitler, A. (1936), *Mein Kampf*, München: Zentralverlag der NSDAP.
Hitler, A. (1937), *Reden des Führers am Parteitag der Arbeit 1937*, München: Eher.
Hobbes, T. ([1651] 1970), *Leviathan or the Matter, Forme and Power of a Commonwealth Ecclesiaticall and Civil*, London: Collier-Macmillan.
Hobson, J. A. (1902), *Imperialism: A Study*, London: James Nisbet.
Hodge, B. (n.d.), "Ideology," *Semiotics Encyclopedia Online*, Short Entry, E.J. Pratt Library, Victoria University, http://www.semioticon.com/seo/I/ideology.html# (accessed August 13, 2013).
Hofbauer, H. (2012), "Civil Society Intervention as a Geopolitical Instrument," *Strategic Culture Foundation*, October 1, 2012, http://www.strategic–culture.org/news/2012/10/01/civil–society–intervention–as–a–geopolitical–instrument.html (accessed August 10, 2014).
Hofbauer, H. (2016), *Feindbild Russland. Geschichte einer Dämonisierung*, Wien: Promedia.
Hofer, J. (1688), *Dissertatio medica de nostalgia oder Heimwehe*, Basel: Bertsch.
Holmén, J. (2015), "History-writing and identity formation in five island regions in the Baltic Sea," in S. Edquist and J. Holmén, *Islands of Identity*, 9–38, Stockholm: Elanders.
Holocaust Museum Houston (n.d.), "History, Humanity, Responsibility: You Can Make A Difference," https://www.hmh.org/ed_Religious_Trunks.shtml (accessed 30 January 2017).
Horowitz, M. (2014), *Identity and the Psychoanalytic Explorations of Self–Organization*, Hove and New York: Routledge.
Horwitz, M. J. (1966), "Tocqueville and the tyranny of the majority," *The Review of Politics*, 28 (3), 293–307.
Howarth, W. (1996), "Some Principles of Ecocriticism," in C. Glotfelty and H. Fromm (eds.), *The Ecocriticism Reader*, 69–91, Athens: University of Georgia Press.
Hugo, V. (1845), *Le Rhin. Lettres à un ami*, vol. 3, Paris: Duriez.

Human Rights Center (2007), *The Responsibility to Protect (R2P): Moving the Campaign Forward*, Berkely: University of California.
Hume, D. ([1740] 1994), "Of the Origin of Justice and Property," in D. Hume, *Political Writings*, 7–20, Indianapolis: Hackett.
Hume, D. ([1754] 1987), "Idea of a perfect commonwealth," in D. Hume, *Essays, Moral, Political, and Literary*, edited by E. F. Miller, 512–29, Indianapolis: Liberty Fund.
Hume, D. ([1777] 1987), "Of National Characters," in D. Hume, *Essays Moral, Political, Literary*, 197–215, Indianapolis: Liberty Fund.
Huntington, S. P. (1993), "The Clash of Civilisations?," *Foreign Affairs*, 72 (3): 22–49.
Hyneman, C. S., and D. S. Lutz (1983), *American Political Writing During the Founding Era, 1760–1805*, vol.1, Indianapolis: Liberty Press.
Ibhawoh, B. (2007), *Imperialism and Human Rights. Colonial Discourses of Rights and Liberties in African History*, Albany: State University of New York Press.
ICTY (2016), *Case number IT-95-5/18-T, prosecutor vs Radovan Karadžić*, March 24, http://www.icty.org/x/cases/karadzic/tjug/en/160324_judgement.pdf (accessed November 19, 2016).
Imposimato, F. (2012), *Repubblica delle stragi impunite*, Roma: Newton Compton.
Isabella, M. (2016), "Mediterranean liberals? Italian revolutionaries and the making of a colonial sea," in M. Isabella and K. Zanou (eds.), *Mediterranean Diasporas. Politics and Ideas in the Long 19th Century*, 77–96, London: Bloomsbury.
Israel, J. (2001), *Radical Enlightenment. Philosophy and the Making of Modernity*, Oxford: Oxford University Press.
Israel, J. (2006), *Enlightenment Contested. Philosophy, Modernity, and the Emancipation of Man 1670–1752*, Oxford: Oxford University Press.
Israel, J. (2014), *Revolutionary Ideas. An Intellectual History of the French Revolution from the Rights of Man to Robespierre*, Princeton: Princeton University Press.
Jackson, R. R. (1993), "Truth and Argument in Buddhism," in R. R. Jackson (ed.), *Is enlightenment possible?: Dharmakīrti and rGyal tshab rje on knowledge, rebirth, no-self and liberation*, 17–145, Ithaca: Snow Lion Publications.
Jacob, M. C. (1976), *The Newtonians and the English Revolution, 1689–1720*, Ithaca: Cornell University Press.
Jahn, B., T. Rahn, and C. Schnitzer (1998), "Einleitung," in B. Jahn, T. Rahn and C. Schnitzer (eds.), *Zeremoniell in der Krise*, 7–15, Marburg: Jonas Verlag.
James, W. (1890), *Principles of Psychology*, vol.1, New York: Holt & Company.
JanMohamed, A. R. (1985), "The Economy of Manichean Allegory: The Function of Racial Difference in Colonialist Literature," *Critical Inquiry*, 12 (1): 59–87.
Jefferson, T. ([1776] 1904), "Proposed Constitution for Virginia," in P. L. Ford (ed.), *The Works of Thomas Jefferson*, vol. 2, 158–83, New York: Putnam's Sons.
Joas, H. (1985), *G.H. Mead: A Contemporary Re–Examination of his Thought*, Oxford and Cambridge: Polity and MIT Press.
Johnson, C. A. (2010), *Dismantling the Empire: America's Last Best Hope*, New York: Metropolitan Books.
Johnson, R. A. (2014), "Predicting Future War," *Parameters*, 44 (1): 65–76.

Joint Chiefs of Staff (2005), *Doctrine for Joint Nuclear Operations. Joint Publication 3–12; Final Coordination (2)* 15 March 2005, http://www.wslfweb.org/docs/doctrine/3_12fc2.pdf (accessed February 16, 2014).
Jolly, R. (2006), *Inequality in Historical Perspective*, Research Paper 32, Helsinki: World Institute for Development Economics.
Jonas, H. (1984), *The Imperative of Responsibility*, Chicago: University of Chicago Press.
Jordan, D. P. (1969), "Gibbon's 'Age of Constantine' and the Fall of Rome," *History and Theory*, 8 (1): 71–96.
Judson, P. M. (2003), "Regionalismus—Nationalismus: Neue Zugänge," *Geschichte und Region/Storia e regione*, 12 (2): 175–89.
Jünger, E. ([1959] 1991), *An der Zeitmauer*, Stuttgart: Klett-Cotta.
Kant, I. ([1777] 2000), "Of the Different Human Races," in R. Bernasconi and T. L. Lott (eds.), *The Idea of Race*, 8–22, Indianapolis: Hackett.
Kant, I. ([1781] 1855), *Critique of Pure Reason*, London: Bohn.
Kant, I. ([1784] 1914), "Idee zu einer allgemeinen Geschichte in weltbürgerlicher Absicht," in J. G. Herder, *Ideen zur Philosophie der Geschichte der Menschheit*, 321–38, Berlin: Deutsche Bibliothek.
Kant, I. ([1785] 1914), "Rezensionen von J. G. Herders 'Ideen zur Philosophie der Geschichte der Menschheit'," in J. G. Herder, *Ideen zur Philosophie der Geschichte der Menschheit*, 297–319, Berlin Deutsche Bibliothek.
Kant, I. ([1790] 2002), *Critique of the Power of Judgment*, Cambridge: Cambridge University Press.
Kant, I. ([1795] 1903), *Perpetual Peace: A Philosophical Essay*, London and New York: Allen & Unwin-Macmillan.
Kennedy, E. (1979), "'Ideology' from Destutt De Tracy to Marx," *Journal of the History of Ideas*, 40 (3): 353–68.
Kennedy, P. (2006), *The Parliament of Man. The Past, Present, and Future of the United Nations*, New York: Random House.
Kermode, F. ([1966] 2000), *The Sense of Ending. Studies in the Theory of Fiction*, Oxford: Oxford University Press.
Killingsworth, M. J. (2004), *Walt Whitman and the Earth*, Iowa City: University of Iowa Press.
King, A. (2012), *The Founding Fathers v. the People: Paradoxes of American Democracy*, Cambridge (MA): Harvard University Press.
Kochi, T. (2009), *The Other's War. Recognition and the Violence of Ethics*, Abingdon: Birbeck Law Press.
Koselleck, R. (2004), *Futures Past. On the Semantics of Historical Time*, New York: Columbia University Press.
Koskenniemi, M. (2015), "Between context and telos: Reviewing the structures of international law," in H. Trüper, D. Chakrabarty and S. Subrahmanyam (eds.), *Historical Teleologies in the Modern World*, 213–34, London: Bloomsbury.
Krepinevich, A. F. (2017), *Preserving the Balance. A US Eurasia Defense Strategy*, Washington: Center for Strategic and Budgetary Assessments.
Kress, G., and B. Hodge (1979), *Language as Ideology*, London: Routledge & Kegan.
Kryshkin, Y. (2010), "NATO seeks unshared responsibility," *The Voice of Russia*, September 16, http://voiceofrussia.com/2010/09/16/20731550/ (accessed January 25, 2014).

Kuklinski, J. H., E. Riggle, V. Ottati, N. Schwarz, and R. S. Wyer Jr (1991), "The Cognitive and Affective Bases of Political Tolerance Judgments," *American Journal of Political Science*, 35: 1–27.

Kurunmäki, J. (2017), "Political Representation, Imperial Dependency and Political Transfer: Finland and Sweden 1809–1819," *Journal of Modern European History*, 15 (2): 243–60.

La Capra, D. (2004), *History in Transit. Experience, Identity, Critical Theory*, Ithaca: Cornell University Press.

La Vopa, A. J. (2009), "A New Intellectual History? Jonathan Israel's Enlightenment," *The Historical Journal*, 52 (3): 717–38.

Laclau, E. (2005), *On Populist Reason*, London: Verso.

Lafraie, A. (2006), "Afghanistan, the 'War on Terror,' and the Continuing Quest for Security," in R. G. Patman (ed.), *Globalization and Conflict. National Security in a "New" Strategic Era*, 114–32, London and New York: Routledge.

Lamb, R. (2009), "Quentin Skinner's revised historical contextualism: A critique," *History of the Human Sciences*, 22: 51–73.

Lang, M. (2011), "Globalization and global history in Toynbee," *Journal of World History*, 22 (4): 747–83.

Lash, S. (1998), "Being after time: Towards a politics of melancholy," in S. Lash, A. Quick and R. Roberts (eds.), *Time and Value*, 147–61, Oxford: Blackwell.

Lawson, S. (2012), *International Relations*, Cambridge: Polity Press.

Le Goff, J. (2001), *Il Medioevo. Alle origini dell'identità europea*, Roma-Bari: Laterza.

League of Nations ([1924] 2008), "The Covenant of the League of Nations," *The Avalon Project: Documents in Law, History and Diplomacy*, Yale Law School, Lillian Goldman Law http://avalon.law.yale.edu/20th_century/leagcov.asp#art22 (accessed March 27, 2017).

Lennox, J. G. (1993), "Darwin was a teleologist," *Biology and Philosophy*, 8 (4): 409–21.

Lentin, A. (2004), *Racism & Anti-Racism in Europe*, London: Pluto Press.

Lentin, A. and G. Titley (2010), *The Crisis of Multiculturalism. Racism in a Neoliberal Age*, London: Zed Books.

Leonhard, J. (2001), *Liberalismus: Zur historischen Semantik eines europäischen Deutungsmusters*, München: Oldenbourg.

Leopold, D. (2012), "A Cautious Embrace: Reflections on (Left) Liberalism and Utopia," in B. Jackson and M. Stears (eds.), *Liberalism as Ideology. Essays in Honour of Michael Freeden*, 9–33, Oxford: Oxford University Press.

Leopold, D. (2013), "Marxism and ideology," in M. Freeden, L. T. Sargent, and M. Stears (eds.), *The Oxford Handbook of Political Ideologies*, 20–37, Oxford: Oxford University Press.

Leroux, R. and D. M. Hart (2012), "Introduction," in R. Leroux and D. M. Hart (eds.), *French Liberalism in the Nineteenth Century*, 1–8, Abingdon: Routledge.

Leslie, M. (1998), *Renaissance Utopias and the Problem of History*, Ithaca: Cornell University Press.

Levi, C. ([1945] 1982), *Christ Stopped at Eboli*, London: Penguin Books.

Levi, C. (1945), *Cristo si è fermato a Eboli*, Torino: Einaudi.

Levis Sullam, S. (2010), *L'apostolo a brandelli. L'eredità di Mazzini tra Risorgimento e fascismo*, Roma–Bari: Laterza.

Levitt, T. (1983), "The Globalization of Markets," *Harvard Business Review*, 25 (May/June): 92–102.
Liakos, A. (2010), "Il passato come utopia e il desiderio di storia," in R. Petri (ed.), *Nostalgia. Memoria e passaggi tra le sponde dell'Adriatico*, 63–74, Roma: Edizioni di storia e letteratura.
Liakos, A. (2011), *Αποκάλυψη, Ουτοπία και Ιστορία: Οι μεταμορφώσεις της ιστορικής συνείδησης*, Athens: Polis.
Lindberg, T. (2004), "Nuclear and Other Retaliation after Deterrence Fails," in H. D. Sokolski (ed.), *Getting MAD: Nuclear Mutual Assured Destruction, its Origins and Practice*, 317–39, Carlisle: Strategic Studies Institute/U.S. Army War College.
Locke, J. ([1669] 2003), "The Fundamental Constitutions of Carolina," in J. Locke, *Political Writings*, 210–32, Indianapolis: Hackett.
Locke, J. ([1690] 1764), *Two Treatises of Government*, London: Millar et al.
Lombroso, C. (1871), *L'uomo bianco e l'uomo di colore*, Padova: Sacchetto.
Losurdo, D. (2011), *Liberalism. A Counter-History*, London: Verso.
Löwenstein, H., and V. Zühlsdorff (1975), *NATO and the Defense of the West*, Westport: Greenwood Press.
Löwith, K. (1949), *Meaning in History*, Chicago and London: University of Chicago Press.
Löwith, K. ([1957] 1981), "Natur und Humanität des Menschen," in K. Löwith, *Sämtliche Schriften*, vol. 1, 259–94, Stuttgart: Metzler.
Lukács, G. (1911), *Die Seele und die Formen. Essays*, Berlin: Fleischel & Co.
Lukács, G. ([1916] 1982), *Die Theorie des Romans. Ein geschichtsphilosophischer Versuch über die Formen der großen Epik*, Darmstadt-Neuwied: Luchterhand.
Lyotard, J. F. (1991), *The Inhuman: Reflections on Time*, Stanford: Stanford University Press.
Machiavelli, N. ([1531] 1971), "Discorsi sopra la prima Deca di Tito Livio," in N. Machiavelli, *Tutte le opere*, 73–254, Firenze: Sansoni.
Mackinder, H. J. (1919), *Democratic Ideals and Reality: A Study in the Politics of Reconstruction*, New York: Holt & Company.
Madsen, D. L. (1998), *American Exceptionalism*, Edinburgh: Edinburgh University Press.
Magalhaes Godinho, V. (2001), "The Portuguese Empire 1565–1665," *The Journal of European Economic History*, 30 (1): 49–104.
Maier, C. S. (2006), *Among Empires: American Ascendancy and its Predecessors*, Cambridge: Harvard University Press.
Mamdani, M. (2000), "Introduction," in M. Mamdani (ed.), *Beyond Rights Talk and Culture Talk. Comparative Essays on the Politics of Rights and Culture*, 1–13, New York: St. Martin's Press.
Mandeville, B. ([1714] 1795), *The Fable of the Bees; or, Private Vices, Public Benefits*, London: Bathurst et al.
Marat, J. P. (1789), "Assemblée Nationale: Séance du Lundi 14 Septembre," *Le Publiciste parisien*, September 15: 43–53, Paris: Hérissant.
Marcuse, L. (1960), "Was ist der Mensch? Die Philosophische Anthropologie antwortet auf ewige Fragen," *Die Zeit*, July 29: 8.
Marramao, G. (2012), *The Passage West. Philosophy After the Age of the Nation State*, London and New York: Verso.
Marx, K., and F. Engels ([1848] 1970), *Manifest der kommunistischen Partei*, Frankfurt am Main: Verlag Marxistische Blätter.

Marx, K., and F. Engels ([1848] 2010), "Manifesto of the Communist Party," in K. Marx and F. Engels, *Selected Works*, 1–68, vol. 1, Moscow: Progress Publishers, transcribed by Marxists Internet Archive, http://www.marxists.org/archive/marx/works/download/pdf/Manifesto.pdf (accessed August 23, 2014).
Marx, K. ([1853] 2005), "The British Rule in India," *New–York Daily Tribune*, June 25, transcribed by Marxists Internet Archive, https://www.marxists.org/archive/marx/works/1853/06/25.htm (accessed August 23, 2014).
Maturana, H. R., and F. J. Varela (1972), *Autopoesis and Cognition. The Realization of the Living*, Dordrecht: Reidel.
Mazzini, G. ([1829] 1939), "D'una letteratura europea," in G. Mazzini, *Opere*, vol. 2, 81–122, Milano: Rizzoli.
Mazzini, G. ([1847] 1939), "Del moto nazionale slavo," in G. Mazzini, *Lettere slave*, 23–74, Bari: Laterza.
Mazzini, G. ([1866] 1939), "Missione italiana, vita internazionale," in G. Mazzini, *Lettere slave*, 97–106, Bari: Laterza.
McAdams, D. P. (1999), "Personal narratives and the life story," in L. A. Pervin and O. P. John (eds.), *Handbook of Personality*, 478–500, New York and London: Guilford Press.
McFarland, D. (1999), *Animal Behaviour: Psychobiology, Ethology and Evolution*, London: Longman.
Mead, G. H. (1912), "The Mechanism of Social Consciousness," *Journal of Philosophy*, 9: 401–6.
Mead, G. H. ([1932] 2002), *The Philosophy of the Present*, New York: Prometheus Books.
Mead, G. H. ([1934] 1974), *Mind, Self, and Society from the Standpoint of a Social Behaviorist*, Chicago: University of Chicago Press.
Merchant, C. (2007), *American Environmental History. An Introduction*, New York: Columbia University Press.
Mettan, G. (2015), *Une guerre de mille ans. La russophobie de Charlemagne à la crise ukrainienne*, Genève: Editions des Syrtes.
Michelet, J. (1846), *Le peuple*, Paris: Hachette.
Michelet, J. (1847), *Histoire de la Révolution Française*, vol. 1, Paris: Chamerot.
Middell, M. (2016), "The French Revolution in the global world of the eighteenth century," in A. Forrest and M. Middell (eds.), *The Routledge Companion to the French Revolution in World History*, 23–38, Abingdon: Routledge.
Mikkeli, H. (1998), *Europe as an idea and an identity*, Basingstoke: Macmillan.
Mikulić, B. (1987), *Sein, Physis, Aletheia: zur Vermittlung und Unmittelbarkeit im "ursprünglichen" Seinsdenken Martin Heideggers*, Würzburg: Königshausen & Neumann.
Milanesi, M. (1988), "Le carte dell'Europa," in G. Bazoli (ed.), *Europa. Storie di viaggiatori italiani*, 13–46, Milano: Electa.
Mill, J. S. ([1859] 1867), *On Liberty*, London: Longmans, Green & Co.
Miller, P. ([1953] 1993), "Errand into the Wilderness," in M. McGiffert (ed.), *In Search of Early America. The William & Mary Quaterly 1943–1993*, 1–12, Williamsburg: Institute of Early American History and Culture.
Milward, A. S. (1992), *The European Rescue of the Nation-State*, London: Routledge.
Mochnatzki, M. (1833), *Über die Revolution in Deutschland*, Dresden-Leipzig: Arnoldische Buchhandlung.

Moïsi, D. (2009), *The Geopolitics of Emotion: How cultures of Fear, Humiliation, and Hope are Reshaping the World*, New York: Doubleday.
Montesquieu, C. ([1758] 1843), "De l'esprit des lois," in *Œuvres completes de Montesquieu*, 289–528, Paris: Didot Frères.
Morison, S. E., H. S. Commager, and W. E. Leuchtenburg (1977), *A Concise History of the American Republic*, New York: Oxford University Press.
Münkler, H. (2004), "Die neuen Kriege. Kriege haben ihre Gestalt fundamental verändert," *Der Bürger im Staat*, 54 (4): 179–84.
Nagel, G. K. (1994), *Alte Landkarten, Globen und Städteansichten*, Augsburg: Battenberg.
Nash, R. F. (1989), *The Rights of Nature. A History of Environmental Ethics*, Madison: University of Wisconsin Press.
Nazemroaya, M. D. (2012), *The Globalization of NATO*, Atlanta: Clarity Press.
Niceforo, A. (1898), *L'Italia barbara contemporanea*, Palermo: Sandron.
Niceforo, A. (1901), *Italiani del nord e italiani del sud*, Torino: Bocca.
Nietzsche, F. ([1886] 1921), *Jenseits von Gut und Böse. Zur Genealogie der Moral*, Stuttgart: Kröner Verlag.
Nietzsche, F. ([1887] 1967), "Book one: European Nihilism 55 (June 10, 1887)," in F. Nietzsche, *The Will to Power*, 35–9, New York: Vintage Books.
Norton, M. B. et al. (2012), *A People & A Nation: A History of the United States*, vol. 1, Wadsworth: Cengage Learning.
Novalis ([1799] 1999), "Christianity or Europe: A Fragment," in F. C. Beiser (ed.), *The Early Political Writings of the German Romantics*, 59–79, Cambridge, Cambridge University Press.
Núñez Seixas, X. M. (2006), "Presentación," *Ayer. Revista de Historia Contemporánea* (64): 11–17.
Obama, B. (2011), "Full text of Obama's speech to UK parliament, May 25, 2011," *CNN Politics*, http://edition.cnn.com/2011/POLITICS/05/25/obama.europe.speech/ (accessed February 5, 2017).
O'Brien, K. (1997), *Narratives of Enlightenment: Cosmopolitan History from Voltaire to Gibbon*, Cambridge: Cambridge University Press.
Oelschlaeger, M. (1991), *The Idea of Wilderness. From the Prehistory to the Age of Ecology*, New Haven–London: Yale University Press.
Oschema, K. (2017), "No 'Emperor of Europe': A Rare Title between Political Irrelevance, Anti-Ottoman Polemics and the Politics of National Diversity," *The Medieval History Journal*, 20 (2): 1–36.
Paine, T. (1776), *Common Sense: Addressed to the Inhabitants of America*, Philadelphia: Carter.
Paine, T. ([1792] 1817), *The Rights of Man. An Answer to Mr. Burke's Attack on the French Revolution*, London: Sherwin.
Parekh, B. and R. N. Berki (1973), "The History of Political Ideas: A Critique of Q. Skinner's Methodology," *Journal of the History of Ideas*, 34 (2): 163–84.
Parker, H. (1642), *Observations upon some of His Majesties late answers and expresses*, Oxford: s.n.
Pasinato, A. (2000), "Introduzione," in A. Pasinato (ed.), *Heimat. Identità regionali nel processo storico*, 3–12, Roma: Donzelli.
Pazé, V. (2004), *Il comunitarismo*, Roma–Bari: Laterza.
Perkins, M. A. (2004), *Christiandom and European Identity. The Legacy of a Grand Narrative since 1789*, Berlin: De Gruyter.

Peters, R. (2001), "Constant Conflict," in R. Peters, *Fighting for the Future. Will America Triumph?*, 133–50, Mechanicsburg: Stackpole Books.
Petri, R. (1999), "Pamphlet per il tempo storico," in S. Bertelli (ed.), *Miti di fondazione e percezione del tempo nella cultura e nella politica del mondo contemporaneo*, 37–68, Roma: Carocci.
Petri, R. (2012a), "The Idea of Culture and the History of Emotions," *Historein*, 12: 21–37.
Petri, R. (2012b), "Cittadinanza, dimora, espulsione. Riflessioni sull'Austria ottocentesca," in H. Obermayer, S. Risse, and C. Romeo (eds.), *Regionale Zivilgesellschaft in Bewegung. Cittadini innanzi tutto*, 32–51, Wien: Folio.
Petri, R. (2017), "Balcani: Teleologia di una regione," in R. Petri (ed.), *Balcani, Europa: Violenza, politica, memoria*, 1–22, Torino: Giappichelli.
Petzen, J. (2012), "Contesting Europe: A call for an anti-modern sexual politics," *European Journal of Women's Studies*, 19 (1): 97–114.
Pietarinen, J. (1990), "Early Liberalism and Women's Liberty," in A. J. Arnaud, E. Kingdom (eds.), *Women's rights and the rights of man*, 125–37, Aberdeen: Aberdeen University Press.
Pocock, J. G. A. (1975), *The Machiavellian Moment. Florentine Political Thought and the Atlantic Republican Tradition*, Princeton: Princeton University Press.
Pocock, J. G. A. (1999), *Barbarism and Religion*, vol. 1, Cambridge: Cambridge University Press.
Pocock, J. G. A. (2003), "Afterword," in. J Pocock, *The Machiavellian Moment*, second edition, 553–87, Princeton: Princeton University Press.
Pocock, J. G. A. (2007), "Barbarians and the redefinition of Europe. A Study of Gibbon's Third Volume," in L. Wolff and M. Cipolloni (eds.), *The Anthropology of the Enlightenment*, 35–49, Stanford: Stanford University Press.
Pocock, J. G. A. (2009), *Political Thought and History. Essays on Theory and Method*, Cambridge: Cambridge University Press.
Polanyi, K. (1957), *The Great Transformation. The Political and Economic Origins of Our Time*, Boston: Beacon.
Pollack, K. M., D. L. Byman, M. Indyk, S. Maloney, M. E. O'Hanlon, and B. Riedel (2009), *Which Path to Persia? Options for a New American Strategy toward Iran*, Analysis Paper 20, Washington: The Brookings Institution.
Pomian, K. (1993), "Nations et religions: l'Occident, l'Europe centrale, l'Europe de l'Est," in P. den Boer and W. Frijhoff (eds.), *Lieux de mémoire et identités nationales*, 47–60, Amsterdam: Amsterdam University Press.
Pratt, A. (n.d.), "Nihilism," *Internet Encyclopedia of Philosophy*, http://www.iep.utm.edu/nihilism/ (accessed February 6, 2015).
Prigogine, I. (1980), *From Being to Becoming. Time and Complexity in the Physical Sciences*, San Francisco: Freeman.
Puar, J. (2010), "Israel's gay propaganda war," *The Guardian*, July 1st, http://www.theguardian.com/commentisfree/2010/jul/01/israels-gay-propaganda-war (accessed August 5, 2014).
Qutb, S. ([1964] 2005), *Milestones*, Birmingham: Maktabah.
Rahn, T. (1998), "Masse, Maske und Macht. Psychologien des Zeremoniells im 20. Jahrhundert," in B. Jahn, T. Rahn, and C. Schnitzer (eds.), *Zeremoniell in der Krise*, 129–48, Marburg: Jonas Verlag.
Rasmussen, A. F. (2016), *The Will to Lead: America's Indispensable Role in the Global Fight for Freedom*, New York: HarperCollins.

Ratzinger, J. C. (2000), *The Spirit of the Liturgy*, San Francisco: Ignatius Press.
Rawls, J. (2005), *Political Liberalism: Expanded Edition*, New York: Columbia University Press.
Reichstag (1916), *Verhandlungen des Reichstags. XIII. Legislaturperiode, II. Session*, vol. 306, Stenographische Berichte, Berlin: Norddeutsche Buchdruckerei und Verlagsanstalt.
Reinhard, W. (2008), *Kleine Geschichte des Kolonialismus*, Stuttgart: Kröner.
Remotti, F. (1992), "Cultura," in *Enciclopedia delle scienze sociali*, vol. 2, 641–60, Roma: Treccani.
Remotti, F. (1996), *Contro l'identità*, Roma and Bari: Laterza.
Renan, E. (1882), *Qu'est-ce qu'une nation?*, Paris: Calmann Lévy.
Reyes Mate, M. (2006), "¿Existe una responsabilidad histórica?," *Claves de Razón Práctica*, 168: 34–39.
Reynolds, S. (2016), "Magna Carta in its European Context," *History. The Journal of the Historical Association*, 101 (348): 659–70.
Ricci, M. (2000), "Kosovo, assolta la Nato: 'Non fu genocidio'," *la.Repubblica.it*, June 2, http://www.repubblica.it/online/mondo/natoassolta/natoassolta/natoassolta/natoassolta.html (accessed November 18, 2016).
Richards, R. J. (2008), *The Tragic Sense of Life: Ernst Haeckel and the Struggle over Evolutionary Thought*, Chicago: University of Chicago Press.
Richards, R. J. (2009), "Haeckel's embryos: fraud not proven," *Biology & Philosophy* 24: 147–54.
Richards, R. J. (2013), *Was Hitler a Darwinian? Disputed Questions in the History of Evolutionary Theory*, Chicago: University of Chicago Press.
Richter, D. (2001), *Facing East from Indian country: A Native History of Early America*, Cambridge (MA): Harvard University Press.
Ricœur, P. (1986), *Lectures on ideology and utopia*, New York: Columbia University Press.
Ricœur, P. (2004), *Memory, History, Forgetting*, Chicago and London: University of Chicago Press.
Roberts, P. G. (2013), "Obama's 'Kill List' Grows," *American Free Press*, March 6, https://americanfreepress.net/obamas-kill-list-grows/ (accessed February 5, 2017).
Robespierre, M. ([1791] 2009), "Discours sur la liberté de la presse," in *The Project Gutenberg EBook of Discours par Maximilien Robespierre*, 5, http://www.archive.org/stream/discoursparmaxim29775gut/pg29775.txt (accessed December 17, 2013).
Robespierre, M. ([1792] 2009), "Discours de Maximilien Robespierre sur la guerre," in *The Project Gutenberg EBook of Discours par Maximilien Robespierre*, 5, http://www.archive.org/stream/discoursparmaxim29775gut/pg29775.txt (accessed December 17, 2013).
Rodbertus–Jagetzow, C. ([1861] 1890), "Seid deutsch!," in C. Rodbertus–Jagetzow, *Kleine Schriften*, 297–306, Berlin: Puttkammer & Mühlbrecht.
Roederer, P. L. ([1800] 2012), "Property Rights," in R. Leroux and D. M. Hart (eds.), *French Liberalism in the Nineteenth Century*, 11–19, Abingdon: Routledge.
Rorty, R. (2003), "Response to Appiah," in M. J. Gibney (ed.), *Globalizing Rights. The Oxford Amnesty Lectures 1999*, 233–37, Oxford: Oxford University Press.
Rosanvallon, P. (1986), "Pour une histoire conceptuelle du politique: note du travail," *Revue de synthèse*, 107 (1–2): 93–105.

Rosenberg Wynne, J. (1798), *Costumi di Morlacchi*, Padova: Conzatti.
Rosenblatt, H. (2000), "The Christian Enlightenment," in S. J. Brown and T. Tackett (eds.), *The Cambridge History of Christianity*, vol. 7, 283–301, New York: Cambridge University Press.
Rosenfeld, M. (2010), *The Identity of the Constitutional Subject: Selfhood, Citizenship, Culture, and Community*, Abingdon: Routledge.
Rossi, P. (1991), "Civiltà," in *Enciclopedia della scienze sociali*, vol. 1, 793–808, Roma: Treccani.
Rossi, P. (1997), "Progresso," in *Enciclopedia della scienze sociali*, vol. 7, 76–88, Roma: Treccani.
Rostow, W. W. ([1960] 1991), *The Stages of Economic Growth: A Non–Communist Manifesto*, Cambridge: Cambridge University Press.
Rousseau, J. J. ([1755] 2000), *Discourse on Inequality*, Oxford: Oxford University Press.
Rousseau, J. J. (1761), *Extrait du Projet de paix perpétuelle de monsieur l'Abbé de Saint-Pierre'*, Paris: N.N.
Rousseau, J. J. ([1762] 1913), *The Social Contract & Discourses*, London, Toronto and New York: Dent & Sons-Dutton & Co.
Rueckert, W. (1996), "Literature and Ecology. An Experiment in Ecocriticism," in C. Glotfelty and H. Fromm (eds.), *The Ecocriticism Reader*, 105–21, Athens: University of Georgia Press.
Runciman, S. (1976), "Gibbon and Byzantium," *Daedalus*, 105 (3): 103–07.
Sachsenmaier, D. (2007), "World history as ecumenical history?," *Journal of World History* 18 (4): 465–89.
Sackey, B. M. (2013), "African Worldviews," in T. Manuh and E. Sutherland–Addy (eds.), *Africa in Contemporary Perspective*, 151–64, Accra: Sub-Saharan Publishers.
Said, E. W. (1978), *Orientalism*, London: Penguin.
Saint Paul, *Romans* 1: 13–6, in *Oremus Bible Browser*, http://bible.oremus.org/?ql=56611346 (accessed September 26, 2016).
Sammet, G. (1990), *Der vermessene Planet. Bilderatlas zur Geschichte der Kartographie*, Hamburg: Gruner & Jahr.
Sandys, G. (1621), *A relation of a iourney begun An: Dom: 1610. Fovrebookes. Containing a description of the Turkish Empire, of Ægypt, of the Holy Land, of the remote parts of Italy, and islands adioyning*, London: W. Barrett.
Sartre, J. P. ([1960] 2004), *Critique of Dialectical Reason*, vol. 1, London: Verso.
Sato, M. (2007), "The Archetype of History in the Confucian Ecumene," *History and Theory*, 46 (May): 218–32.
Sato, M. (2015), "Historical Thought and Historiography: East Asia," in J. D. Wright (ed.), *International Encyclopedia of the Social & Behavioral Science*, 2nd edition, vol. 11, 48–53, Oxford: Elsevier.
Schama, S. (1995), *Landscape and Memory*, London: HarperCollins.
Schattkowsky, R. (2002), "Nationalismus und Konfliktgestaltung. Westpreußen zwischen Reichsgründung und Erstem Weltkrieg," in M. G. Müller and R. Petri (eds.), *Die Nationalisierung von Grenzen*, 35–79, Marburg: Verlag Herder Institut.
Schaub, J. F. (2015), *Pour une histoire politique de la race*, Paris: Éditions du Seuil.
Schelling, F. W. J. ([1799] 1858), "Einleitung zu dem Entwurf eines Systems der Naturphilosophie," in *Friedrich Wilhelm Joseph von Schellings sämmtliche Werke*, vol.3, 269–326, Stuttgart: Cotta.

Scherer, A. (1860), *Geographie und Geschichte von Tirol. Ein Lehrbuch für die vaterländische Jugend*, Innsbruck: Wagnersche Buchhandlung.

Scheye, E., and L. Andersen (2007), "Conclusion," in L. Andersen, B. Møller and F. Stepputat (eds.), *Fragile States and Insecure People? Violence, Security, and Statehood in the Twenty-First Century*, 237–46, Basingstoke: Palgrave Macmillan.

Schmitt, C. (1923), *Römischer Katholizismus und politische Form*, Hellerau: Hegner.

Schmitt, C. ([1932] 1991), *Der Begriff des Politischen*, Berlin: Duncker & Humblot.

Schneidmüller, B. (1997), "Die mittelalterlichen Konstruktionen Europas," in H. Duchardt and A. Kunz (eds.), *"Europäische Geschichte" als historiographisches Problem*, 5–24, Mainz: Institut für Europäische Geschichte.

Schönichen, W. (1929), *Umgang mit Mutter Grün*, Berlin: Bermühler.

Schönichen, W. (1934), *Naturschutz im Dritten Reich*, Berlin: Bermühler.

Schönichen, W. (1950), *Natur als Volksgut und Menschheitsgut*, Stuttgart: Ulmer.

Schultz, H. D. (2007), "Die Platzierung der Türkei: ein Fall für den Geographen?," *Geographische Revue*, 9 (1–2): 17–48.

Schulze, H. (1999), *Staat und Nation in der europäischen Geschichte*, München: Beck.

Seeger, S. A. (2010), *Verantwortung. Tradition und Dekonstruktion*, Würzburg: Königshausen & Neumann.

Serna, P. (2016), "The sister republics, or the ephemeral invention of a French Republican Commonwealth," in A. Forrest and M. Middell (eds.), *The Routledge Companion to the French Revolution in World History*, 39–59, Abingdon: Routledge.

Serrier, T. (2004), "'Lavoro culturale tedesco nella marca orientale.' Il mito del primato tedesco e il problema del confine in Posnania (1871–1914)," *Memoria e Ricerca*, 15: 27–48.

Shafer, B. E., ed. (1991), *Is America Different? A New Look at American Exceptionalism*, Oxford: Clarendon Press.

Shils, E. A. (1968), "The Concept and Function of Ideology," *International Encyclopedia of the Social Sciences*, vol. 7, 66–76, New York: Macmillan & Free Press.

Sieyès, E. J., ([1789] 2002), *Qu'est–ce que le Tiers état?*, Paris: Éditions du Boucher.

Silvera, I. (2016), "Guy Verhofstadt: EU can become 'empire of the good' after Donald Trump's election," *International Business Times*, November 29, http://www.ibtimes.co.uk/guy–verhofstadt–eu–will–be–empire–good–opposition–donaldtrumps–america–1593862 (accessed January 14, 2017).

Simal, J. L. (2016), "Letters from Spain: The 1820 revolution and the liberal international," in M. Isabella and K. Zanou (eds.), *Mediterranean Diasporas. Politics and Ideas in the Long 19th Century*, 25–41, London: Bloomsbury.

Simon, R. I. (2005), *The Touch of the Past: Remembrance, Learning, and Ethics*, Basingstoke: Palgrave Macmillan.

Skinner, Q. ([1998] 2012), *Liberty before Liberalism*, Cambridge: Cambridge University Press.

Skinner, Q. (2002), *Visions of Politics*, vol. 1, Cambridge: Cambridge University Press.

Slaughter, T. P. (2003), *Exploring Lewis and Clark: Reflections on Men and Wilderness*, New York: Knopf.

Spinoza, B. ([1670] 2003), "A Treatise on Religion and Politics," in J. B. Schneewind (ed.), *Moral Philosophy from Montaigne to Kant*, 239–46, Cambridge: Cambridge University Press.

Spinoza, B. ([1677] 2003), "Ethics. Fourth Part of the Ethics: On Human Bondage, or the Powers of the Affects," in J. B. Schneewind (ed.), *Moral Philosophy from Montaigne to Kant*, 246–55, Cambridge: Cambridge University Press.

Spirkin, A. (1983), *Dialectical Materialism*, Moscow: Progress Publishers; digital transcription by R. Cymbala, https://www.marxists.org/reference/archive/spirkin/works/dialectical-materialism/ch05-s07.html (accessed January 30, 2017).

Spranger, E. (1923), *Der Bildungswert der Heimatkunde*, Berlin: Hartmann.

Spykman, N. J. (1942), *America's Strategy in World Politics: The United States and the Balance of Power*, New York: Brace and Company.

Sreedharan, E. (2004), *Textbook of Historiography. 500 BC to AD 2000*, Hyderabad: Orient Longman.

Stambaugh, J. (1969), "Introduction," in M. Heidegger, *Identity and Difference*, 7–18, New York: Harper & Row.

Stavenhagen, K. (1939), *Heimat als Grundlage menschlicher Existenz*, Göttingen: Vandenhoeck & Ruprecht.

Stephens, G. M. (n.d.) "John Locke: His American and Carolinian Legacy," *John Locke Foundation*, https://www.johnlocke.org/john-locke-his-american-and-carolinian-legacy/ (accessed October 3, 2016).

Stepputat, F., L. Andersen, and B. Møller (2007), "Introduction: Security Arrangements in Fragile States," in L. Andersen, B. Møller and F. Stepputat (eds.), *Fragile States and Insecure People? Violence, Security, and Statehood in the Twenty-First Century*, 5–13, Basingstoke: Palgrave Macmillan.

Stewart, G. T. (2011), "The Scottish Enlightenment meets the Tibetan Enlightenment," *Journal of World History*, 22 (3): 455–92.

Stråth, B. (2013), "Ideology and conceptual history," in M. Freeden, L. T. Sargent and M. Stears (eds.), *The Oxford Handbook of Political Ideologies*, 3–19, Oxford: Oxford University Press.

Strier, R. (2004), "Against the Rule of Reason: Praise of Passion from Petrarch to Luther to Shakespeare to Herbert," in G. K. Paster, K. Rowe and M. Floyd-Wilson (eds.), *Reading the Early Modern Passions. Essays in the Cultural History of Emotion*, 23–42, Philadelphia: University of Pennsylvania Press.

Subrahmanyam, S. (2015), "The politics of eschatology: a short reading of the long view," in H. Trüper, D. Chakrabarty and S. Subrahmanyam (eds.), *Historical Teleologies in the Modern World*, 25–45, London: Bloomsbury.

Sutherland, M. (2012), "Populism and Spectacle," *Cultural Studies*, 26: 330–45.

Tagore, R. ([1941] 2002), "Historicality in Literature," in R. Guha, *History at the Limit of World-History*, 95–99, New York: Columbia University Press.

Taylor, A. (2011), "Squaring the Circles: The Reach of Colonial America," in E. Foner and L. McGirr (eds.), *American History Now*, 3–23, Philadelphia: Temple University Press.

Taylor, C. (1995), "Ursprünge des neuzeitlichen Selbst," in K. Michalski (ed.), *Identität im Wandel: Castelgandolfo-Gespräche 1995*, 11–23, Stuttgart: Klett-Cotta.

Taylor, R. (2012), "Predator Drone Strikes: 50 Civilians Are Killed For Every 1 Terrorist," *Policy.Mic*, October 20, https://mic.com/articles/16949/predator-

drone–strikes–50–civilians–are–killed–for–every–1–terrorist–and–the–cia–only–wants–to–up–drone–warfare (accessed July 7, 2013).
Teilhard de Chardin, P. ([1959] 2004), *The Future of Man*, New York: Image Books Doubleday.
Thiesse, A. M. (1999), *La création des identités nationales*, Paris: Éditions du Seuil.
Thiesse, A. M. (2006), "Centralismo estatal y nacionalismo regionalizado. Las paradojas del caso francés," *Ayer. Revista de Historia Contemporánea* (64): 33–64.
Thomson, A. (2008), *Bodies of Thought: Science, Religion, and the Soul in the Early Enlightenment*, Oxford: Oxford University Press.
Thrower, J. (1983), *Marxist-Leninist "Scientific Atheism" and the Study of Religion and Atheism in the USSR*, Berlin: De Gruyter.
Thumboo, E. (1996), "Essential space and cross–cultural challenges," in B. Bennet, J. Doyle and S. Nandan (eds.), *Crossing Cultures. Essays on Literature and Culture of the Asia–Pacific*, 11–24, London: Skoob Books.
Tocqueville, A. ([1835] 2012), "The Liberty of the Press" (1835), in R. Leroux and D. M. Hart (eds.), *French Liberalism in the Nineteenth Century*, 89–96, Abingdon: Routledge.
Tocqueville, A. ([1835] 2010), *Democracy in America: Historical-Critical Edition*, Indianapolis: Liberty Fund.
Todorov, T. (1984), *The Conquest of America: The Question of the Other*, New York: Harper & Row.
Tolstoy, L. N. ([1889] 1997), "The Kreutzer Sonata," in L. Tolstoy, *The Kreutzer Sonata and other Stories*, 85–177, Oxford: Oxford University Press.
Toynbee, A. J. (1948), *A Study of History*, vol. 1, London: Oxford University Press.
Tricoire, D. (2015), "Die Selbstkolonisierung Europas oder: Wie lässt sich eine andere Geschichte der Aufklärung erzählen?," in Jürgen Heyde et al. (eds.), *Dekonstruieren und doch erzählen. Polnische und andere Geschichten*, 25–31, Göttingen: Wallstein.
Tromnau, A. (1889), *Der Unterricht in der Heimatskunde*, Halle an der Saale: Heynemann.
Trüper, H. (2014), "Löwith, Löwith's Heidegger, and the unity of history," *History and Theory*, 53 (February): 45–68.
Trüper, H., D. Chakrabarty, and S. Subrahmanyam (2015), "Preface," in H. Trüper, D. Chakrabarty and S. Subrahmanyam (eds.), *Historical Teleologies in the Modern World*, xi, London: Bloomsbury.
Tugendhat, E. (2010), *Anthropologie statt Metaphysik*, München: Beck.
Tugrul, S. (2013), "Invisible Sovereign: Nation. Visible Power: People," *International Journal of Business, Humanities and Technology*, 3 (4): 77–86.
Tully, J. (1993), *An Approach to Political Philosophy: Locke in Context*, New York: Cambridge University Press.
Turner, F. (1991), *Rebirth of Value. Meditations on Beauty, Ecology, Religion, and Education*, Albany: State University of New York Press.
Turner, F. J. ([1893] 2005), "*The significance of the frontier in American history. Address to the American Historical Association, Chicago, 12 July 1893*," Research Triangle Park (NC): National Humanities Center; available online nationalhumanitiescenter.org/pds/gilded/empire/text1/turner.pdf (accessed October 4, 2016).

Tyrrell, I. (2010), *Reforming the World: The Creation of America's Moral Empire*, Princeton: Princeton University Press.
U.S. Congress ([1830] 1846), "An Act to provide for an exchange of lands with the Indians residing in any of the states or territories, and for their removal west of the river Mississippi," *Public Statutes at Large of the United States of America*, edited by R. Peters, vol. 4, 411–12, Boston: Little & Brown.
Uexküll, J. von (1934), *Streifzüge durch die Umwelten von Tieren und Menschen. Ein Bilderbuch unsichtbarer Welten*, Berlin: Springer.
UNESCO (1950), *UNESCO and its programme*, III, The Race Question. Statement Issued 18 July 1950, p. 6, available online: http://unesdoc.unesco.org/images/0012/001282/128291eo.pdf (accessed July 24, 2014).
Vacante, S. (1963), "La situazione economica dell'Alto Adige," in C. Battisti (ed.), *L'Alto Adige nel passato e nel presente*, 170–95, Firenze: Istituto di studi per l'Alto Adige.
Valentine, D. ([1990] 2000), *The Phoenix Program*, Lincoln: iUniverse.com.
Vasoli, C. (1977), "The Machiavellian Moment: A Grand Ideological Synthesis," *The Journal of Modern History* 49 (4): 661–70.
Vico, G. ([1744] 1816), *Principi di scienza nuova d'intorno a una comune natura delle nazioni*, vol. 1, Milano: Silvestri.
Vincent, A. (2012), "Political Ideology and Political Theory: Reflections on an Awkward Partnership," in B. Jackson and M. Stears (eds.), *Liberalism as Ideology. Essays in Honour of Michael Freeden*, 159–77, Oxford: Oxford University Press.
Virilio, P. (2005), *The Information Bomb*, London and New York: Verso.
Vogler, G. (1997), "'Europa' an der Wende vom Mittelalter zur Neuzeit," in M. Řezník (ed.), *Nations, Identities, Historical Consciousness*, 289–307, Praha: Charles University.
Voltaire, F. M. ([1751] 1779), *The Age of Louis XIV*, London: Fieldings & Walker.
Voltaire, F. M. (1759a), *An Essay on Universal History*, vol. 1, London: Nourse.
Voltaire, F. M. (1759b), *An Essay on Universal History*, vol. 2, London: Nourse.
Voltaire, F. M. (1761) "A Recapitulation of the whole of the Foregoing History," in *The Works of M. de Voltaire*, vol.9, 142–52, London: Newbery et al.
Voltaire, F. M. (1764), "General History," in *The Works of M. de Voltaire*, vol. 23, 89–99, London: Newbery et al.
Walliss, J. (2004), *Apocalyptic Trajectories. Millenarism and Violence in the Contemporay World Context*, Bern: Peter Lang.
Ward Scaltsas, P. (1990), "Women as Ends—Women as Means in the Enlightenment," in A. J. Arnaud, and E. Kingdom (eds.), *Women's rights and the rights of man*, 138–48, Aberdeen: Aberdeen University Press.
WikiAnswers® (s.d.), "Why we are calling human and not huwoman?," *The WikiAnswers® Community*, http://www.answers.com/Q/Why_we_are_calling_human%27_and_not_huwoman (accessed August 8, 2014).
Wintle, M. (2009), *The Image of Europe: Visualizing Europe in Cartography and Iconography Throughout the Ages*, Cambridge: Cambridge University Press.
Wittgenstein, L. (1922), *Tractatus Logico–Philosophicus*, London: Kegan, Trench, Trubner & Co.
Wolff, L. (2010), "Nostalgia antropologica. Venezia e la Dalmazia," in R. Petri (ed.), *Nostalgia: Memoria e passaggi tra le sponde dell'Adriatico*, 107–22, Roma: Edizioni di storia e letteratura.

Wolff, L. (2016a), *The Singing Turk: Ottoman Power and Operatic Emotions on the European Stage from the Siege of Vienna to the Age of Napoleon*, Stanford: Stanford University Press.

Wolff, L. (2016b), *Mental Mapping and Eastern Europe*, Huddinge: Södertörn University.

Wolin, R. (2001), *Heidegger's children*, Princeton: University of Princeton Press.

Wood, G. S. ([1966] 1993), "Rhetoric and Reality in the American Revolution," in M. McGiffert (ed.), *In Search of Early America. The William & Mary Quaterly 1943–1993*, 54–77, Williamsburg: Institute of Early American History and Culture.

Wopfner, H. (1921), "Tirols Eroberung durch deutsche Arbeit," in *Tiroler Heimat. Beiträge zu ihrer Kenntnis und Wertung*, 5–38, Innsbruck: Tyrolia.

Wörsdörfer, R. (2004), "'Italiani' e 'sloveni': concetti d'identità nazionale nell'area alpina e adriatica tra metà Otto e metà Novecento," *Memoria e Ricerca*, 15: 49–78.

Young, R. (1992), "Colonialism and humanism," in J. Donald and A. Rattansi (eds.), *"Race," Culture and Difference*, 243–51, London: SAGE.

Žižek, S. (2008), *The Sublime Object of Ideology*, London and New York: Verso.

Index

Abbas, Asma 54
Abbott, Carl 68
Acadia 60
Achleitner, Wilhelm 84
Ackerly, Brooke A. 140
Adam (figure of the Genesis) 62, 146
Aegean 17
Aesthetics 81, 89, 91, 120, 122
Afghanistan 129, 147, 158, 167
Africa 10, 25–9, 38, 56, 70, 109–10, 114–15, 118, 127, 136–9
  Central 165
  East 21
  North 21, 112
  South 70, 109, 111
  Southwest 165
African Americans 64, 67–70, 108, 174
Agazzi, Elena 45
Ahmad, Aijaz 130
Akkadian 19
al-Awlaki, Anwar 156
al-Awlaki, Nasser 156
al-Awlaki, Nawar 156
Albright, Madeleine Korbel 150
Albrow, Martin 142–3
Alexander III of Macedon (the Great) 20, 22
Algeria 150
Althusius, Johannes 72–3
altruism 132, 142–3, 149, 153, 162, 167, 177
Amadori Virgilj, Giovanni 84, 149, 154–7, 160, 162–3, 168
America (continent) 1, 22, 29–31
  Latin 70, 129
  North 60–1, 149
America (United States)
  colonies 37–8, 51, 55–7, 60–6, 108–9, 113–14

constitution 66–72, 92, 94, 96–7, 111
ecological thought 173–5, 178
exceptionality 67–71, 199
foreign policy 15, 110, 138, 143, 147, 150–64, 167–9
society 106, 132
American Colonization Society 110
American Revolution 49, 62–7, 71, 75–6, 94
Amerindians 56, 62–4, 68–9, 102, 108–9, 111, 120
Amuzegar, Jahangir 143
Anabaptism 121
Ancien régime 29, 68, 77, 80–2, 87–8, 94
Andersen, Louise 166–7
Anderson, Benedict 82, 166
Anderson, Tim 158
Andes 133
Anglo-American alliance 1, 38, 151
Anglo-Saxons 57–8
animal 31, 35, 41–3, 51, 114–16, 122–4, 146, 174–80, 190–3
anti-Semitism 119–21
apocalypse 2, 11, 40, 65, 158, 171–99, 201
Appalachian Mountains 64–5
Appiah, Kwame Anthony 136, 139
Arab(s) 20–1, 23, 28, 76, 118, 142–3
Arendt, Hannah 77
aristocracy 26, 33, 42, 57, 63, 71–2, 81, 90–2, 161, 163
Aristotle 66, 79, 90
Armageddon 15, 198–9
Arndt, Ernst Moritz 119
Aron, Stephen 68–9
Arrighi, Giovanni 150
Aryans 117

Asia 13–15, 18–19, 21, 25–9, 104–8, 129–30, 138, 151, 199
  Southeast 129
Asia Minor 18, 21
Astell, Mary 144
atheism 26, 32, 37, 40–1, 51, 70, 76, 83, 195
Athens 70
Atlantic Ocean 13, 15, 23–4, 30, 61, 150, 168
Auckland 141
Auschwitz 123
Australia 56, 70
Austria 84, 119
authoritarianism 49, 52, 76–8, 190

backwardness
  political 87, 159–61
  racial 114, 116, 120, 127
  spatial 13, 30, 78, 102, 106–7
  temporal 5, 28–9, 55, 102–4, 143–5, 183
Bacon, Francis 31
Baker, James Addison 151
Baldwin, Richard E. 131
Baledrokadroka, Joeli 141
Balibar, Étienne 101, 119, 172
Balkans 23, 78, 105
Baptism 63–4, 67
Baraka, Amiri 101
barbarity 22, 38, 63, 75–6, 106–8, 114–16
  antiquity 18, 24
  lawlessness 54–7, 91, 109
  rudeness 12, 25, 27, 145, 156, 164
  stage of development 9, 28, 33, 40, 129–31, 145, 147,
  threat 30, 56, 63
Barbeyrac, Jean 114
Barcellona, Pietro 19
Barents, Willem 25–6
Barker, Ernest 83
Bassin, Mark 13
Bastiat, Frédérik 58
Bate, Jonathan 178–80, 187
Bauman, Zygmunt 131, 133, 184–5, 190
beast 27, 32–3, 35–7, 101, 110, 173, 192, 194
Beck, Ulrich 139, 141–2

Belgium 109, 160–1, 164
Benhabib, Seyla 78
Benjamin, Walter 189–90
Bentham, Jeremy 58
Berki, Robert Nandor 9
Berlin, Isaiah 58
Bernier, François 113–15, 118
bestiality 36, 41, 44, 113
Bible 40, 62–3, 84
bin Laden, Osama 155, 157
Black, Will 195
Blair, Anthony Charles Lynton 131
Bloch, Ernst 188, 190
Blount, Henry 105
Blumenbach, Johann Friedrich 116
Blumenberg, Hans 39
Boer, Roland 188
Bolshevism 13, 120
Borgna, Eugenio 187–8
Borgolte, Michael 21
Boschman, Robert 62, 176, 199
Boston 63
Boucheron, Patrick 5–6
Bourdieu, Pierre 182
bourgeoisie 72, 77–9, 86, 97, 129, 132, 188
Bové, José 133
Boyer, Paul Samuel 60–4
Boym, Svetlana 45, 81, 89, 91, 106, 188
Bradstreet, Anne 171
Bretton Woods 131
Brice, Catherine 6
Brissot, Jacques Pierre 75
Britain 30
  British 28, 55, 58, 67, 76, 97, 151, 162, 178
  colonies 55–6, 60–4, 67–8, 71, 109, 114, 129–30, 174, 199
  empire 150
  England 49–50, 71–2, 83, 92, 103
  English 13, 27, 57, 67–8, 106, 154, 173
  Great Britain 55, 57, 64, 71, 106, 108–9, 111, 114, 131, 156
  United Kingdom 154, 162
Bron, Gregoire 58, 97
Brunner, Otto 6
Brussels Treaty 167
Brzezinski, Zbigniew Kazimierz 151

Buddhism   14–15, 25, 42
Burke, Edmund   74
Bush, George Walker   147, 155, 163
Bushmen   110
Butler, Judith   146
Byzantine Empire   22, 105

Campanella, Tommaso   32
Camus, Albert   189
Cana, Frank Richardson   110
Canaan   63
Canetti, Elias   88
Cape Town   110
capitalism   59, 58, 63, 130, 132, 172
Cardini, Franco   23
Carolina   55–6
Carolingian period   17, 20
Catholicism   20–4, 40, 58, 64–5, 71, 83–4, 160
Caucasus   21
Celts   80–1, 117
Cervantes, Miguel   111–13, 143
Chakrabarty, Dipesh   2, 194
Chan, Sewell   139
Chanock, Martin   48–9, 127, 133, 143
chaos theory   10
Charles I (Charlemagne, the Great)   20
Charles Martel   20
Chechens   106
Chesapeake   60, 68
Chile   150
China   10, 14, 29, 102, 129, 151, 161
Chomsky, Noam   93–4, 131, 138, 150, 152, 155–6
Christian Democrats   59, 120
Christianity   15, 20–7, 32–5, 39–3, 47–9, 63–7, 70, 74, 112, 120–1, 144, 169
    beliefs   68, 82–3, 111, 121, 141, 173, 195, 199
    politics   58–9, 82–4, 120, 160–1
    traditions   51, 65, 103, 105, 123, 143, 153
citizen   29, 85, 87, 120, 144, 150, 156, 166, 172
citizenship   50, 59, 65–7, 71–80, 90, 94, 159, 162–3
civil society   27, 66, 87, 141–3, 152, 167
civility   3, 19, 27, 63, 105

civilization   68, 70, 78, 81, 104–8, 120–1, 165, 191, 195
    concept   1–3, 5, 12–14, 28
    disease   45, 173, 177–8, 190
    stages   115–18, 123–4, 131–2, 145, 147, 166, 183
civilizing mission   25–6, 30–4, 37, 40, 55, 58, 61, 76, 102, 109, 111, 129, 154–5, 159–61, 164, 175
clash of civilizations   1, 13–14
clergy   58, 65, 72
climate   113–15, 174, 194
Cobain, Ian   157
Cockburn, Catherine   145
Cold War   1, 12, 58, 158, 169, 199
Collins, Dana   140, 147
colonialism   13, 28–30, 42–3, 53, 113, 116–18, 123, 127, 149, 155, 160
    American   110
    Belgian   109, 161
    British   55–6, 60–8, 71, 109, 114, 129–30, 174, 199
    colonization   33, 60–5, 67–72, 108–11
    decolonization   149–50, 152, 164, 202
    Dutch   55, 60, 68, 108–10
    French   57–8, 60, 64–5, 68, 71, 109, 163
    German   108–9
    Iberian   22–3, 25, 68, 104, 108, 113–14, 160,
    Italian   105, 109
    mandate system   165–7
    neocolonialism   125–9, 133–4, 139, 147
    postcolonial states   125, 128, 133–4, 137, 166–7
Commager, Henry Steele   61, 65, 68
communication   6, 79, 82, 89, 128–9
communicative rationality   3, 5
communism   15, 50, 142, 171–3, 202
community
    animal   179
    ideal   78, 80, 97, 106, 130, 133–7, 182–5, 188–91
    national   70, 82, 85–6, 104, 111–12, 125–6
    primitive   33, 56–7, 109, 125, 165–8, 176, 179

scientific   11, 174
virtual   146
western   13, 55, 166–8
Comte, Auguste   38
Comte, Charles   98
conceptual history   4–11, 74
Condorcet, Marie-Jean-Antoine-Nicolas   28–9, 37–8, 57, 70, 76–7, 104, 110, 145, 160
Confino, Alon   85–6
Congo Free State   161
conquest   21–5, 28–30, 56, 62–5, 69, 77, 80–1, 96, 103–4, 107–8, 149, 160, 164, 168
consciousness   3–4, 8, 30, 43–5, 60, 89, 125, 130, 133, 136–7, 151, 169, 177, 182, 191, 195, 198
consent   3, 45, 49, 52, 60, 64, 73–4, 81–2, 87, 94, 155, 168, 202
conservatism   50, 59, 74–5, 83, 137, 153, 158–9, 177, 188
Constant, Benjamin   52, 57
Constantinople   21–3, 26
constitution   36, 50, 52, 55–9, 65–6, 71–3, 76, 78, 84, 88, 92–9, 119, 143–4, 154, 160, 163, 168
consumption   128–9, 131, 171–2, 184, 192–3
Conze, Werner   6
Cooke, Charles W.   174
Cooper, Robert   131
Cormack, William S.   163
Cortelazzo, Manlio   20
cosmopolitism   114, 125, 129, 137–9, 142
Cotton, John   62
Crafts, Nick   130
Crete   18
Croatia   83
Croce, Benedetto   58
Croghan, George   65
Crouch, Colin   89
crusades   20, 23, 104, 157
culture   2–9, 13, 113, 116–17, 119–28, 176, 185, 193–5
customs   33–4, 49, 64, 69, 114, 189
diversified   1, 135–41, 167, 189
heritage   17–18, 49, 133–4, 184
land cultivation   62–3, 107, 131

national   166, 197
othering   141–7
political   67, 79–80, 107–9, 173–4, 177, 188–9
religious   64
western   12, 28, 121, 153–4, 158, 190
Curry, Judith A.   174
Czechoslovakia   164
Czechs   106

Danzer, Gerhard   187
D'Arcy McGee, Thomas   72
Darwin, Charles   115, 119, 123, 175, 177–8
Darwinism   119, 123, 178
Dasgupta, Surendranath   134
Davies, James B.   149
de Clootz (du Val-de-Grâce), Jean-Baptiste   76
de las Casas, Bartolomé   113
de Staël, Germaine   98
Debord, Guy   89
Defoe, Daniel   27
Degler, Carl Neumann   51, 62–3, 67
Delanty, Gerard   104
Delaware   68
democracy   9, 75–80, 87–92
American   61, 67–8
constitution   59, 90–9, 138
movements   11, 51, 59, 120, 158, 196
western   2, 55, 92, 125, 131, 138, 142–3, 154–8, 161–2, 166–8
Democratic Party (USA)   51, 156, 158
Derrida, Jacques   191
Descartes, René   31, 47
despotism   14, 18–19, 28–30, 55, 72, 76–7, 92–6, 104–7, 120, 130, 134, 197
Destutt de Tracy, Antoine-Louis-Claude   3–4, 52, 98
Devji, Faisal   15
d'Holbach, Paul Henri   75
dialectics   7, 10, 39, 44, 101, 104, 186, 193, 196
Diderot, Denis   41, 57, 57
Diesterweg, Adolph   85
Dobbins, James   166
Don (river)   21

INDEX

Donnelly (general)   169
Dostoyevsky, Fyodor   106
Douglas, Roy   51
Douzinas, Costas   140
Dreyfus, Alfred   119
Duara, Prasenjit   102
Dubuisson, Daniel   13–14, 24–5, 41–2, 121, 173
Dunn, John   59
Dunoyer, Charles   98
Duso, Giuseppe   73–4
Dutch   55, 60, 67–8, 76, 108, 110

East   13–14, 19, 24, 28, 78, 143
East India Company   60
Eboli   123
ecology   135, 173–81, 185, 189
economy   9, 57, 102–3, 105, 122, 126, 165–6
   bio-economy   178–9, 194
   change   7, 31, 80, 102, 114
   colonial   25, 60–1, 68, 79, 107–8, 114, 133, 135–7
   growth   87, 171–2, 174
   international   1, 13, 15, 59, 126, 128–32, 142, 149–52, 154, 158–62, 197–8
   thought   48–9, 53–5, 58–9, 133
Egypt   118
Ehrenberg, John   141–2
Elba (river)   108
emotions   11, 14, 33–5, 44–8, 70, 75–9, 82–90, 117, 142, 153–4, 159–68, 198
Engels, Friedrich   129, 173
Enlightenment
   anthropology   44, 53, 101, 106, 130, 145
   expectations   2, 37–8
   geography   28, 106
   historiography   26–7, 33–4, 38, 41–2, 102, 135, 169
   philosophy   7, 10–11, 15, 32, 40–1, 44, 142
   political ideas   3, 74–9, 83–7, 90, 104, 153–7, 193–6
equality   28, 72, 94, 97, 101, 105, 138
   gender   126, 142–7
   international   15, 114, 131, 137–9, 165, 167

interpersonal   19, 33–5, 49, 57–9, 114
   social   35, 54, 67, 73, 109, 141
Erikson, Erik H.   182–3
Eritrea   109
eschatology   2, 12, 15, 39–42, 70, 75, 106, 121–2, 140, 152, 157–8, 177, 187, 191, 201
   religious   14–15, 24, 33, 83, 198
   secular   40, 147, 169, 172, 193–4
Esposito, Roberto   88, 97, 141, 184
ethnicity   77–80, 86–7, 97, 103, 114, 117, 124–7, 132, 139, 166
Eton, William   28
Etruscans   80
Ettinger, Maia   146
Eurasia   13, 28, 151, 199
Europe
   Central   107
   Christian   20–33, 84
   Eastern   106–8, 119, 143, 151
   European settlers   60–3, 68–70, 110–11, 160
   European Union (EU)   107, 143, 160
   European wealth   149
   Europeanness   1, 13, 104–7, 116, 120, 153–4
   Europeans   63, 67
   mission   36, 55, 70–1, 104, 107–13, 160, 164
   myth   17–19, 80
   Northeastern   17
   Northern   17, 21, 25–6
   Northwestern   105
   Old   61, 71, 103, 132, 125
   Southeastern   105, 107–8
   Western   15, 28, 102, 106, 128
European politics   50–3, 58–90, 96–9, 102–11, 119, 123–8, 131–5, 143–5, 164
Eve (figure of the Genesis)   146
evolution   6–7, 25, 86, 109, 116, 127, 138, 146, 172, 178, 192, 195, 198

Fakhraie, Fatemeh   147
Falk, Richard   139
Fanon, Frantz   13, 116
fascism   93, 123
Fauchet, Claude   75
Fauriel, Charles-Claude   103

fear 26, 28, 40, 42, 63–4, 82, 88, 94, 98, 134, 153–4, 159, 191–3
Febvre, Lucien 26–7
feminism 126, 140, 144–7, 174
Ferguson, Adam 3, 27–8
Fichte, Johann Gottlieb 38, 121
Fiji Islands 141
Flemish 57
Fordism 59
Forrest, Alan 105
Forsythe, David P. 137–8, 155
Fortunati, Vita 45
Foster, Robert Fitzroy 72
Foucault, Michel 4–5, 74, 82, 86, 145–6
France 30, 45, 49–50, 85, 96–7, 109, 119, 132, 166, 182, 186
Franchetti, Leopoldo 109
Franconia 81
Frank, Robert 105
Franklin, Benjamin 56, 65
Franks 20, 81
Freeden, Michael 6–7, 50, 52, 58–9, 91
freedom
  concept 90–1, 180
  economic 53, 129, 131
  free state 50, 72–3
  free will 35–6, 39, 41, 47, 51–2, 73, 193–6
  individual 48, 52, 55–7, 87, 90–4, 99, 133, 137–8, 168
  natural 35–7, 43, 49, 51, 73, 144
  political 18–19, 53, 55, 73–4, 92–3, 99, 106, 133, 137–8, 168, 197, 202
  reasonable 39, 91, 98, 122, 196
  religious 64–5, 165
  western 29, 58, 125, 150–2, 157–3
Freemen 30, 57, 61–5, 71, 174
French Revolution 7, 11, 45, 49–50, 71–87, 89, 92, 94–7, 104–6, 163
Freud, Sigmund 182–3
Fried, Alfred H. 76
Fröbel, Friedrich 85

Galilei, Galileo 31
Galimberti, Umberto 43
Gallant, Thomas W. 84
Gamble, Andrew 1–2
Garden of Eden 40, 42–3, 188, 191
Gauls 81
Geertz, Clifford 3, 122
Gelernter, David 70
Gemelli, Agostino 84
gender 117, 126, 128, 142–7
General Motors Corporation 138
general will, *esprit général* 27, 52, 97
Geneva 34–5
genocide 56, 139, 166, 168
geopolitics 12, 14, 68, 128, 132, 142, 150–3, 165
Georgescu-Roegen, Nicholas 194, 199
Germanic Confederation 80
Germanics 80
Germans 106, 116, 119–21
Germany 6, 30–1, 58, 72–81, 85, 95, 107–9, 142, 155, 164, 166, 177–8, 183–5, 196
Ghiselin, Michael T. 179
Gibbon, Edward 22, 29–30, 32–3, 114
Gibney, James 161, 163, 169
Gibraltar 17
Gilbert, Roger 178
Gilroy, Paul 125–8, 155
Gladstone, William Edwart 51
globalization 31, 60, 87, 125–36, 141, 153–4, 166–7, 184, 189
Glorious Revolution 72
Goa 25
Gobineau, Joseph Arthur 118–19
God 180–1, 193
  apotheosis 40, 43, 191, 199
  chosen people 69–70
  creationism (soul) 26, 34, 38, 41, 57, 145–6
  death of god 187–8
  deism 44
  divine love/justice 67, 75
  godlikeness 36, 40
  gods 174
  gospel 20, 24–5, 121, 160
  omnipotence 39, 121
  pantheism 32, 34, 176, 179–81, 196
  providence 30–41, 56, 62, 155
  redemption 69, 121, 190–1
Golden Age 43, 47–8, 172

INDEX

Goldgeier, James M. 151
good and evil 15–16, 32–5, 39, 51, 102, 112, 121, 157–9, 189, 193, 197–8, 202
Goodhart, Michael 52, 54, 135
Gorbachev, Mikhail Sergeyevic 151
Gott, Gil 161
Grand Canyon 174
Graumann, Carl Friedrich 19
Gray, John 1–2, 12, 15, 39–41, 53, 78, 93, 103, 121, 152–3, 157–8, 176, 195, 199
Gray, Thomas 103
Greece 17–19, 22, 79, 84, 105, 142, 178
Greeks 18, 24, 27–8
Greenland 133
Greenwald, Glenn 156
Grimm, Dieter 95–6
Grossman, Zoltán 150–1
Grotius (Huig de Groot) 31–4, 48, 55, 114
Grundtvig, Nikolaj Frederik Severin 83–4
Guha, Ranajit 134–5
Gut, Przemysław 9, 32
Gyekye, Kwame 136–7
Gypsies 112–13, 143–4

Habeas corpus 48, 92–3, 155, 202
Habermas, Jürgen 3, 60
Haeckel, Ernst 178–80
Haken, Jeremy 129
Hall, Stuart 117, 125
Haller, Albrecht von 103
happiness 30–5, 37, 42–4, 52, 54, 56, 66, 76–7, 122, 171, 183
Hapsburg Empire 103, 120
Haritaworn, Jinthana K. 147
Harrington, James 50, 65–6
Harris, Angela P. 146
Harris, Matthew L. 64
Hart, David M. 57–8
Harvey, David 131–2, 161–2
Haumann, Heiko 42
Hegel, Georg Wilhelm Friedrich 38, 121, 196
hegemony 13–14, 24, 95, 102, 125, 128, 131–3, 136, 150–3, 162, 167, 202

Heidegger, Martin 14, 134, 177–8, 183–8, 190
Heisig, James W. 14
Helvétius, Claude-Adrien 75
Henry, Patrick 64
Heraclitus 9, 175
Herder, Johann Gottfried 36–7, 40, 43, 70, 103, 120, 196
Herodotus 18–19
Hertner, Peter 154
Hesmivy D'Auribeau, Pierre 75
Hessel, Stéphane 90
Heywood, Colin 146
Higuchi, Yoïchi 78
Hinduism 15, 25, 130
history of events 5
history of ideas 5–11
history of mentality 6–8
Hitler, Adolf 119–21, 161, 197
Hoagland, Edward 178
Hobbes, Thomas 34, 48, 51–2, 66, 73–4, 89, 118, 144, 151, 174
Hobsbawm, Eric 166
Hobson, John Atkinson 161–2
Hodge, Bob 4, 12
Hofbauer, Hannes 14, 142–3
Hofer, Johann 44
Holmén, Janne 185
Holocaust 119, 123, 174, 196
Holy Land 21
Holy Roman Empire 20, 80
home 42–4, 80–1, 86, 118, 178–80, 185
homecoming 42–5, 172–3, 179, 183–9
homeland, *Heimat* 42, 80, 85–6, 102, 177, 179, 183–5, 188–9
Horowitz, Mardi 182
Horwitz, Morton J. 93
Hottentots 110
Howarth, William 178
Hudson River 60, 68
Hugo, Victor 13
human rights 16, 33–4, 84, 92, 102, 137–42, 147, 155, 163, 166–8, 189, 197
Humanism 17, 23, 44, 65, 90, 130
humanitarianism 12, 29, 105, 108, 142, 151, 155, 157, 161, 167, 197–8

humanity 2, 39, 60, 75, 122, 141–2, 193–6
 dehumanized 91, 116, 140
 differentiated 82, 118, 146, 189
 full, true 44, 70, 113–14, 130, 191, 198
 inhumane 28, 127, 140, 155–7, 176, 189, 197
 predestined 24–6, 36, 62, 69–71, 102, 116, 121, 176–7
 progressing 27, 42–4, 84, 115, 153, 163, 183, 193, 198
 responsible 35, 196
 unconscious 25, 27
 universal 36, 128, 139, 149, 161, 163, 167–8
humanization 38, 40, 42–4, 194, 198
humankind 1, 14, 31–2, 36–7, 42–4, 79, 82, 87, 113, 121, 180, 190, 194–6
 human species 36–7, 48, 116, 160, 173, 175–6
 mankind, man 3, 15, 17, 31–45, 66, 70, 73–4, 91, 104, 114–25, 130, 134, 171–7, 182–99
 nonhuman 176
Humboldt, Alexander von 31
Hume, David 27, 53–4, 91, 98, 114–15
Hungarians 164
Huns 23, 114
Huntington, Samuel P. 1–2, 12–13
Hussein, Saddam 161
Hutchins, Robert 93
Hyneman, Charles S. 63

Iberian Peninsula 25, 108, 113
Ibhawoh, Bonny 109
identity 2, 19, 59, 69, 104, 114, 125–6, 133, 136, 153, 180–7, 195
imperialism 13, 109, 128, 131–3, 149, 152–4, 159–63, 167–9
Imposimato, Ferdinando 150
Incas 102
indentured laborers 63, 67, 71–2 (see also serfdom)
India 29, 60, 118, 129, 134
individualism 48–9, 54, 58, 109, 135–6
indoctrination 2, 84–5
Indonesia 150
intellectual history 5–11, 127, 201

International Criminal Court 139, 157
International Criminal Tribunal for the former Yugoslavia (ICTY) 138–9, 157
intolerance 24, 78, 127, 137
Iran 143, 150, 158, 161, 167
Iraq 152, 155, 158, 161, 166
Ireland, Irish 13, 28, 67, 71, 83, 105–6, 120
irreversibility 10, 38, 43, 50, 185, 201
Isabella, Maurizio 58
Ishmaelites 110
Islam, Muslims 14–15, 21–3, 111, 113, 126, 143, 147
Israel 62–3, 83, 147, 199
Israel, Jonathan 7–10, 32, 75–6
Italy 22, 58, 76, 83–4, 93, 106–7, 109, 116–17, 123, 154, 162

Jackson, Robert Houghwout 155
Jackson, Roger Reid 14
Jacob, Margaret C. 40–1
Jacobinism 58, 77
Jahn, Bernhard 89–90
James, William 8
Jamestown 61
JanMohamed, Abdul R. 128, 133
Jefferson, Thomas 65–6
Jehovah 63, 70
Jerusalem 21, 25
Jesus 75, 101
Joachim of Fiore (Gioacchino da Fiore) 121
Joas, Hans 192
Johnson, Chalmers Ashby 150, 159
Johnson, Robert A. 14
Jolly, Richard 149
Jonas, Hans 196
Jordan, David P. 22
Judaism, Jews 24, 39–40, 62, 111, 113, 119–21, 145,
Judson, Pieter M. 146
Jünger, Ernst 183

Kant, Immanuel 26, 35–7, 44, 47, 54, 57, 91–2, 95, 114–16, 122–3, 125, 127, 195–6
Karelia 17
Kennedy, Emmet 3
Kennedy, Paul 108, 138, 164–5

INDEX

Kermode, Frank 187, 193
Keynes, John Maynard 59
Kidd, Thomas S. 64
Killingsworth, M. Jimmie 178
King, Anthony 66–7, 72–3
Kochi, Tarik 108
Komenský, Jan Amos (Comenius) 26
Koselleck, Reinhart 6, 30–2, 38–9, 41–2, 193
Koskenniemi, Martti 137, 139
Kosovo 157
Krepinevich, Andrew F. 199
Kress, Gunther 4, 12
Kryshkin, Yevgeny 150
Kuhn, Thomas Samuel 11
Kuklinski, James 87
Kurunmäki, Jussi 50
Kuwait 161

La Capra, Dominick 191
La Fayette (du Motier), Gilbert 163
La Vopa, Anthony J. 10
Laclau, Ernesto 88
Lafraie, Najibullah 167
Lake Peipus 108
Lamb, Robert 9
Lang, Michael 31, 162
language 4–11, 59, 62–4, 77, 80, 85–6, 112–13, 119, 122–5, 168, 175
　imperial 58, 133
　reasoning 51, 192
　western 45
Lash, Scott 190
Latin 2, 7, 22–4, 58, 70, 78, 81, 103, 152
Lawson, Stephanie 151–2
Le Goff, Jacques 102
League of Nations 164–6
Lebanon 158
Leibniz, Gottfried Wilhelm von 31–2
Lenin (Ulyanov), Vladimir Ilyich 188
Lennox, James G. 179
Lentin, Alana 101, 113, 119, 123, 125, 127–8, 147
Leonhard, Jörn 50
Leopold II of Belgium 161
Leopold, David 3, 59
Lepanto 23
Leroux, Robert 57–8

lesbian, gay, bisexual, transgender (LGBT) 126, 146–7, 168
Leslie, Marina 41
lethargy 25, 107, 120
Leuchtenburg, William Edward 61, 65, 68
Levant 19–22, 27, 60, 105
Levant Company 60
Levi, Carlo 123–4
Levis Sullam, Simon 83
Levitt, Theodore 128
Lewis, Henry Morgan 173
Liakos, Antonis 2, 41
liberalism 12–13, 48–60
　American 67, 174
　Anglo-Saxon 57–8
　European 58
　French 57, 96, 98, 109
　German 58
　Italian 58, 93
　liberal geopolitics 151
　liberal governments 71, 98
　liberal movements 50, 57, 91, 98
　liberal thinkers 3, 52, 57, 98, 109, 136
　liberal thought 48–57, 72, 92–8, 137–9, 144–5, 149, 175, 178
　liberalization 131, 133
　neo-liberalism 59, 88, 125, 128, 131–2, 135, 138, 184
Liberia 110
liberation 76, 91, 172
liberty 35, 38, 49–58, 62, 64–5, 68, 70, 73, 77, 83, 91, 97, 105, 114, 159, 168
Libya 152, 158, 166
Lindberg, Tod 198–9
List, Friedrich 58
Livy (Titus Livius) 50, 66
Lluberas, Rodrigo 149
Locke, John 41–2, 48–56, 59, 62, 65–6, 73, 109, 130, 135–6, 144
Lombroso, Cesare 118
Losurdo, Domenico 55–8, 63, 67, 72, 97, 110, 114
love 25, 35, 48, 75, 112
Löwenstein, Hubertus zu 166, 169
Löwith, Karl 12, 39–40, 42, 176–7, 195
Lueger, Karl 120

Lukács, György 188
Lunacharsky, Anatoly Vasil'evich 188
Lusatia 108
Lusitania 20
Luther, Martin 182
Lutz, Donald S. 63
Lycia 18
Lyotard, Jean-François 189

McAdams, Dan P. 183
McDonald's Cooperation 133
McFarland, David 122
Machiavelli, Nicolò 23, 33, 50, 65
Machiavellian moment 65–6
Mackinder, Halford John 14, 151–2, 199
McKinley, William 155
Macpherson, James 103, 135
Madsen, Deborah L. 69, 199
Magalhaes Godinho, Vitorino 25, 160
Maghreb 21
Magna Carta 71, 72, 174
Maier, Charles S. 152
Malcolm X (*alias of* Malcolm Little) 101
male chauvinism 146
Mallet, Paul Henri 103
Malouet, Pierre-Victor 57
Mamdani, Mahmood 137
Mandeville, Bernard de 47–8, 50, 136
Marat, Jean-Paul 97
Marcuse, Ludwig 176–7
Marramao, Giacomo 1, 16, 31, 132
Martin, Philippe 131
Marx, Karl 3, 12, 38, 129–30, 134, 172–3
Marxism 12, 121, 171–3, 188
Maryland 60
Massachusetts 60–2
materialism 32, 40, 196
Maturana, Humberto R. 191
Mazzini, Giuseppe 83–4, 106
Mead, George Herbert 45, 177, 180, 191–2
meaning in history 2, 5, 11, 30–3, 39–43, 57, 66, 70, 116, 132, 173, 187–9, 192, 195, 202
meaninglessness 11, 51, 187–9, 195, 199, 202

Mediterranean 18, 21, 23–4, 28, 117, 124
melancholy 42–5, 130, 135, 190, 192
Melanesia 142
memory 11, 42–5, 55, 69, 75, 103, 122, 135, 180, 184, 189–92, 196
Merchant, Carolyn 174, 176
Mesopotamia 21
Methodism 63–4
Mettan, Guy 14
Mexico 67–8, 138, 140
Michelet, Jules 81, 84
Middell, Matthias 50, 72, 76
Middle Ages 17, 20–5, 61, 83, 102, 107, 111
Middle East 23, 161
Mikkeli, Heikki 20–1
Mikulić, Borislav 175
Milanesi, Marica 21
Mill, John Stuart 55, 58
Miller, Perry 70
Milošević, Slobodan 139
Miltiades the Younger 22
Milward, Alan Steele 87
mission 14–15, 19–20, 24–5, 29–30, 40, 43, 61, 65, 70, 76, 104–8, 129, 132, 153, 160–1, 169, 175, 178, 196
Mississippi 64
Moby Dick 101
Mochnacki, Maurycy 84
modern society 3–5, 52, 56, 91, 96, 112–13, 117–19, 124, 131–3, 136–9, 145, 152, 173, 183, 189, 191
modernity 2, 13, 28–31, 38, 52, 56, 73–4, 78–9, 82–3, 87, 105–6, 109, 122, 125, 131–5, 159, 164, 168, 184–6 (*see also* post-modernity)
  modern communication 89–90
  modern Europe 18–19, 22, 24, 28, 61, 164
  modern history 55–9, 103
  modern temporality 2, 38, 194
  modernization 2–3, 31, 40, 42
  pre-modern times 34, 136, 183
Moïsi, Dominique 153
Møller, Bjørn 166
monarchy 26, 50, 66, 72, 76, 81, 90–8, 103–4, 111–12

Mongols 120
Monroe, James 110
Montesquieu, Charles de Secondat 27, 50, 57, 65, 76, 94–9
morals, ethics 32, 161, 174–6, 196
 amorality 151
 Christian moral 41
 immorality 174, 176
 moral duty 14, 59, 70, 84–6, 109, 146–7, 151, 174–8
 moral judgment 35, 44, 58, 64, 67, 69, 84, 102, 122, 129, 136–41, 151, 175, 189
 moral laws 35–6, 50, 115, 140–1, 165, 195–6,
 moral sentiments 44, 48, 50, 59, 74–5
 moral superiority 160–3, 168
 morality 35, 48, 75, 84, 120, 136–7, 151, 187
More, Thomas 32, 73
Morison, Samuel Eliot 61, 65, 68
Morlachs 28, 105
Moscow 22, 26
Muir, John 175, 178
Munich Agreement 164
Münkler, Herfried 197
Muralt, Béat-Louis 103
Muscovy Company 60
Mussolini, Benito 123
myth 11, 22, 69–71, 77, 87, 96–9, 111, 114, 168, 173, 176, 188, 202
mythical origin 17–19, 40–4, 79–82, 85–6, 103, 135, 173, 190, 195

Nagel, Gert K. 21
Napoleon Bonaparte 3, 50, 53, 96, 98
Nash, Roderick Frazier 174–6
nation 27, 29, 33–4, 37, 47, 55, 62–3, 95–9, 124, 129, 138, 145, 154–7, 161–2, 168–9, 174, 177
 concept 76–91, 103–9, 118, 133–4
 nation building 79, 83, 166
 nation state 71–2, 78–9, 87, 91, 102, 105, 118–19, 142
 national character 60, 111–13, 115
 nationalism 11, 47–9, 57–8, 83–4, 87, 107, 118–20, 126–7, 135, 151, 166, 188–9, 199

National Socialism (Nazi Party) 77, 93, 119–21
natural justice, law 47–9, 51–7, 65–6, 72–7, 81–6, 91, 96–8, 102–5, 108, 113–14, 144–5, 130, 202
nature 2–3, 31–44, 60, 70, 75–6, 84, 113, 120–3, 133, 127, 163, 173–83, 186–8, 191–6
 natural border 28, 105
 natural conditions/phenomena 78, 112, 115, 137, 166, 193–4, 199
 natural environment 115, 117
 naturalization 67, 103
 state of nature 31, 34–5, 40, 42–5, 48, 54, 73, 91, 105, 118, 135, 164
Nazemroaya, Mahdi
 Darius 129, 150, 157
negro, moor 55, 57, 62–3, 66–7, 114–20, 145
New England 60–1, 68, 199
New World 1, 29–30, 34, 63, 68–9, 114
New York 60
New Zealand 141
Newton, Isaac 31, 40–1
Niceforo, Alfredo 116–17, 123–4
Nicholas of Cusa 23
Nietzsche, Friedrich 14, 119, 187–9
Nieuwveld 110
nihilism 14, 187, 189, 199, 202
Nile 21
Nixon, Richard Milhous 131
Noah (biblical patriarch) 62
nobility 20, 30, 56, 63, 72, 75, 80–1, 94, 103
non-governmental organizations (NGOs) 137, 141–3, 158, 160–1, 167
North 21, 25, 29, 68, 78, 106, 117–18, 138
North Atlantic Treaty Organization (NATO) 12–13, 143, 150–1, 157, 165, 167–8
North Korea 167
Norton, Mary Beth 63–4, 67, 69
nostalgia 43–5, 62, 79, 86, 106, 145, 171–3, 179–81, 188, 191–2
Nova Scotia 60
Novalis (Georg Friedrich Philipp von Hardenberg) 45, 74–5, 77, 82, 84, 188

Núñez Seixas, Xosé M.   85–6
Nuremberg Trials   155

Obama, Barack   153–7, 162
O'Brien, Karen   34
Occident   1, 19, 31, 106
Odessa   119
Oelschlaeger, Max   175, 178, 190–1
Old World   68, 129
Orange (river)   110
Orient   19–23, 29–30, 114, 120–1, 130, 134, 145
Orthodox Church   22–3, 83–4
Orwell, George (*alias of* Eric Arthur Blair)   159
Oschema, Klaus   20
Ottoman Empire   22–3, 27–8, 30, 103–5, 112, 164–5

Paine, Thomas   64, 66, 70
Pakistan   156
Paley, William   97
Palmerston (Temple, Lord of), Henry John   129–30
Parekh, Bhikhu   9
Paris   64, 76, 84, 86, 163
parliament   61, 64, 71, 75, 96, 103, 128, 156, 160
Pasinato, Antonio   185, 189
Patras   84
Pazé, Valentina   184
pedagogy   45, 85–6, 122, 179–80
Perkins, Mary Anne   26
Persia   18–19, 76, 114, 118
person   35, 42, 45, 49–55, 58, 65, 85–7, 90–1, 129, 137–8, 141, 168–9, 176–7, 180, 182, 185–6, 202
Pestalozzi, Johann Heinrich   85
Peters, Ralph   158
Petri, Rolf   2, 10, 78, 91
Petzen, Jennifer   126
Philippines   154–5
philosophy of history   30–48, 77, 99, 130, 145, 171, 193, 202
Phoenicia   18
Physis (Φύσις)   175–7, 192, 194
Pietarinen, Juhani   144
Pius II (Pope, Enea Silvio Piccolomini)   23, 113

Plato   22, 34, 42–3, 90, 173
Pocock, John Greville Agard   5, 8, 10–11, 24, 40, 43, 65, 159
Poland   26, 83–4, 103, 106–7, 164
Polanyi, Karl   130, 135
politics   1, 3–8, 34, 45, 48–61, 69–89, 102–10, 118–19, 123, 140, 166–9, 196
  international   128, 142–7, 151–3, 158, 198–9
  political realm   15–16, 60, 75, 81–2, 89–99, 119, 201–2
Pollack, Kenneth M.   143
Polybius   65
Polynesia   118, 142
Pomerania   108
Pomian, Krzysztof   107
Popper, Karl   3, 58
populism   49, 76–7, 90
Portugal   108, 160
post-modernity   128, 132, 146, 173, 186, 189–91 (*see also* modernity)
power   74, 86–92
  absolute   52, 55–6
  balanced   50, 55, 66, 159, 202
  discursive   4, 74, 89, 93–4, 142, 184
  economic   131, 135, 142, 162
  evolutionary   175
  geopolitical   22–6, 33, 128, 131–3, 137–40, 151–4, 157, 164–5, 168–9, 189, 197–9
  human   37–8
  ideological   15, 44, 48–9, 69, 74–5, 132, 153, 163, 174, 198
  military   15, 25, 68, 104, 142, 162, 198–9
  political   20, 45, 49, 52–3, 59, 64, 71, 76–83, 89–99, 102–4, 120, 124, 156, 159, 162, 168, 174
  religious   20, 23–4, 83, 102
  social   3, 33, 52, 76, 117, 131, 144, 146
  state   14, 23, 109
Pratt, Alan   189
pre-Christian period   11, 23, 65, 103
prehistory   31, 33
Prigogine, Ilya   191
privilege   25, 51, 71, 80, 89–94, 104, 134, 137, 139

INDEX

progress 13, 29–30, 38–44, 75, 83, 101, 123–4, 127–30, 135, 168, 172–3, 190, 194–6
  American 69
  European 30, 104–9
  human 29, 37–8, 44, 104, 114–17, 153, 160, 163–4, 198
  western 31
propaganda 4, 12, 147, 197
property rights 35, 48, 53–4, 56–9, 62–6, 70–2, 98, 109, 172
Protestantism 40, 60–5, 67, 83
Prussia 76, 107
Puar, Jasbir 147
Pufendorf, Samuel 48
Puritanism 60–6, 69–70, 75, 83
purpose of history 1–2, 6, 11, 14, 26, 31–6, 39, 62, 108, 127, 182, 188, 192–6, 202
purposelessness 177, 179, 187–9, 202
Pushkin, Alexander Sergeyevich 81, 106

Qutb, Sayyid 15

race 55, 67, 76, 83, 108, 111–29, 140, 146–7, 174, 177–8
Rahn, Thomas 82, 89–90
Rasmussen, Anders Fogh 159
rationalization 31, 74
Ratzinger, Joseph 149
Rawls, John 60
reason 2, 26–38, 41, 44, 47, 51–60, 66, 73–6, 81, 87, 91–2, 98, 114, 122–7, 163, 183, 187, 193
redemption 36–7, 40–3, 69, 121, 158, 187–90, 193
Reformation 23, 60, 121, 133
Reinhard, Wolfgang 108
religion 11, 34, 41, 55, 60–7, 86–7, 111–13, 119, 137, 140, 145–7, 151, 160–1, 165–9, 188
  Abrahamic 15
  apocalyptic 2, 14, 192–8
  concept 3, 13–15, 41, 121
  monotheistic 15, 19–27, 169
  non-revelatory 14
  political 58, 70–7, 82–3, 94, 158, 169

Remotti, Francesco 3, 19, 122, 186
Renaissance 17, 22, 41, 50, 111
Renan, Ernest 82, 168–9
republic 11, 26, 34, 50, 65–6, 73–6, 84–5, 89–98, 106, 158–9
Republican Party (USA) 156, 158
revolution 10, 29, 55, 74, 84, 94, 97, 101, 115, 130, 143, 151–2 (*see also* Glorious Revolution; American Revolution; French Revolution)
Revolution of 1848 50, 58, 72
Reyes Mate, Manuel 196
Reynolds, Susan 71
Ricci, Maurizio 138–9
Richards, Robert J. 178–9
Richter, Daniel K. 68
Ricœur, Paul 173, 191
Riebeek, Jan van 110
rights 31, 57–9, 80, 84, 89, 92, 96–9, 109, 128, 135, 145, 198 (*see also* human rights; property rights)
  civil 57, 72–3
  individual 31, 58, 99, 109, 137–8, 202
  natural 48–9, 52–3, 65, 73, 81, 103, 144, 174–5
  political 71–2, 97, 110
  social 91, 138, 143
Roberts, Paul Craig 157–8
Robespierre, Maximilien 75–7, 84–5, 96
Robinson Crusoe 9, 27
Rodbertus-Jagetzow, Carl 108
Roederer, Pierre-Louis 53
Roman Empire 20–2, 29, 33, 81
Roman Law 50, 109, 141
Romanticism 58, 74, 78–9, 84, 135, 173, 179, 188
Rome 21–2, 24, 26, 29, 33, 50, 76, 81
Roosevelt, Theodore Jr. 156
Rorty, Richard 142
Rosanvallon, Pierre 6, 8–9
Rosenberg Wynne, Justine 145
Rosenblatt, Helena 41
Rosenfeld, Michel 79
Rossi, Pietro 27–8, 43
Rostow, Walt Whitman 171–2, 192

Rousseau, Jean-Jacques 27, 34–5, 41, 43–4, 52, 73, 76, 97, 172, 179
Rueckert, William 176
rule of law 50, 52, 74, 90–9, 139, 168, 202
Runciman, Steven 22
Russia 13–14, 26, 30, 58, 81, 106–8, 120, 151, 161, 197
Ruthenians 106

Sachsenmaier, Dominic 134
Sackey, Brigid M. 136–7
sacredness 21, 25, 34, 60–4, 74–7, 82–6, 96–8, 111, 164, 169
Said, Edward W. 19, 30
Saint Augustine of Hippo 21
Saint John the Apostle 121
Saint Lawrence (river) 68
Saint Paul the Apostle 24
Sammet, Gerald 21
Samoyedes 118
Sandys, George 27
Saracens 114
Sartre, Jean-Paul 57, 189
Sato, Masayuki 14
savagery 40, 68, 78, 106, 115, 130–1, 145
savages 27–30, 33, 38, 53–7, 70, 81, 91, 105–6, 109–11, 151, 159, 163, 175
Say, Jean-Baptiste 58
Scandinavia 26
Schama, Simon 176
Schattkowsky, Ralph 107
Schaub, Jean-Frédéric 111–13, 115, 117
Schelling, Friedrich Wilhelm Joseph 121, 194–5
Scherer, Augustin 86
Scheveningen 139
Scheye, Eric 167
Schmitt, Carl 83, 155, 161
Schneidmüller, Bernd 20
Schnitzer, Claudia 89–90
Scholasticism 90
Schönichen, Walther 177
Schultz, Hans-Dietrich 1
Schulze, Hagen 103–4
Scotland, Scots 27, 53, 67, 72, 163, 178
Scott, Walter 103
Seckinelgin, Hakan 142–3
secularization 2, 12, 23, 25, 32, 38, 60, 65, 70–1, 83, 104, 194–5
Seeger, Stefan A. 196
selfishness 104–5, 135, 153, 161, 174–7
sense of superiority 25, 29–30, 97, 106, 108, 114, 119, 126, 142, 152, 163, 201
Serbia 107, 139, 157, 164
serfdom 27, 56, 63, 67–8, 106, 108, 112, 144 (*see also* Indentured laborers)
Serna, Pierre 76
Serrier, Thomas 107
sexuality 126, 143, 146
Shafer, Byron E. 69
Shakespeare, William 153, 178
Shambala (mythical kingdom) 42
Shils, Edward Albert 3–4
Shorrocks, Anthony 149
Shultz, George Pratt 138
Siberia 70
Sicambrians 81
Sicily 116
Sieyès, Emmanuel Joseph 41–2, 76–8, 81, 96
Silesia 108
Silvera, Ian 160
Simal, Juan Luis 50
Simon, Roger I. 45
Simons, Marlise 139
Singapore 133
Skinner, Quentin 5–6, 9–10, 50–1, 66, 71, 73, 97
Slaughter, Thomas P. 68
slavery
  institution 30, 43, 55–7, 62–3, 66–70, 108, 110, 113–15, 144, 165, 174
  submission 29, 38, 72, 124, 145
Slavs 106, 117, 120
Slovaks 106
Smith, Adam 57, 163–3
Sneeuwberg 110
social contract 32, 35, 43, 48–9, 53–4, 57, 72–4, 77–8, 92, 98, 118, 136
Social Democrats 59, 120, 196–7

INDEX

socialism 50, 59, 87, 172, 188
sociobiology 117
Somalia 152, 158, 166
Sophocles 22
soul 26, 40–7, 75, 86, 141, 169, 187–8, 192–4
South 78, 106–7, 116–17, 123–4, 143
South Pacific 133, 141, 165
sovereignty 26, 41, 51–2, 60, 71, 90–2, 95–7, 99, 107, 109, 144, 151, 155–8, 165–6, 202
sovereignty of the people 35, 45, 49, 66, 71–99, 103–4, 162–4, 168
Soviet Union 12, 15, 59, 128, 147, 150, 158, 165–7, 188
Spain 50, 68, 108, 111–12, 118, 160
Spinoza, Baruch 32, 176
spirit 8, 34, 41, 57, 81, 84–5, 121, 124, 175, 180–1, 192
spirituality 18, 20, 24, 41–2, 49, 60–1, 64, 69, 84, 113, 122, 172, 176, 192–5, 199
Spirkin, Alexander 196
Spranger, Eduard 177, 179, 183
Spykman, Nicholas J. 151
Sreedharan, E. 34
Stambaugh, Joan 186
state of nature 31, 34–5, 40–4, 48, 54, 73, 91, 118, 164
Stavenhagen, Kurt 183–4
Stephens, George M. 56
Stepputat, Finn 166
Stewart, Gordon T. 42
Stoicism 32, 142
Stråth, Bo 4
Strier, Richard 44
subjectivity 8, 38, 47–9, 51, 73, 88–9, 122, 125, 184–5, 191
Subrahmanyam, Sanjay 2, 15
Sudan 158
suffering 38, 42, 45, 54, 83, 124, 142
Sutherland, Meghan 89
Sweden 26
Switzerland 44, 85, 103
Syria 152, 158

Tagore, Rabindranath 134
Talcott, Molly 140
Taliban 147, 167
Tartars 22, 26, 28, 30, 114, 120, 152

Tasso, Torquato 23
Taylor, Alan 62, 68–9
Taylor, Charles 183
Taylor, Robert 156
Taylor Mill, Harriet 144–5
Teilhard de Chardin, Pierre 172, 192–5, 198–9
teleology 1–2, 9–10, 14, 32–40, 61, 65, 118, 134–8, 171, 187, 201
temporality 38–9, 45, 88, 102, 106, 121–2, 134, 173, 177, 187, 193
terrorism 92, 120, 126–8, 140, 147, 150, 154–9, 166–8
Texas 67
The Hague 157
theology 15, 21, 39–40, 62, 137, 173
Thermodynamics 10, 201
Thiesse, Anne-Marie 80–1, 85–6, 103
third estate 42, 77, 80–1
Third World 125, 128, 134, 137, 150, 167
Thomson, Ann 40
Thoreau, Henry David 175, 190
Thrower, James 188
Thumboo, Edwin 133
Tibet 42
Titley, Gavan 123, 128, 147
Tocqueville, Alexis de 53, 57, 93, 106, 169
Todorov, Tzvetan 56
tolerance 2, 52, 63, 83, 127, 139, 163
Tolstoy, Lev Nikolayevich 17
Tönnies, Ferdinand 133, 184
Tories (party) 50
Toynbee, Arnold Joseph 63
transcendence 14, 30–2, 47, 60, 71, 87–8, 96, 169, 173, 177, 182, 191–6, 202
  lacking 38, 187–8
  legitimizing 25, 79, 83, 94, 104,
  meaningful 57, 83, 104, 141, 173, 187–8, 192, 195
  purposeful 14, 26, 30–2, 36–9, 187–8, 193, 202
Transvaal 154
Treaty of Paris 64
Tricoire, Damien 33, 65, 75–6
Tromnau, Adolf 85
Trotter, Catherine 145
Trump, Donald John 156, 159

Trüper, Henning   2, 12, 40
Tsarist Empire   103, 107
Tugendhat, Ernst   39
Tugrul, Saime   78
Tully, James   109
Turin   123
Turkey, Turks   22, 27–8, 76, 104–6, 114, 145, 165
Turner, Frederick   175
Turner, Frederick Jackson   68–9
Tuscany   117
Tyr   18
tyranny   30, 51–2, 55, 77, 90, 93–9, 160, 168, 175–6
Tyrol   86, 107
Tyrrell, Ian   152, 161

Uexküll, Jakob von   179–80
Ukraine   143
United Nations (UN)   92, 108, 137–8, 150, 157, 164–5
United Nations Educational, Scientific and Cultural Organization (UNESCO)   124–5
universalism
  American   69–70
  Christian   20–5, 195
  humanitarian   91–2, 102, 105, 128, 132, 137, 147
  imperial(ist)   19, 151–9, 167–9
  liberal   59, 91–2, 143
  missionary   43, 83–4, 174, 191
  presumptuous   13–14, 79, 101–2, 109, 121–3, 139–42, 191
  revolutionary   76, 83, 104, 163–4
  secular   34–6, 76
  western   2, 15–25, 30–6, 43, 101–8, 134, 151–9
Urals   28
utopia   2, 30, 32, 35, 41–5, 48, 59, 61, 67, 73, 84, 102, 106, 138, 142, 173, 180–1, 188, 191

Vacante, Salvatore   107
Valentine, Douglas   150
Vandalia Company   65
Varela, Francisco J.   191
Vasoli, Cesare   65
Venables, Anthony   130
Verhofstadt, Guy   160

Versailles Peace Treaties   164
Vico, Giambattista   26, 33–4, 85
Vienna   120
Vietnam   150
Vincent, Andrew   4–5
Virginia   60, 66–7
Virilio, Paul   189
virtue   11, 18, 27, 29, 33, 47, 65, 76, 147, 159
Vogler, Günter   22
Voltaire (Aroue), François-Marie   3, 22, 26–9, 32, 34, 76, 113–14, 145

Walliss, John   193
Wanna (principal town of South Waziristan)   156
war   29, 56, 62, 96, 104, 112, 138–9, 154–8, 167 (*see also* Afghanistan; Cold War; Iraq; Somalia; Syria)
  American War of Independence   64–6, 94
  asymmetrical   197–8
  colonial, neo-colonial   110–11, 123, 147, 150, 161
  confessional   23, 104
  English Civil War   61, 71
  First Opium War   129
  First World War   71, 84, 86, 96, 109, 131, 164, 188, 196–7
  French Revolutionary Wars   104
  holy   22–3
  hybrid   151–2
  Korean War   131
  nuclear   150–2, 193, 198–9
  perpetual   34, 48, 150, 158
  Persian Wars   18–19
  proxy   158, 166
  Second World War   3, 56, 77, 96, 123–6, 131, 155, 164–5, 171, 197
  Seven Years War   64
  Thirty Years War   26
  tribal   166, 168
  Yugoslav War   108, 138–9, 152, 157, 164, 166
Ward Scaltsas, Patricia   144
Weber, Max   120
Webster, Peter J.   174
Welches   81

welfare state 48, 58–60, 87–8, 125, 131–3, 136, 184–5
West Indies 68
Westphalia Peace Treaties 26, 151
Wharton, Thomas 65
Whig Party 49–51, 67
wilderness 13, 27, 62, 70, 102, 105–6, 110, 120, 174, 178, 190
Williamson, Richard S. 150
Winthrop, John 61–2, 70
Wintle, Michael 20, 22
Wittgenstein, Ludwig 5, 185–6
Wolff, Larry 13, 28, 44, 106
Wolin, Richard 177
Wollenstonecraft, Mary 144
Wood, Gordon S. 68
Wopfner, Herrmann 107

workers 55, 72, 118, 143, 145, 172–4, 182
Wörsdörfer, Rolf 107

Xerxes I of Persia (the Great) 18

Yisroel ben Eliezer (Rabbi, Ba'al Shem Tov) 42
Young, Robert 121
Yugoslavia 108, 138, 152, 157, 164, 166

Zimbabwe 167
Žižek, Slavoij 5, 12
Zoroastrianism 15
Zühlsdorff, Volkmar von 166, 169

www.ingramcontent.com/pod-product-compliance
Lightning Source LLC
Chambersburg PA
CBHW071825300426
44116CB00009B/1445